Massimo Gargia holds a doctorate in law. He has written for *Paris Vogue* and for nearly twenty years has published the magazine *The Best*. He heads the Committee for The Best, which includes leading members of the fashion and entertainment world. He also runs a public relations firm which represents many members of the aristocracy as well as such stars as Gina Lollabrigida and Ursula Andress. He has residences in Rome, Paris, and Miami Beach.

Allan Starkie, Ph.D. is a West Point graduate who has had a multi-faceted career. He served in Army Intelligence and was an officer of the Defense Intelligence Agency, where he was decorated for his undercover operations in Korea, Granada, and Chad-Libya. He later became CEO of one of the largest European construction and development corporations, and co-founder of a children's charity in Germany. Allan and Massimo have been longtime friends as well as collaborators. He lives in New York City and maintains a home in Frankfurt, Germany.

JET SET

In the early sixties, Massimo Gargia became a member of the group known as the Jet Set. Here is the account of his adventures as an international playboy to his current career as a writer, public relations expert, and publisher of the magazine *The Best*. With his extraordinary good looks and sexual charisma, Massimo became the lover of many beautiful and socially prominent women, including Baroness Cecile de Rothschild and Greta Garbo. He had a romantic relationship with the heiress Lady Lydia Deterding when he was in his late twenties and she was past eighty. This revealing memoir contains explosive material involving many famous people and even offers startling new information about Princess Diana's death.

MASSIMO GARGIA
as told to Bestselling Author
ALLAN STARKIE

◆

JET SET

Memoir of an International Playboy

Complete and Unabridged

CHARNWOOD
Leicester

First published in Great Britain in 1999 by
Barricade Books Inc
New York

First Charnwood Edition
published 2001
by arrangement with
Barricade Books Inc
New York

British Library CIP Data

Gargia, Massimo
   Jet Set.—Large print ed.—
Charnwood library series
   1. Gargia, Massimo
   2. Celebrities—United States—Biography
   3. Large type books
   I. Title II. Starkie, Allan
   973.9′092

   ISBN 0–7089–9213–7

Published by
F. A. Thorpe (Publishing)
Anstey, Leicestershire

Set by Words & Graphics Ltd.
Anstey, Leicestershire
Printed and bound in Great Britain by
T. J. International Ltd., Padstow, Cornwall

This book is printed on acid-free paper

To the memory of His Royal Highness
The Duke of Windsor,
an eternal symbol of grace and elegance
June 23, 1894 – May 18, 1972

Escorting Gina Lollobrigada and ex-Indonesian First
Lady Dewi Sukarno, South of France, 1976.

1

SETTING THE STAGE

The phones simply stopped ringing. It doesn't really matter as I am forbidden to answer them anyway. My servants have been turned into jailers. They monitor my actions ensuring that I communicate with no one and most of all that I do not leave the apartment. I am under house arrest in my home in Rome. It is a pleasant enough prison as prisons go. I live across from the Roman Colosseum. From my window box, I sit and stare endlessly at the ravaged ruin. I count the columns. Eighty-six across, three rows high. The sun sets over the arch of Constantine, and I know I have survived another day of captivity — now I must survive the night.

I await the daily visits of my lawyer with enormous expectation. He comes with both the typically tentative hope of the legal world as well as the latest press clippings of my fall from the current headlines. Hundreds of stories, each filled with partial truths and sensational speculation. Yet despite their individual inaccuracies, together they form a strangely accurate mosaic. As I look down at the pile of clippings a picture forms of my life and of the strange history of the Jet Set in which I have lived. A pantheon of famous faces from my past stare at me in black and white, each a chapter and a milestone in my journey through forty years of life within the world elite.

The headlines are full of their normal combination of trite alliteration combined with misleading sensationalism:

All his life in the Jet Set

Two hundred stars plucked

The secret of Mozzarella, friend of the Divine

Rien ne va plus, For the Great Playboy

The Party Lion roars no more

It is a field day for the yellow press. Names and families that still carry magic and had only appeared in the society pages have finally made their way to the scandal sheets. The loves of my life, my closest friends, and even the people I have launched into society are neatly listed and put on parade. The press has accused me of using my role as a leader and organizer of the Jet Set to become their pied piper of financial ruin. I had allegedly lured scores of trusting socialites and movie stars to a casino which attracted heavy surveillance from federal law enforcement for its questionable ownership and rigged games, in Morocco. It seems I had the odd sense of judgment to jeopardize my freedom, vast network of friends, and social position to assist such a hairbrained scheme.

The days pass slowly, and the future seems rather empty and uncertain now. I am drawn to a past that was not so much a continuous party as an almost infinite collection of individual parties in diverse locations that painted the picture of the world that I have watched from

2

its infancy to the present.

I would like to tell that story now. It is a story of my life, but also the history of my world — a history that is often misunderstood and perhaps never clearly defined. There seems to be so much uncertainty over what the Jet Set really is that one cannot be certain even how the term is spelled. Is JET SET one word or two — or perhaps it's hyphenated. Should it be placed in quotations or capitalized? A quick perusal of a telephone book from any international capital will reveal Jet Set used as the name of various businesses ranging from travel agents and ladies apparel, to escort agencies; yet try to find it in a library, and you will be disappointed. The Internet has seen fit to allow the existence of a Website that chronicles the parties of a Lhasa apso and famous Jet Setter named Lady Gizmo LeBratt. Yet perhaps these clues do not lead us closer to a clear definition.

Maybe it is easier to begin with describing what the Jet Set is not. The Jet Set is not comprised of people who travel in airplanes. A frequent-flyer card does not guarantee membership nor is the first-class lounge the meeting point. The Jet Set follows a fairly regimented travel circuit primarily dictated by particular events in a prescribed series of locations each year. Yet were one to follow this itinerary and even to stay in the obligatory hotels, one would sadly still not be counted among the members of this group. The Jet Set is simply another term for a mobile segment of high society, recently augmented with entertainment and fashion luminaries. Neither extensive traveling nor enormous wealth guarantee acceptance within this society. Entry is very restricted, but possible. My story illustrates how this can be accomplished and perhaps even answers the question of why one would want to be.

The Jet Set as a recognized element of society began shortly after the Second World War. The early Jet Set of the fifties was called café society and was essentially a subset of the international high-society families who had existed in their segregated sphere for generations. It was comprised of roughly 200 titled families mixed with the fresher blood of industrial giants. The industrialists had been able to thus upgrade their social status and sophistication, and the old families had acquired new wealth. An excellent example of this is the Rothschilds. This enormously powerful industrial and banking family had begun to develop in the early 1800s from very bourgeois origins. By the turn of the century, they had become not only one of the richest and most powerful international financiers, but also aristocrats. Another example is the fabulously wealthy owners of Fiat, the Agnellis. For the last two generations, the Agnelli men have married princesses, thus, adding nobility to wealth.

It was my good fortune to be adopted socially by senior members of both these families. During the sixties, I thus had the opportunity to watch the early Jet Set as it began its evolution to the socially more multifaceted constellation it enjoys today. But more than just being a

4

participant in this world, I was able to benefit from the social education that I received from these two families.

As I mentioned, physical mobility and wealth certainly do not connote acceptance within the Jet Set. Nevertheless, wealth is certainly an asset in attempting entry. If one wishes to be accepted in this circle and is not born with great family wealth, then other talents are required to compensate for this liability. It is not enough to be good looking, although it certainly is an enormous asset in such an aesthetic-oriented world.

What is required is a cultivated charm and an understanding of the rules of engagement on the social battlefield upon which the life of the Jet Set is played. I was fortunate to be blessed with good looks and truly lucky to have been chosen by members of two such great families to be the recipient of a complex social education that has enabled me to survive in this precarious world for more than three decades.

By the time I entered the world of the Jet Set in the early sixties, the habits of the social elite were undergoing the initial changes that would earn them that title. Formerly the great families exchanged visits to each other's palaces, summer homes, and yachts. With the inception of commercial air-travel, distances were naturally less prohibitive, and the younger socialites began to develop a jet-oriented travel circuit. What evolved was a group whose self-definition was linked to an uninterrupted participation in this annual circuit. It is this prerequisite and the life-style and values that are required to fulfill it that form the ultimate definition of the Jet Set. It requires a total time commitment that does not allow for the interruptions of business or career. When I entered this group in the early sixties, an almost formal travel schedule had been developed in a de-facto way that resulted from participation in particular events.

Christmas and New Year's Eve was always a choice between sun and snow. The winter sport enthusiasts had either Gstaad or St. Moritz. For those who selected St. Moritz, the key event was the formal New Year's Eve party thrown by the great shipping magnate, Stavros Niarchos, at the Chesa Veglia Club. It was a wonderful party, but did carry a great risk should you not receive an invitation for some reason. This would mean facing the socially devastating prospect of simply having nowhere to go.

In general St. Moritz had the reputation of being the snootiest place in the world. There was simply one 'A' group and nothing else. Princess Milana Furstenberg to this day leads this social segment. If she did not like you, St. Moritz was clearly out. During the day, Princess Furstenberg's group dominated the beautiful Corviglia Club on the mountaintop, which was the only 'in' place to break from your ski runs. At night her tightly controlled social circuit required invitations to the various chalet parties. Without them, you became a member of the lonely occupants of the dining room of the Palace Hotel — as if you were exiled to a leper colony. Clearly St. Moritz is a dangerous choice.

That left Gstaad for the slightly less-courageous winter enthusiasts. Gstaad social life offered at least a selection of nationality groups. The Greek group was led by the Greek tycoon, Basil Goulandris, and featured the frequent appearance of King Constantine and his family. The German group was led by the Mercedes heirs, Mick and Muck Flick, with their respective wives. There were some smaller segmented groups, but they were a little unsure socially. Even in Gstaad, one risked not being invited to the major event, the New Year's Eve party of the Prince and Princess of Savoy, hereditary King and Queen of Italy.

The Savoys have long enjoyed an elevated status among the Jet Set for a somewhat romantic reason. After the Second World War, Italy became a republic and forbade the Savoys to return. They were essentially an exiled royal house. This is, of course, very intriguing. Were they to be demoted to simple princes of a once-royal family (like the Bourbons), they could have enjoyed an acceptable, but unremarkable existence in Italy. But exiling them implied that their mere presence was a danger to the republic. It made one think of the exiled Napoleon planning his return from Elba or perhaps of Charles II staring across the Channel at an England he would soon reconquer. Such images intrigued and impressed the other members of the Jet Set. The very fact that the Savoys were exiled resulted in their unobstructed participation in the Jet Set's intricate travel circuit. To this day, the Savoys are prohibited from returning to

Italy and consequentially remain very involved in the Jet Set.

For those who preferred the sun, Acapulco was the destination of choice. Here, too, there was only one group. Their exclusive villas were all built together in a large complex on the hill of Las Brisas, by the sea. The complex felt almost like a prison in that it was enclosed and constantly patrolled by police. One needed special permission even to visit. Although there was only one group, at least one had three chances to be invited to a New Year's party. Lowell and Gloria Guinness (of the beer empire) hosted the most restrictive party with a microscopic guest list, which included Frank Sinatra and Henry Kissinger. The most outrageous party was at the home of Baron and Baroness Rick and Sandra Portanova. There one could mingle with a more avant-garde guest list, which included actresses such as Joan Collins and Linda Christian, as well as grand aristocrats like Prince Michael of Kent with his German wife, Christina. The third party was for a younger, but nevertheless socially prominent crowd hosted by the French millionaire Tony Murray.

Usually the daytime was dominated by Warren and Yanna Avis, of the rent-a-car company. Margaux Hemingway, George Hamilton, and other Hollywood people could be found at the Avis's palatial hilltop home. I particularly relished the exercise value of their long stone stairway down to the sea.

In early March, we would migrate to the warm

elegance of Palm Beach. Palm Beach has a culture and social world of its own. The international Jet Set simply visits with Palm Beach society, and for that matter, very few members of the Palm Beach elite actually are members of the Jet Set. It is an insular society made up of the Old Guard families, generously mixed with the nouveau riche. It tends to overcompensate a little for that fact in ways that Europeans often find to be quite cute. For example, Zsa Zsa Gabor's husband sells European aristocratic titles to the newly wealthy. Nevertheless, for spectacles of sheer extravagance, Palm Beach cannot be beat.

April brought us back to Europe for the Feria of Seville. The Feria is a week-long, uninterrupted party, which takes place in very diverse locations. There is constant partying along the street in small wooden stands where one drinks and dances the flamenco throughout the day. Frequent bullfights attract the sporty, while wonderful parties are thrown in the old palace for the elite. There is one hotel frequented by the Jet Set, the Alfonso XIII. However, it is more chic to arrive by yacht and return to it each night in the harbor. The Duchess of Alba presides over the social portion of this festival and throws lavish parties for the visiting elite.

The great summer migration generally begins in July when the move is to St. Tropez. The chic section of St. Tropez is les Parcs, where most of the private villas are located. The harbor is dominated by the assembly of yachts. The enormous yachts of Hollywood producers such as Sam Spiegel and Darryl Zanuck were moored next to the vessels of Greek tycoons and old socialites. Brigitte Bardot could be seen at the in-vogue clubs, and a slightly less discreet Rock Hudson could often be spotted with a handsome escort like the Italian actor, Fabrizio Miani. The fabulous yachts were used to host the daily beach parties.

Here a truly odd phenomenon would occur. The massive boats would go through the elaborate and costly process of pulling anchor, starting their powerful engines, or even hoisting their sails simply to cruise a couple of hundred yards out of the harbor to stop in front of the adjacent beach. The guests would then disembark from the immense luxury and fantastic cuisine offered by these pleasure craft to partake of the poor food of the tiny beachfront restaurants. This sacrifice was made for the compensation of admiring the many topless beauties sunning themselves on the beach.

I often would select a restaurant adjacent to the beachfront home of the ultimate 1960s vintage playboy, Gunter Sachs, who single-handedly defended the honor of German playboys against the then-dominant Italians. This one-time husband of Brigitte Bardot had outfitted his home with a Moroccan-style tent by the beach. I would enjoy watching the stream of beautiful women who walked in and out of his house. The nights were filled with wonderful parties at the various villas. A great hostess of that period was the Italian actress, Elsa Martinelli, who starred with Kirk Douglas in

The Indian Fighter.

Of course, the quintessential Riviera destination was Monte Carlo in August. The Red Cross Ball held the first Saturday in August kicked off the season. Prince Rainier and Princess Grace held court over the most complete assortment of Jet Setters imaginable. Monte Carlo life is much more elegant that St. Tropez. The sun is superfluous to the scene. Bathing suits are not required. Even at lunch, one wears a jacket, and beginning at 7:00 P.M., one finds oneself already in black tie in an endless progression through various cocktail parties until one reaches the dinner location. Dinner takes place either at a private villa or on the terrace of the exclusive rooftop Winston Churchill room of the Hotel de Paris. The roof opens so one can eat under the stars and enjoy the panoramic view of the harbor filled with beautiful yachts, which were illuminated at night.

The newest discovery made by no less a personage than His Highness Karim Aga Khan was the Costa Smeralda of Sardinia. The natural beauty of this island made it very appealing. Although lacking in natural beaches, it offered majestic, granite cliffs that dropped dramatically into a clear, blue sea. Porto Cervo offered adequate facilities to accommodate the yachts that began to follow the Aga Khan's discovery. Soon Sardinia was to be the choice resort for the end of August. Before long, magnificent villas sprung up along the coast, built of the natural stone and blending subtly into the landscape. It was in these homes that the closed social life of

11

the Costa Smeralda was acted out. During the day, the yachts carried us to islands that offered better beaches. It was here through my friendship with Amyn Aga Khan that I first met Princess Margaret of England and Crown Prince Carl Gustav of Sweden. And it was to be here that I would spend some of my fondest days with Gianni Versace.

Capri had been a longtime favorite of the Jet Set. September always brought us back to the beautiful island with its eccentric assortment of characters. For some reason, the island of Capri brought out the strangest behavior in some of Italy's most aristocratic families. The Prince Dado Ruspoli was generally to be found walking about with a red parrot on his shoulder. He usually took these strolls wearing specially made trousers that had legs of different and often clashing colors.

On the other hand, the Princess Pignatelli was an elegant lady of sixty who insisted on constantly wearing the same black funeral shroud with a black shawl worn as a hood over her head. She would encrust her face with white powder and took to sleeping in a coffin in her ancient villa. This bizarre scene was presided over by the uncrowned social Queen of Capri, Duchess Elena Serra Di Cassano, who in addition to being a duchess, boasted the dubious title of the Queen of the Italian DDT Industry. This, of course, is nothing less than the aerosol poison used to kill cockroaches. The duchess lived in a beautiful villa that is today owned by the designer Valentino. She would make her

12

nightly after-dinner appearance on the terrace of the Hotel Quisisana, which was the meeting point at that time. Upon sighting her, everyone present would rise and holding up their goblets, shout 'Viva Elena, Queen of Capri' — they were dead serious, too. It was exactly like watching a Cecil B. DeMille film about Tiberius Caesar during his years in Capri.

Although an angry Italy executed Mussolini, his daughter, Edda Ciano, for some reason, was admired and loved by the simple inhabitants of Capri, who enthusiastically shouted out her name when she passed. She somewhat devalued the Mussolini mystique by choosing as a boyfriend a jeweler sporting the name of Chanteclair (which, of course, means morning cock in French). I dated her daughter, Dindina, who struck up a great friendship with the daughter of Generalissimo Franco.

Eccentric Capri was a lucky place for me. It was here in 1965, as a very young man, that I broke into the ranks of the Jet Set. In fact, one might say that I was discovered. The designer Pierre Cardin took a liking to me, and we became friends. While visiting him in Paris some time thereafter, I had the great fortune to begin my relationship with Countess Cristiana Brandolini, née Agnelli, heiress to the Fiat empire. As I mentioned earlier, acceptance in the Jet Set requires a carefully cultivated charm. Cristiana was to become my first tutor.

Our life-style was an upscale gypsylike existence that seemed almost a social reaction to the postwar, conservative values, as well as disgust with the nuclear age. In a sense, it was a similar reaction to that of the 'Lost Generation' following the First World War, in which characters like Hemingway traveled extensively, orienting his life around the running of the bulls at Pamplona and other such events. The early development of the Jet Set was met with as much scorn as it was with fascination. Perhaps the first article about this phenomenon, and credited with coining the term 'Jet Set,' was written in 1965 by the Italian intellectual and author, Alberto Moravia. He defined the Jet Set as 'a group of parasites who should all be placed on an island and uniformly annihilated with the exception of one young man from Naples named Massimo.' Although I was grateful that Alberto saw fit to spare my life, I was disturbed by the hatred that the Jet Set seemed to generate from some spheres.

Although the early 1960s brought the development of an extensive travel itinerary, the Jet Set was at this time still very homogeneous in its social structure. The guest list of most parties contained the same names one might have found in a prewar social register or the first-class lounge of the *Titanic*. There were, of course, exceptions to this. The most notable non-aristocratic/non-industrialist member was Greta Garbo. Strangely, her acceptance into the Jet Set was not because she was a great movie star, but because she was Greta Garbo. Her very eccentric behavior not only appealed to the Jet Set, it even intimidated it. Although completely disinterested in her own influence, Garbo was a trendsetter.

She was adopted by Cécile de Rothschild, as was I, and became an unpredictable and sporadic member of the Jet Set. Garbo's inherent behavior greatly influenced the style of the group. She naturally embodied characteristics that were admired and often copied. I was lucky to witness these qualities firsthand as a result of my great fortune to have enjoyed a relationship with this truly unique lady.

Vulgar displays of wealth were never encouraged within European high society, but Garbo carried her notions of minimalism to a new extreme. She wore absolutely no jewelry, no makeup, and an androgynous uniform consisting of gray trousers and a simple blouse or turtleneck sweater. It was a very poignant statement. In addition to her understated wardrobe, Garbo was essentially rather stingy. Her frugal existence was construed to imply a distaste for ostentatious wealth, a scorn for showiness. Her contemporaries began to become apologetic of any show of splendor and either toned down their appearance or tried to understate their possessions. Those like Marella Agnelli, who sent teams of jewelers around the globe to search for matching rubies, pretended to have 'picked up the little things in a bazaar in India.' Collections of Picassos were described as 'a couple of modern paintings,' while Marie-Héléne de Rothschild's palatial country mansion would be depicted as a 'little cottage.'

The repercussions were widespread. The most chic hostesses began to serve the fewest courses and the smallest servings. Smaller parties with more exclusive guests were preferred. Understated quality instead of lavishness was the ideal. Less was definitely more.

Garbo pretended to neither know nor remember anyone. When trying to describe to her where we were going or whom we would see, regardless of the person's notoriety, Garbo would invariably ask, 'who is he?' in her lyrical, mystified way. If you responded with surprise, she would simply add, 'I know nobody. I only know three or four people.' Whether real or contrived, this translated to the ultimate degree of chic snobbery. The most pretentious people were simply destroyed by her innocent question of 'who are you?' It implied that one is so important that one really does not have the time or interest to keep track of anyone else. This, too, would set a trend. Dropping names was now decidedly gauche. On the contrary, one had to feign nonrecognition of the most famous names.

Finally, Garbo went out of her way to discourage the use of even her own name. Except in our most intimate moments, Garbo, who truly disliked the name Greta, would insist on being called Miss. G. Coming from the ultrasnob, this, too, set a trend. It was understood that the really important people were to be called something else or be given an abbreviated nickname. For example, His Royal Highness Karim Aga Khan was known as 'K,' while Gianni Agnelli went by the nickname of 'L'Avvocato' (the lawyer). The most significant person in the next step of the evolution of the Jet

Set was therefore to be known simply as Ari.

Aristotle Socrates Onassis was peculiar in a number of ways. Unlike the former industrial members of the Jet Set, he was a self-made tycoon of very recent vintage. Onassis is the most prominent of a number of the Greek tycoons known as 'the Golden Greeks' who began to infiltrate the Jet Set in the mid-1950s and actually achieved social acceptance and prominence in the 1960s. By the mid-1960s when I became acquainted with Onassis and his girl-friend, the opera star Maria Callas, he had achieved a level of personal sophistication and social respectability that left no question that he belonged in the center of the most exclusive society. But in the early days, Onassis lacked the sophistication that was generally required and compensated with a degree of lavishness that was previously unknown.

Perhaps the best example of his extravagant imagination was the creation of the definitive luxury yacht, the *Christina*. The ship was a sixteen-hundred-ton Canadian frigate called the *Stormont* when Onassis bought her for $ 45,000. He sent her to the finest German architects and designers in 1954, and $6 million later, picked up the most decadently beautiful yacht in the world. A crew of fifty served the needs of this floating pleasure palace, which featured a swimming pool that could be raised to create a dance floor, an English-style paneled study with a lapis-lazuli fireplace, solid-gold faucets in the bathrooms, and old-master paintings on every wall. In honor of Onassis's whale-fishing fleet, he had the bar stools constructed from various whale parts. The footrests were massive whale teeth, while the enormous mammals were encouraged to sacrifice their foreskins for the honor of upholstering the stools. This allowed the eccentric Greek to enjoy his joke of asking elegant socialites if they knew they were sitting on the largest penis in the world.

In addition to filling the yacht with every imaginable luxury, Onassis was equally extravagant with his choice of guests. Soon Greta Garbo became a frequent passenger. What could it mean? The Queen of Minimalism befriended by the King of Ostentation? Such a riddle was not to be ignored by the astonished Jet Set. Cautiously other members began to visit Onassis, as secretly as they could manage it. There they discovered bizarre spectacles such as Garbo playing cards with Winston Churchill and Cécile de Rothschild. If this were not amazing enough, it seemed that the *Christina* was the venue of an increasing number of historic introductions. Among the more memorable meetings was that of the young Senator John Kennedy and his wife, Jackie, who came for a short visit to meet Churchill. Noticing Churchill's lack of enthusiasm, Jackie told her husband that perhaps the great prime minister had thought he was a waiter. In 1952, Onassis made a decision that set a chain of events in motion that was to forever alter the structure of the Jet Set as well as Onassis's position within it.

As a young refugee, Onassis had passed the

magical port of Monte Carlo on his journey to freedom. It was a place that held great sentimental value for him, and he wished to restore it to its former splendor. In the early 1950s, he began to quietly buy an interest in the rather unprofitable Societé des Bains de Mer. He arranged to meet the recently crowned Prince Rainier III, a descendant of the original Grimaldi princes who, disguised as monks, had captured the Rock of Monte Carlo in 1291. The two men hit it off, and with Rainier's consent, Onassis obtained controlling interests in the SBM by 1952.

Onassis had great plans for the rebirth of Monte Carlo. Yet by 1954, he was still dissatisfied with the profitability of the SBM. Onassis decided that what Rainier needed was a charismatic American movie star to be his wife and the princess of their fairytale land. Aboard the *Christina*, Onassis hatched his plan and confided it to Greta Garbo and her boyfriend, George Schlee.

Accepting this as an Onassis commission, Schlee returned to America and began searching for the appropriate bride. Amusingly, one of his ports of call was Marilyn Monroe, who was visiting friends in Connecticut. Monroe was intrigued and dubbing the monarch 'Prince Reindeer,' suggested that a romantic weekend be scheduled prior to matrimonial decisions.

Also in 1954 two events were occurring in parallel. Alfred Hitchcock was conducting on-location filming of his Jet Set tale *To Catch a Thief*, starring Cary Grant and Grace Kelly.

19

Concurrently the formerly staid and somewhat unnoticed Cannes Film Festival heated up when the French actress Simone Sylva removed her bikini top and startled actor Robert Mitchum. The south of France was finally being noticed by the American public. During the filming of *To Catch a Thief*, *Paris Match* was cooperative enough to persuade Grace Kelly to pose for a photo shoot at Grimaldi Palace with Prince Rainier. Were Onassis to have drawn up specifications for the requirements he had defined for Prince Rainier's bride, he could not have met them any closer than with Grace Kelly. Gorgeous in an elegant, cool way, she possessed breeding, charm, intelligence, and an ice-queen sensuality. It was small wonder that Rainier became enchanted, and a correspondence developed that resulted in their engagement.

Now the newly discovered south of France was the topic of American attention. The final stages of the courtship, the cruise from New York to Monaco, and the ensuing wedding were the most highly covered news events of the day. The wedding itself received the largest television coverage up to that time. MGM even got permission to have the civil ceremony done a second time for their cameras. Fashion magazines competed to define the Grace Kelly look. NBC added Monte Carlo time to their studio clocks. Grace's mother, Margaret Kelly, wrote a series of articles that ended with her encouraging belief that any nice American girl could find her prince.

America was enthralled, the world was

charmed, and the Jet Set now had its first family.

As Onassis cleverly predicted, the selection of an American movie star changed the complexion of Monte Carlo. Changes were swift and significant. Tourism increased dramatically, and the revenues of the SBM grew steadily. Prince Rainier was so delighted with his wife's success that in 1958 he appointed her chairman of the Monte Carlo Red Cross. This was significant in the world of the Jet Set.

Grace turned the Red Cross Ball into the premier social event of the Riviera. She invited swarms of Hollywood stars like David Niven, Sammy Davis, Jr., Cary Grant, and Frank Sinatra. It was truly the direct result of this event that movie stars became regarded as members of the Jet Set. Before this, Garbo was the exception. Grace Kelly altered the closed society of the Jet Set as effectively as if she had called out the Monte Carlo National Guard (if one had existed) to desegregate the pompous Hotel de Paris. She created a trend that would continue and eventually completely alter the configuration of the Jet Set.

One of Grace's best friends was Countess Donina Cicogna. I had the privilege of living for many years with Donina during which time we spent a great part of each year in Monte Carlo. By virtue of this relationship, I was able to watch the evolutionary process that Grace Kelly had begun in 1958 as it continued on its own steam. By the midsixties, it would have been unusual not to find at least one movie star at a Jet Set party. In fact this trend was to continue throughout the next decade until the overall mixture at the parties began to reflect an acceptance of outstanding people (or as some put it, of 'international protagonists.')

The social changes precipitated by Grace Kelly were not simply limited to the constellation of the Jet Set. After having to deal with six thousand journalists during their 1956 wedding, Prince Rainier and Princess Grace decided that they would control the future press coverage of their children. They naively believed that if they granted two intimate personal interviews each year regarding the development of their family, they would be able to accommodate the public's curiosity while still maintaining privacy. This proved to be a fallacy. The public wanted intimate details of the Grimaldi family life and royal life in general. Teased by the bi-yearly interviews, they hungered for more.

In the past, most European countries that still maintained royal families controlled press coverage. A prime example was the Duke of Windsor's relationship with the American divorcée, Wallis Simpson, when he was the Prince of Wales. Although the world press was writing voluminous stories about the affair and even managed to publish a picture of the two in Villa D'Este on Lake Como, the English press staunchly remained silent. Even today, countries like Holland and Sweden try to control the press invasions into the lives of their royal families. The trend to increase the degree of observation that now borders on espionage was begun by the Grimaldi attempt to control the media.

What began innocently enough in 1957 with the birth of Princess Caroline of Monaco would continue to the point where the press would become the battlefield on which royal families would act out their personal wars. Charles and Diana — the Prince and Princess of Wales — were the most extreme example. Granting a number of private interviews and even individually appearing on national television, both the prince and princess individually appealed to the world to pardon their errors, excuse their infidelities, and side with one against the other. This 'War of the Tabloids' was won by the Princess of Wales. The extreme accessibility of the private lives of the royals added to the popularization of high society and Jet Set life.

Nothing was off limits. The public hungered for and received transcripts of private telephone conversations, confessions of the royal wish to be used as a tampon, and even photos of untimely death. The world of the Jet Set was to become a global soap opera. Far from the discreet aristocrats and industrialists who had initially dominated the Jet Set, the players of the developing Jet Set were to become an increasingly diverse group of protagonists on an obsessively watched world stage.

The road to the desegregation of the Jet Set that resulted in the culturally multifaceted group of today might have begun with the acceptance of particularly sophisticated movie stars, but other groups were soon to challenge the restrictions of the socialites. Outstanding intellectuals were historically sprinkled in the parties of the Jet Set. They were chic to have around, perhaps as a reminder of the café society days. But one very special intellectual was to go one step further than allowing herself to be the token genius. Françoise Sagan, the woman who shocked the world by writing *Bonjour Tristesse* at the age of eighteen, attacked and changed the configuration of the Jet Set with a subtle, yet militant intellectualism. She simply created an alternative social structure, which was to subtly taunt and eventually alter the Jet Set. It was called la bande Sagan.

La bande Sagan was composed of a diverse group, which included Yves St. Laurent, Bettina Graziani (girlfriend of Ali Khan), movie director Roger Vadim (who discovered and married Brigitte Bardot, Catherine Deneuve, and Jane Fonda), the dashing playboy Porfirio Rubirosa, Helene Rochas (owner of the cosmetics house), Genevieve Fath (wife of the famous designer), Juliette Greco (girlfriend of Darryl F. Zanuck), and the famous model Annabelle. For a time, this group of socialites, intellectuals, and artists was virtually inseparable and spent their evenings in Paris at the entrance of Regine's Jet Set hangout called Jimmy's — apparently too chic to actually enter.

This movement predated the social acceptance of the majority of the groups represented by its members and constituted an avant-garde movement. The ability to create social change should come as no surprise to those like myself who had the privilege of enjoying a relationship with Sagan. A woman who as a teenager was able to paint the definitive picture of Parisian life while directly influencing the evolution of the novel was not a person who necessarily had great patience for social pretensions. By creating a stylish group with even more restrictive entry than the Jet Set, she mocked the socialites with an intellectual and artistic snobbery that at once threatened and fascinated them. For many years, la bande Sagan was to be seen at many of the haunts of the Jet Set, never really entering the room, but waiting tauntingly at the entrance content with their own company. In a sense, it was gang warfare. It predated, but foreshadowed the next step in the development and integration of the Jet Set.

By the late 1960s, the once homogenous Jet Set had been out-snobbed by Garbo, inundated with Hollywood stars transplanted by Grace Kelly, reluctantly wined and dined by Onassis, and pursued by a more invasive press. They had faced the nightly tauntings by la bande Sagan and now were shell shocked enough for even further liberalization.

In the past, fashion designers had been the people who simply made one's clothes. But by the midsixties, the great fashion designers were becoming stars on the world stage. And perhaps even more significantly, they were becoming very rich. Of course, there were always some exceptions. Oleg Cassini boasted an aristocratic background, and as a former fiancée of Grace Kelly and confidant to Jackie Kennedy, certainly was accepted in the highest circles as early as the midfifties. Givenchy was very sophisticated and through his friendships with important people including Audrey Hepburn, was often seen at elegant parties. And we could devote an entire book to the social and amorous exploits of Coco Chanel. But they were notable exceptions. For the most part, future fashion icons like Valentino were sewing their own creations in the sitting rooms of their two-room walk-up apartments and not mingling socially with the Jet Set.

Slowly, this began to change. In addition to a now-wealthy, famous, more-glamorous image, the designers (and finally even their models) began to participate in a newly emerging social phenomenon. A number of after-hours clubs had opened that provided a mixing ground for a variety of formerly isolated groups. The most famous among the clubs of the 1970s was Studio 54 in New York. Here one would find a truly bizarre mixture. The club was a social blender. Debutantes and society people mixed with movie stars, designers, and the newest cult hero, the supermodel.

It was not easy to get in, so it still allowed a certain necessary feeling of exclusivity. Once inside, the next hurdle was to be admitted into the VIP area. Inside the enormous space of Studio 54, a new wave of Jet Setters was cross-pollinating — literally. In the dark mezzanine, many sexual trysts were consummated in this pre-AIDS era, while the *Metropolis*-like basement was the chosen location for partaking of the new flavor of the month — cocaine. Drug use reduced the social barriers to an even-greater degree. The combination of sex, drugs, and alcohol with every form of celebrity created a carnival-like atmosphere that had gotten out of hand by the late 1970s.

Within this strange world, roamed such characters as Andy Warhol — silently chronicling it all with his Polaroid and tape recorder. (I still have the signed Polaroid he snapped of me.) One would see writers such as Truman Capote mixing with fashion stars like Halston and Calvin Klein. Actors would be talking to debutantes like Cornelia Guest.

Now fame and not family name was the price of membership. A form of status inflation began to occur in the ensuing frenzy for fame-induced social acceptance. Everyone who made a TV commercial was a star. Each pretty girl was a supermodel. And of course, those who purchased a Concorde ticket were Jet Setters. One lost track of a real sense of a social aesthetic. Elegance had died of an overdose of cocaine. Manners were the things one's parents had employed. It was in this melee that I decided to create some mechanism in which the endangered concept of elegance could be somehow preserved. Eleanor Lambert had long published her list of ten best-dressed people. I believed that were the criterion to be expanded and internationalized, one could identify the people who overall demonstrated the best elegance in their total life-style. I thought that like la bande Sagan, such a group would be a living reminder and also a challenge against a social liberalization that I felt had gotten out of control.

In 1976, I established *The Best* Award. As opposed to the haphazard way that best-dressed awards were determined, I opted for the creation of an international jury comprised of the presidents of the French and Italian fashion syndicates as well as a selection of personalities whom I felt represented the best of what the Jet Set could be. These people included Pierre Cardin, Hubert de Givenchy, Claude Montana, Gina Lollobrigida, Ursula Andress, Princess Marina de Savoy, Duchess d'Orléans, Franco Zeffirelli, Françoise Sagan, Roger Peyrefitte, Buzz Aldrin (anticipating the Rocket Set), Roman Polanski, Princess Soraya, Krizia, Duchesse de la Rochefoucauld, Alberto Sordi, and Ivana Trump.

Social change is cyclical, and the elegance that once dominated the life of the Jet Set will experience a form of renaissance in the next century. The problem that will be faced in the further evolution of elegant society might be the rediscovery of an almost extinct and yet very intricate system of behavior. Perhaps it will be necessary to redefine etiquette in the computer age. Maybe we have so outgrown Emily Post's concepts of politeness that we must create rules to govern modern questions ranging from the appropriate time and place to use a mobile phone to the polite, but insistent demand for safe sex. The creation of an award for the best members of the Jet Set and my magazine *The Best* has been my effort to perpetuate the social aesthetic that we once enjoyed. Naturally the members of the social elite need to use their power and the prestige to support worthy causes and not simply to search endless sources of personal pleasure.

I have provided you with this background so you can listen to the story of my life inside this group without being interrupted by the need to explain the historical context of the experiences. Each of the characters I have so far mentioned plays some role, major or minor, in the story you are about to read.

2

GRETA GARBO: LESS THAN A MIRACLE

Even among the most rarified circles of high society, there is an accepted hierarchy in which some names take on almost mythical proportions. Each country has its famous families and cultural icons. Throughout the Western World, one of the names that has held the most magic has been that of the Rothschilds. It was my good fortune to become intimately acquainted with the most senior members of this family.

By virtue of this relationship, I would be guided through invisible portals into an inner sanctum of power and intrigue. I would come to learn of the extraordinary interconnections of the elite that transcend national boundaries and define their own morality. I would acquire wealth, prestige, and all the trappings of superficial success. The price of these treasures was to be the loss of something one does not even miss until it is irretrievably gone.

It all started in Capri in the early sixties when I was befriended by Pierre Cardin. I was only twenty-four years old and was considered to be handsome, and having completed a doctorate in law, it was generally assumed that I would be clever enough not to embarrass powerful friends.

As a result, I was considered to be more than just one of the many pretty faces that are found at the periphery of the Jet Set.

During my early years of attempting the elusive entry into the ranks of this rarified crowd, I had the good fortune to begin a close relationship with the owners of Fiat — the Agnelli family. Gianni, the prototype European tycoon, took a liking to me, and his sister, Cristiana, became a close friend. Now with powerful sponsors, I was able to receive invitations to the most exclusive balls in which the Jet Set plays out its ritualistic scenarios. For me, the embarkation point into the inner sanctum of the world elite occurred in Portugal at the Patiño Ball. It was here in 1968 that I would meet one of the most powerful matriarchs of European high society, Baroness Cécile de Rothschild, the sister of Élie and the cousin of Guy de Rothschild.

Although enormously wealthy, elegant, and still very beautiful at sixty years, she remained unmarried. She had by this time somewhat withdrawn from the Parisian social world and occupied herself with acquiring one of the finest private art collections in the world. Her eighteenth-century mansion in Paris at Faubourg St. Honoré, adjacent to the gardens of the British Embassy, was filled with antique furniture. The walls were crowded with paintings by Goya, Gauguin, and Picasso. Yet in a sense, it was an empty, lonely house. Like the powerful, but pitiful Miss Havisham in *Great Expectations*, Cécile was trapped in decaying splendor

31

and the memories of lost love. Once engaged to a powerful and handsome prince, Cécile ended the relationship as a result of her fiancé's decision not to convert to Judaism and Cécile's fear of her family's reaction to marrying a Catholic.

I welcomed the patronage of my benefactor, who was very generous with her tutelage, and eagerly accepted her introductions to art, music, culture, and other socialites. She seemed to enjoy the role of teaching me and introducing me to the cultural world. I'm sure she enjoyed being seen with me in public for she began to reenter society with me always on her arm.

I pursued her friendship with great resolve, and after six months, we became sexually intimate. At that time, I could perform several times a day, and I loved to exercise my sexual power over women. It excited me to see how aroused I could get them. As a result, the stimulation that I felt at my use of power was a genuine sexual response that was quite flattering to a sixty-year-old woman. Our friendship was a relaxed one without pressure or jealousy, and the sexual component was always secondary to the over-riding theme of the relationship, which was one in which Cécile tried to mold and refine me.

For my part, I tried consciously not to fall into the pattern of a standard gigolo. Although I accepted gifts from her, I did not let her support me. After father died in 1966, I inherited enough money to live independently for at least a limited time. I was fascinated with the society in which I was becoming more and more accepted, and I was totally obsessed with climbing ever further up the social ladder. In this respect, I was willing to use Cécile and any others who might be useful, but I knew that if I began to accept support from such people, I would sacrifice acceptance in their world. So I contented myself in being Cécile's escort at cultural exhibitions where she explained the significance of the various works of art, and to restaurants where she taught me how to select wines, and at parties where she showed me how to interact with intellectuals. She enjoyed the role of teacher in many ways, and it became almost a ritual of seduction for her to guide me through art and literature and then back to one of her fabulous homes.

Our sex life often incorporated ingredients that I had formerly associated with love between women while the more conventional act was invariably mechanical and cold. So it came as no big surprise when she confessed that she was often attracted to other women. However, I was shocked to discover that her greatest love was none other than Greta Garbo. This fascinated me.

Despite my devoted participation in the full travel circuit of the Jet Set for the past several years, I had never seen her once. Garbo, understated in all things, even displayed minimalism in her appearances. Garbo spottings were similar to sightings of the Loch Ness monster. One never could be quite sure. Since the fifties, her primary mode of transport within the world of the Jet Set was on Onassis's floating palace, the *Christina*. Thus was her beloved privacy protected.

Ensconced in one of his six palatial staterooms named after the Greek islands (she preferred Lesbos), Onassis respected and protected her need for complete isolation. She would suddenly appear at a formal party in Monte Carlo calling herself Mrs. Smith. Clad in a simple black dress and sandals with not a single piece of jewelry, she would taunt and shame the overdressed bejeweled socialites. Then a tiny photo of her would appear playing cards with Winston Churchill, and the world would be in a frenzy of speculation.

Her irregular participation in the life of the Jet Set was pure Garbo. It led to expectation, speculation, and most of all adulation — because it implied that she was too good for us. We who would not truly welcome movie stars into our ranks until the mid-sixties were falling over ourselves to get Garbo to participate in any function she might consider and under any terms she chose. Without ever consciously flexing her muscles, Garbo was an icon and a trendsetter among us, and I had to meet her.

At this point, Garbo was in one of her more extreme reclusive periods. She saw almost nobody and refused all invitations. Nevertheless she frequently visited Cécile in Paris and every summer would accompany Cécile on Élie de Rothschild's yacht, the *Bibo*, for several weeks in the Mediterranean. When I learned this, I begged Cécile to introduce us.

'It simply is not possible, Massimo. She

34

refuses to meet new people,' Cécile replied firmly.

I was unwilling to accept this for an answer. I was determined to become a collector of celebrities, and I was not about to lose the opportunity for this rare specimen. In fact I had always had a great desire specifically to meet the elusive Garbo, and I insisted that Cécile at least try. Cécile finally conceded. 'All right, I will arrange a tea and invite her. I simply will not tell her in advance that anyone else will be in the room. When she enters and sees you Massimo, we will see what happens. I cannot promise anything more than that.'

Several days later, Cécile called to invite me to tea at her Paris home. I arrived at five and sat down across from her in her drawing room, with the tea service already set out in front of our sofa. Someone knocked on the door, and Cécile got up to open it herself. I will never forget my first glimpse of Garbo. She did not so much enter the room as she made the entrance of a queen. Her demeanor was so regal and overpowering that it took a second glance to realize that she was actually a rather small woman. She wore what I was to learn was her standard garb: gray trousers (of which she possessed twenty identical pairs), a gray Korean jacket, and flat shoes — almost moccasins.

In her hand, she carried a cigarette in a long holder. Her hair was pulled back severely in a bun, accentuating the dramatic bone structure of a face she felt required no makeup. She strolled in and froze when she realized that Cécile was not the only one in the room.

'Oh, I am sorry, I will go,' she announced as if she were interrupting something private.

'No, no stay, you must stay,' replied Cécile reaching out toward her.

It was clear that Garbo was torn. She looked at me then at Cécile, and although she did not withdraw, she said in a tone of fear mixed with curiosity, 'Oh no I can't, I can't . . . ' Cécile grabbed hold of her and exclaimed, 'You stay!'

She responded pathetically in a small voice, 'OK . . . ' and sat down. She regarded me silently for a few seconds then asked, 'Who *are* you?'

It is difficult to describe how much cuteness and vulnerability can be conveyed with such a simple phrase. Perhaps it is in the Garbo intonation, the way her voice lifted and lingered with wonder in the middle of the phrase. The way she made the word 'are' hold such music and such expectation.

I was surprisingly relaxed and decided to try to keep the conversation light, so I simply responded, 'I am a person from Naples.'

I did not intend this to sound enigmatic, but I believe it was just the mystery of promising her that I was 'a person' that seemed to answer the longing of her pathetic question. She immediately brightened up and became quite animated. 'Naples in Italy,' she exclaimed with excitement, then paused for a second to consider this and added suspiciously, 'which Naples?' apparently concerned that I might have meant Naples, Florida.

I immediately acknowledged that it was indeed the Italian Naples, at which point she bent her head to one side, raising her eyebrows as she smiled and sang, 'Ooohh, I love Naples.' She paused as if she were inventorying her beautiful Neapolitan memories, then added, 'I was there four years ago with a Greek friend.'

'Oh yes. You were with Ari,' supplied Cécile.

'Yes,' agreed Garbo. 'We sailed to a beautiful little harbor filled with fishing boats and many little boys.'

'That is just across from the street where I was born, in Mergellina,' I exclaimed.

I told her how I would often take my dinghy out into the harbor, and perhaps I was one of the boys she had seen. We talked for almost an hour about Italy before she asked, 'Why are you in Paris?' I laughed and responded that 'it is great to be born in Naples, but much better to live in Paris.' She looked at me appraisingly then asked, 'Do you work?' and seemed pleased when I told her that I did not. She gave me another of her rare smiles and said she had to leave.

The next day, an excited Cécile called and said, 'It was a great success, in fact it was a miracle.' I knew that it had gone well, but it would have been just as possible that I never heard another word about that afternoon. 'Massimo, she thinks you are charming,' Cécile said, 'and that you are the most beautiful young man she has seen for many years.'

Then came the shocker. 'She is coming with me to my home in Saint-Raphaël and perhaps you can join us for the weekend.' This was more than I hoped was possible. After one meeting, I had somehow penetrated the barrier of the world's most pursued recluse. This was truly happy news. I canceled my existing plans and drove to the south of France. It would turn out to be something more than a weekend and something less than a miracle.

It was a long drive, and I arrived in time to have dinner with Cécile and Garbo. I joined them in the dining room at seven. They were seated, waiting for me. Garbo was dressed almost exactly as she had been during our first meeting with one exception. In place of her gray Korean jacket, she now wore a gray high-neck sweater that covered her wrists and even part of her hands. She was forever freezing. Perhaps in my honor, she had let her hair down. It curved at the sides and came down to her neck in the back.

Again she wore absolutely no makeup. She was sixty-four years old at this time and looked absolutely beautiful — almost childlike as she smiled shyly at me. The two women were drinking, and I soon learned the Garbo alcohol ritual — whiskey before and after dinner with wine sandwiched in during the meal. Garbo refused to go to restaurants, and so it was planned that we would take all our meals at home.

What was supposed to be a three-day weekend lasted ten days. Each day I was drawn more deeply into Garbo's quiet, strange world with its endless ritualization of her unreal existence, and each night we would somberly eat dinner at seven so that Garbo could go to bed by nine, 'or the Sandman won't come.'

She invited me to join her on her walks each morning and each afternoon. Although I accompanied her on the afternoon walks, I initially declined those in the morning, as I would go out to St. Tropez at night after the ladies had gone to bed. These were long walks that lasted up to three hours in which we would talk about everything but the past.

Discussion of her former life was taboo. She was fascinated with nature and would stand silently for long periods of time admiring the coloring of the sky at sunset or regarding a particular flower. She would get excited when she saw animals and at one point spent fifteen minutes stroking a horse.

When I mentioned this to Cécile, she told me that it's a good thing we were not in Switzerland where there were cows. Apparently Garbo would caress the cows and speak softly to them for hours. Garbo seemed to enjoy an almost-enchanted relationship with animals of all kinds as if she were a pure force of nature to which they were drawn. Insects would sometimes fly onto her hand and seemed completely unafraid of her. Even if she were to gently close her hand, they would remain contently after she opened it again.

During these walks, Garbo showed great interest in what I did after she went to bed. 'What have you done yesterday night?' she would ask each afternoon. She would be hungry for every detail and would sometimes cry out 'how I love the lights of St. Tropez . . . oh, and young people . . . and how I love to dance.' It was as if she was paralyzed and could only live vicariously through my experiences.

She was a good listener and seemed to hang on each word I said. Yet she certainly was not afraid of long periods of silence, either. What I soon realized is that she detested forced small talk and had no interest in gossip. She enjoyed listening to me recall my youth in Naples. I amused her with stories of the famed Neapolitan propensity to act macho and street smart. You see, although I pretended to be both these things, she saw right through it and enjoyed her cleverness. I think Garbo was more comfortable with the company of women in a social as well as a sexual sense. But when she did choose to be with men, they seemed to fall into one of two very different categories. She wanted either a man who completely dominated and controlled her or someone with whom she could be completely at ease. I guess I belonged to the second category, and she got a great laugh out of any attempt I made to pretend that I belonged to the first. I found it was easy to talk to her about myself. It filled the void in our conversations left by her decision to never speak of her own past.

As the weekend ended, there was no mention of returning to Paris and no possibility of leaving the house. I was reminded of the film *Sunset Boulevard*, and in my imagination I began to feel as if I were trapped in a strange world inhabited by both Norma Desmond as well as Miss Havisham. After several days, I received a call from my friend, Princess Ismene Chigi, who was staying at the nearby Metropole Hotel at Beaulieu with her wealthy boyfriend. She was about to throw a party and invited me. 'I would love to come,' I admitted, 'but I really can't leave Saint-Raphaël because I am with Greta Garbo.'

I could hear her laughter immediately. 'Oh come on Massimo! I don't believe that. If it's true, why not bring her along?'

'Are you crazy?' I replied. 'You know she never goes out to parties. It's not possible.'

Ismene was skeptical, but practical. 'Massimo, I will bet you ten thousand dollars that you can't bring her to lunch tomorrow.'

Now this was a lot of money in 1969, and I was sorely tempted. The money was certainly an attraction, but also I wanted to somehow break the spell that was holding us all captive. I decided to try to persuade Garbo, but felt that imagination as opposed to pleading would be the only chance for success. So I embellished upon the situation to appeal to those elements of Garbo's personality that I had learned about during our arduous walks and guarded conversations. Greta Garbo loved a good love story, and if the story involved a beautiful princess, all the better.

In this particular case, another element was in my favor. For many years, Garbo's best friends were a married couple. The woman, a famous and very beautiful designer named Valentina, had been one of the great loves of Garbo's life. A beautiful Russian aristocrat with blonde hair flowing down to her ankles, Valentina was an imposing sight. She emigrated from Russia at a young age and married an unattractive and controlling older man named George Schlee. The Schlees adopted Garbo, and the three remained virtually inseparable, often seen in public with the women dressed identically, attached to either arm of the small, but gloating Schlee. To this day, great speculation exists as to the nature of their relationship. Most people assume it to have been a sexual threesome, but the diminutive and unattractive Schlee did not strike me as the type of man to have pulled it off.

It was the Schlees, in fact, who persuaded Garbo to purchase a seven-room apartment in their building on Fifty-second Street in Manhattan. Somehow the ménage got out of hand, and Mr. Schlee, who apparently was smitten, left his wife to devote himself to Garbo. For the rest of their lives, the two women no longer spoke to each other and would actually call down to have the concierge of their building make sure that the other was not standing in the lobby before even leaving their respective apartments.

George bought a fifteen-room villa called le Roc for Garbo and himself in Cap d'Ail (which literally means Cape of Garlic), which he filled with her favorite works of art. He took charge of her business and personal life to a degree that most people would have found claustrophobic. Garbo seemed to love being so controlled and obeyed his every command. Perhaps it reminded her of her early career when she was created and controlled by the eccentric, but strong-minded silent-movie director, Mauritz Stiller. In any case, Schlee remained true to his plan and devoted himself entirely to her happiness for the rest of his life, which unfortunately was shorter than anyone expected.

One evening in the fall of 1964, Schlee and Garbo were dining with Cécile in Paris when Schlee began to feel ill. Returning to their hotel, Garbo suggested that a walk might be helpful. Unfortunately, Garbo's elixir for long life did nothing but shorten George's, who collapsed with a heart attack. He died that night, and Garbo disappeared, spirited away in the Rothschild private plane — leaving Schlee's estranged wife to deal with the final arrangements. I thought it odd that Garbo would react in such a way. Unfortunately for me, it would prove to be a pattern.

Valentina flew to Paris for her husband's body and testament. As it turned out, the Cap d'Ail house as well as a great deal of Garbo's art collection had been registered in the name of George Schlee. The vengeful Valentina immediately ordered the house off limits to Garbo and spent the next several months 'exorcising' it from 'the vampire.' She had all of Garbo's photos, antiques, clothing, and memorabilia removed from the house then burned. When she had completed the purge to her satisfaction, she sold the house where Garbo had known some happiness. This very house was virtually within eyeshot of the Metropole Hotel.

That evening after Garbo had begun to drink heavily, I told my story about the beautiful Roman princess. I related her doomed marriage to an Italian prince — of the vulgar variety — and how she finally left him in despair and was staying of all places in the Metropole Hotel. 'Is it not a funny world, really?' I mused. The story of the princess's various ordeals held Garbo's interest, and when I got to the Metropole Hotel, she sighed and said, 'The Metropole, I could almost see it from my house . . . I used to sail there sometimes from my house . . . could we go and look at it?'

'Of course,' I answered. 'Princess Ismene has a beautiful boat, and we could cruise by the house and have lunch afterward.'

Garbo looked at me in that confused uncertain way and said, 'Oh no, I can't go back to the Metropole. People will see me, they will recognize me, they will torture me . . . '

'Oh no,' I said quickly. 'Nobody will recognize you. We will take my Porsche, and we'll be there in an hour and a half and will board the boat immediately.'

I could tell that she really wanted to go, but the terror she felt was enormous. She began to stroke her face with her hands, pulling downward on her cheeks, and muttered, 'They will recognize my face. It is my curse. They will torture me.'

Cécile joined in with more reassurances, no doubt also pleased with the prospect of getting her friend out of the house. Finally Garbo agreed.

'But you must tell your friends I am someone else or that you are going alone.'

So I called Ismene from the sitting room

because Garbo wanted to make sure I really did as I was told and said, 'I will arrive tomorrow alone at noon.'

I ran outside, found a telephone booth, and called to say, 'I am bringing her along, but be secretive about her identity.'

The next morning, Garbo was nervous, but also excited. She was rather daring with her wardrobe in that she had substituted her usual choice of gray tops with an attractive red blouse that tied at the throat in a ribbon. We decided to leave at ten and drive along the Corniche. It was a beautiful sunny day, and the sky seemed the exact shade as those indescribable eyes on which my attention was riveted. As we drove, I was amazed at how exuberant and vivacious she became. She was so charming and talkative that before I knew it, we had driven past St. Tropez and were entering Italy.

I turned around, but this detour resulted in us being so late that the boat left without us. Thinking fast, I sent the hotel motorboat to look for them and sat with Garbo by the pool. I could sense her mounting terror as she looked around at the strangers nearby. 'They are looking at me. They recognize me,' she began to drone in that shrill whisper she reserved for her attacks of paranoia.

'No, no,' I tried to assure her. 'It is only that you are so well dressed and look so pretty that they are staring. Let's have lunch,' I suggested.

'But if they don't come, we have to pay,' lamented the frugal movie star. 'Do you have money, Massimo?' she asked sheepishly. 'We must eat only little things. It is so expensive here.'

Fortunately my friend's boat appeared, and we were saved further exposure to inquisitive eyes and expensive menus.

Princess Ismene and her lover were amazed, but tried to remain calm and charming. We went on board at once and headed for Garbo's old house. When we were directly in front of it, she asked us if we would mind stopping the boat so she could look at the house once more. We left one sailor on board with instructions to ring the bell when she was finished, and we went to shore and waited. She made quite a sight standing straight with arms crossed in front of her chest and the breeze blowing her hair. It reminded me of that famous scene at the end of *Queen Christina* where she stands at the prow of a boat heading away from her past and her dead lover. I wish I could have seen her eyes to see if they held that same empty stare. Later we asked the sailor, and he said she had been quietly weeping. She remained staring at the house for over half an hour, and the sailor never did get to ring the bell. Finally we returned to the boat and sailed away from Garbo's past and her dead lover. As the house shrunk out of sight, she looked over at us and said, 'Thank you.'

It was time to go back for lunch. 'I can't return to the Metropole for lunch,' she said firmly. 'Let's go to the village and eat at a simple bistro in the harbor.' She suggested that we ask the sailors for their favorite inexpensive restaurant. In the end, we agreed, and although we went to a bistro, we had them send out for fine wines and lobster. She was too good a connoisseur of wine to be fooled by this trick, but she was delighted with the meal. 'Lobster? We eat lobster?' she exclaimed like a child being offered a great treat. 'But it is so expensive,' she remarked.

It was a beautiful sunny day, and we were sitting in the open air drinking the delicious wine and eating our lobster without a care in the world when disaster struck. Three students approached her with paper in hand. 'Miss Garbo, can we have your autograph?' one asked. She reacted as if she were a wife discovered in flagrante delicto. 'No, no,' she cried covering her face. 'I am not what you think, I am not . . . leave me in peace.' Then to us, 'Please, please, take me away from here.' Her reaction brought her to the attention of others who had not yet recognized her, and soon the streets resounded with her name.

We managed to get her back to the hotel where I deposited her in the safety of my car, quickly said good-bye to my friends, and collected the winnings on my bet. On the drive back, she thanked me for what she described as the best day she'd had in many years.

We resumed our secluded routine of daily walks and early nights, but I could tell that the day on board the boat had awakened Garbo's interest in the outside world. She asked me about nightclubs and new dances as if she were slowly recovering from amnesia. I encouraged her reviving interest in the world and decided that she was ready for another outing. My motives rarely have been exclusively altruistic. Nevertheless, I had fallen under her charms and wanted her to have a happier, fuller life. For my part, I welcomed the thought of what being seen as Garbo's consort would do for my reputation. And so, when a second invitation arrived, I was prepared.

That afternoon I received a call from a well-known socialite named Princess Giovanna Pignatelli Aragona Cortez. She was rich, beautiful, and had a taste for beautiful women. News had spread about our previous sojourn at the Metropole, and Giovanna was frantic to have Garbo and me make our first real public appearance at one of the daily parties at her home in St. Tropez. The home was already filled up with such notable houseguests as Soraya, the Shah of Iran's ex-wife, and a number of movie directors and producers.

At tea, I broached this to Garbo who, not surprisingly, reacted with her usual expression of horror and flat refusal. It was quite ironic that a woman who insisted on ignoring her movie-star past would invariably behave so theatrically. Cécile, as always, came to my rescue. She said, 'Come on, darling, it will make Massimo happy.'

Cécile must have already known that making me happy was somehow important to Garbo, who now began to come around. 'A party . . . ,' she mused, 'what time does it start?'

'Tomorrow at nine,' I lied, knowing that Garbo would not be pleased to hear that most parties did not begin until at least ten. 'We should leave here at eight-thirty,' I added hopefully. 'Eight-thirty!' she cried. 'So late . . . we must eat something here first . . . it is so late . . . Massimo, please call her and have her make the party earlier . . . at eight.'

I was delighted with this success and even agreed to go through the motions of making the impossible request of rescheduling a party for 100 people just one day before the event.

Needless to say, our host was ecstatic that we were coming and said that the party could start for us at any time we liked, but her guests would arrive as they had planned.

'Look, Massimo,' she said, 'most of my guests are on their boats all day long and need time to get ready. Even if I could get them to come earlier, there is the possibility that Garbo will not show. Come whenever you like. I don't give a shit!'

I put down the receiver and smiling widely at Garbo and Cécile, announced, 'It is settled. The party will start at eight.'

The next evening, I passed the sitting room on my way to take a nap before the party, and there she sat, nervously waiting. She was dressed in her usual androgynous uniform, but on her head, she wore a black hat that concealed part of her face. She was sitting upright, with a look somewhere between childlike excitement and mortal terror. I glanced at my watch. It was only six o'clock. I dressed quickly and told the ladies that it might be fun to drive into St. Tropez and visit some of the shops before arriving at the party. So we took Cécile's car and drove into town. We began at an exclusive store for women's apparel where Garbo discovered a pretty silk blouse, which in dramatic deviation from the norm was in white. 'Oh, it is so beautiful!' she crooned, stroking it longingly. 'May I try it?' she asked sheepishly.

'Please. You will look beautiful in it,' I encouraged.

I had to wait to know how she would look in it for she remained sequestered alone in the dressing room for close to half an hour in lonely deliberation about the magnitude of such a purchase. When she finally came out, she said sadly, 'It is so beautiful, but too expensive.' Actually, it was about $300, which admittedly was not cheap in 1969, however, was this not the woman for whom the matinee idol John Gilbert built a waterfall?

Despite her protests, I bought the blouse for her, which had several interesting side effects. The immediate reaction was one of disproportionate gratitude. She accepted the blouse with pure disbelief and was not even able to utter her thanks audibly. 'For me?' she whispered. 'I can't, I can't accept this . . . ' She was really only mouthing the words. I insisted that it was nothing and begged her not to make a scandal out of a small gift. For the first time, she touched me and then asked incredulously, 'But how can you spend so much on me?' I thought she must be teasing me, but she was completely serious. It was then that I understood that she simply wished to feel that someone else wanted to look after her, perhaps that she wanted to be kept. It seemed that this role somehow excited her. And this strange excitement was to be her second reaction.

Garbo was so happy after this tiny gesture that I suggested we go to another store. 'Only if you promise that you won't buy me anything else,' she said, again clasping my hand. I agreed to respect her frugality, although I never really understood its source. It is true that when George Schlee died, much of Garbo's wealth, which he'd managed, was lost. It seemed possible that she had very little money left, but it is just as likely that her desire to protect what she had was linked to her terror of having to deal with other human beings. Her apparent thriftiness was so extreme that Cécile took to tipping her own servants on behalf of Garbo. After Garbo's death, I learned that her estate was worth a little more than thirty million dollars of which two-thirds was invested in her art collection and the remainder in stocks and securities. But at that time, I would not have been surprised to learn that her net worth totaled twenty pairs of gray trousers, two sweaters, and now one white blouse.

In the second shop, Garbo found a silk scarf in white and gray. This was a perfect combination between her standard color and tonight's flamboyant choice of white. She picked it up reverently then draped it over her head, pulling the corners over her face, allowing only her eyes to remain exposed. It was as if she found a security blanket in which she could hide from a world that held the constant risk of impending recognition. To her delight, I broke my promise and bought it for her. She accepted it with even more exaggerated gratitude than the first gift, and perhaps even more astonishingly, she had not noticed that it was already nine o'clock.

Cécile's chauffeur was waiting outside the shop and drove us straight to the party. Princess Giovanna was good to her word that the party could begin anytime we arrived, and when we were announced, she came down in her bathrobe to greet us. She introduced us to Princess Soraya before returning upstairs to finish her shower.

Princess Soraya was an interesting and very beautiful woman who would play a large role in my life many years later. At eighteen, this daughter of a Baktiar tribal leader and a German woman became the second wife of the Shah of Iran. Her beauty was legendary as much for its coldness as its perfection. Together she and the Shah made an imposing and fun-loving couple who skied in Switzerland and threw masked balls in Teheran. Unfortunately, the Shah needed a successor, and Soraya could not conceive. She complained to a specialist that they did it 'four times a night and twice every afternoon . . . still I don't have a baby.'

The Shah divorced her in 1958. From that point on, Soraya became a very active member of the Jet Set, or as one journalist put it, 'the cynosure of all eyes about the empty halls of international pleasure.'

One or two other guests drifted in, and a

movie producer joined us. I watched as Garbo spoke about films for the first time. I was relieved to see that she was still well aware that she was a movie star. We sat in a group of five, the only guests in a huge home elaborately prepared for a large party.

Giovanna told the servants to bring us food right away, and oblivious of the emptiness of the room and blind to its subsequent filling with a growing number of admiring guests, we chatted and listened to Garbo's stories. As one of the conditions for Garbo's visit, it had been agreed that she did not wish to be introduced to the other guests. The guests had apparently been told this, and so they silently gazed at the star without daring to approach our table too closely until the sheer number of other humans in the room aroused her alarm.

'Massimo!' she wailed suddenly. 'So many people! You said there would only be twenty . . . take me home . . . please . . . I am so tired, so tired . . . ' We bid a hasty good night to our group and drove back to Cécile's house where it turned out Garbo was not as tired as she had thought.

Cécile excused herself, leaving Garbo and me alone in the sitting room where we sat drinking whiskey. Clearly Garbo was in a strange state of agitation. The combination of social interaction and receiving gifts from a young admirer had probably reawakened many dormant memories. She joked and laughed allowing her arm to brush against mine. I placed my left arm around her shoulders and drew her against me

53

so that our faces almost touched. As I brought my lips toward her, she leaned away and giggled, 'Stop . . . don't be crazy . . . you are crazy . . . crazy!'

She was laughing and protesting, but her weight still rested against me. I began to kiss her on the lips. I felt her mouth open and her tongue brush against mine — then she pulled away again protesting, 'Massimo, I could be your mother.'

Silently I stood up. Helping her to her feet, I escorted her to the bedroom. At the door, she paused either for effect or out of genuine indecision. Then suddenly she sprang into the room and closed her door. I pushed it open, entered, then slammed it shut behind me. She stood motionless as I embraced her, all the while whispering weakly, 'No, Massimo, no!' until our mouths met with a tentative hunger. We stood there kissing for a moment, and then I began to lead her to the bed.

She stopped me and said, 'Under one condition . . . no light.'

As I fumbled with the curtains, she climbed into bed where she would periodically utter, 'Dark . . . Massimo . . . dark.'

She was not satisfied until I had placed the bedspread over the crack of the door so no light could enter from the hallway. Through the absolute blackness, I fumbled for the bed and the body lying upon it. Kissing her again, I ran my hand along her body. Her breasts were surprisingly small, almost like a young boy, but when I touched her sex, there was no question that she was a very aroused woman. Yet, when I entered her, the act became at once perfunctory. She seemed to take no real pleasure in it, and when it was over, she asked me to leave the room.

3

THE OUTINGS

The next morning, I thought it might be wise to accompany Greta on her morning walk. I dragged myself out of bed at a quarter to six and resigned myself to the three-hour death march that lay ahead. After the events of the previous night and the extraordinary manner in which it ended, I believed that it would be good to discuss our relationship. I had not slept well that night, trying to figure out what really went on in that dark bedroom. I felt pretty sure that she was attracted to me. Yet, why would she demand such darkness that my presence in her bed was completely obscured? And why had she shown such little enthusiasm during the act and then such coldness when we finished? I naively hoped that these questions could be answered this morning.

Greta was ready to begin at six o'clock sharp. Her costume and expression had returned to their usual shades of gray, and she greeted me without a word. We walked slowly through the forest, and finally I tried to break the ice. 'Greta . . . about last night . . . it was . . . '

'Massimo, please!' she interrupted. 'I prefer not to speak of it.'

She had a way of frowning in which you could

almost calculate her degree of annoyance by the number of lines that creased her forehead. At this particular moment, I was confronted by an imposing number of horizontal lines. I was to learn from Cécile that Greta disliked her first name, and the combination of the subject matter as well as my form of address had really made her cringe.

We walked on in silence for the next hour, and finally she began to make the occasional observations of nature that were the hallmark of these expeditions. I tried to reply enthusiastically to each thing she said. Perhaps it seemed contrived for she studied me for a moment then asked, 'Do these walks tire you?' I understood that she was asking if I were bored.

'Not at all,' I responded too quickly.

She raised her eyebrows in a threateningly skeptical arch and even smiled slightly. 'I had to walk much more to win my first girlfriend,' I explained. This seemed to please her. I think it appealed to her interest in love stories while at the same time it implied that she, too, was a girlfriend whom I was trying to win. 'Tell me about her, Massimo,' she asked quickly, and as she did, I realized that her negative mood had been immediately replaced with eager curiosity.

So I began to tell her about my first love. In Naples society, a small ball would be thrown for the society children each weekend. They were called balletti, which literally means 'little balls.' It was a sort of black-tie kindergarten. At one such ball, I met a beautiful nineteen-year old Neapolitan princess named Ianuaria Carafa. I was only thirteen, and to me, she seemed very mature. These harmless, cute dances would begin at 6:00 P.M. and go on for two or three hours. I danced with her and even found myself flirting. The next day, she invited me to meet her mother. As it often turns out in these small circles, her mother had taken a lover who turned out to be one of my best friends. His name was Enzo, and he was only ten years older than I was. Ianuaria's mother was a great dog lover and had five corgies — little dogs favored by the Queen of England. Each morning she would walk the dogs for two hours and each evening for three. Enzo and I would accompany Ianuaria and her mother on these long walks.

My father was pleased that I had made friends with such a notable family and permitted me to visit them in the evenings after the long walks. There, in the great hall of their palace, we would put the newest records on their phonograph, and I would dance cheek to cheek with Ianuaria while Enzo did the same with her mother. After a couple hours of this, some unspoken signal was exchanged and we simply went off to our respective rooms across the hall from each other. It was like a Fellini movie really — a mother and daughter seducing two best friends as if it were the most normal thing in the world.

The first night this occurred, Ianuaria and I were both nervous and pressured by the knowledge that Enzo and her mother were deep in the throes of love. After some nervous kissing, we undressed and finally admitting that we were both virgins, tentatively discovered what was expected in such situations. We continued this strange routine of marathon dog-walking, dancing in the palace, then exploring our bodies and the various possibilities of how to make love. This innocent if somewhat odd situation went on for several weeks, and as a result, my first introduction to love has always carried with it an association with long walks.

After I completed my story, I looked at Garbo to see if she would have any reaction at all. She stood perfectly still and stared at me almost searchingly for a moment as if she were trying to understand something. Then thrusting her head back, she burst into the deepest laughter I had ever heard from her. To this day, I am not exactly sure what she found so amusing about my little story, but at least it broke the ice.

Trying to use this moment of levity to return to more sensitive subjects, I cautiously ventured again into the issue of the night before. 'Well Greta, last night was very enjoyable,' I offered. She seemed to take no notice of this for a moment and then finally admitted that she had enjoyed drinking late in the night with me. Regarding what had followed, she made no comment nor even acknowledged in any way that it had happened.

Upon our return to Cécile's house, we spent the remainder of the day in our normal, self-inflicted state of imprisonment. That night I tried to seduce her, but she showed no interest and at the nine-o'clock witching hour went alone to bed. I was to learn that our sessions of sex would always remain tied to the meager moments of escape from her very private prison and often to some small act of generosity on my part.

I had an event to attend in Paris, and the weekend in the country had already grown to ten days. I bid the ladies good-bye the following day and flew to Paris. The occasion was something I simply would not miss. It was a party thrown in honor of a man I greatly admired — the Duke of Windsor.

The story of how I got to know the Duke is somewhat amusing in that it offers an interesting insight into the question of how one breaks into the Jet Set in the first place. In the early sixties when I entered this society, it was still a place for socialites. A typical party might include as diverse a list of people as an ambassador, a chairman of a foundation, and even a playboy. Yet each of these would invariably come from the same elevated social background. Garbo had created a beachhead in this restrictive structure that would allow the movie-star invasion precipitated by Grace Kelly. But even the early movie stars who were slowly gaining acceptance were extraordinary and very sophisticated people. Audrey Hepburn and David Niven had come from aristocratic families. So one could argue that they were just socialites who happened to be actors. Elizabeth Taylor, like Garbo before her, was so eccentric and interesting that one simply had to invite her. The only other exception was Rita Hayworth. Born of humble origins as Margarita Carmen Cansino of the Dancing Cansinos, she gave up her movie career to marry Ali Khan, the father of Karim, the current Aga Khan. Karim is the forty-ninth descendent of Mohammed, spiritual leader of fifteen million Shia Muslims in twenty countries and one of the richest and most powerful men in the world. Yet these were a mere handful of exceptions to a society that was locked shut with a polite, but resolute snobbery that kept it hermetically sealed.

If one did not come from an immediately recognizable family, one really had to work hard to break in. I believe there were certain ingredients that were important in achieving this. What I have always believed to be the right formula is composed of the following qualities: a gimmick, a patron, persistence, and patience. By gimmick I mean something that would make these very snobby people interested in having you around. For me, it was good looks, the reputation that I was good in bed, and the perception that I was intelligent and sensitive. Other gimmicks such as the great wealth of Onassis and Niarchos, or the enormous intelligence of Sagan, or great success in a particular field have also worked.

Above all, one needs the right patron. The patron is someone of impeccable social status whose judgment is accepted as sound. The patron tutors you, introduces you to society, and acts as a silent guarantor of your social credentials. I was lucky enough to have two great patrons. My first was Countess Cristiana Brandolini, the heiress to the Fiat fortune. Through her I was to meet my second benefactress, Baroness Cécile de Rothschild. It was Cécile who taught me how to identify fine art, select good wines, and understand great literature. But it was Cristiana who instructed me how to behave. If I had to sum up the general principle to what secrets she imparted on how to navigate through the labyrinth of excruciatingly complex, but unwritten social rules, I could do it in one phrase. Cristiana showed me how to pretend to ignore all the things Cécile had taught me to appreciate. The trick is to subtly imply that you are far too sophisticated to openly acknowledge what is so obviously the quality one should naturally expect. In other words, you pretend to be bored with the fantastic things that are presented to you. Garbo would prove to be my post-graduate tutor in this fine art of cultivated ennui. Both my patrons made an effort to introduce me to the Jet Set and high society, and their good names provided me with the unwritten letters of introduction that one needs to obtain invitations.

My final ingredients for acceptance are persistence and patience. I think you can already see my early track record in these categories. I called Cécile daily and visited her frequently for six months before we became intimate. You have witnessed how persistent I was in obtaining the introduction to Garbo and how persistently I tried to push her to make more public appearances (not to mention the private one). This persistence was especially necessary in winning the support of my first patron, which was by no means an easy task.

I met and was befriended by Pierre Cardin in Capri in the early sixties. Cardin invited me to Paris to visit him and was a perfect host. I felt certain that he found me very attractive, but not wanting me to feel that my invitation was representative of anything but simple friendship, I was given the use of his home and servants, and the gentlemanly designer relocated to his second Parisian home. He invited me to one of his shows, and there I spotted Cristiana. I recognized her immediately as the sister of the Fiat tycoon, Gianni Agnelli. We had good eye contact, and she even returned my smile. But when I greeted her later at the doorway, she did not even answer. 'Wait,' I yelled, 'I met you once at a party in your home.' She looked at me doubtfully and kept walking. I simply walked quietly along side her.

'Where are you going?' she finally asked.

'I have nowhere to go,' I answered sadly, but resolutely. Finally, maybe just to break the silence, she offered to let me walk her home.

'May I come in?' I asked.

'No' was the simple answer.

'Then when can I see you again?' I asked, as if she might want to.

'Tomorrow, come for lunch,' she said as the butler slammed her door.

The next day, I called for her at one o'clock to find her Parisian mansion filled with more than 100 people. Later the actress Elsa Martinelli was to make fun of me in her memoirs, recalling that she 'spotted a young Massimo Gargia quietly hiding in the corner.' This, unfortunately, was true, but here is where the patience comes in. I waited in that corner until all the other guests left. I waited until I could be alone with her, and then came the persistence again. Maybe I wore her down, or maybe she was impressed with my stamina, but she agreed to see me again, and we began a relationship that was to last many years.

Through Cristiana, I first met the Duke and Duchess of Windsor at the home of the socialite Countess Jacqueline de Ribes. Here began a comical misunderstanding that would haunt all my future encounters with the charming Duke.

The Duke of Windsor is perhaps best known as the former King Edward VIII who made the astonishing decision to abdicate as the King of England so that he could marry the American divorcée Wallis Simpson to whom he referred as 'the woman I love' during his famous abdication speech. The Queen, at that time, would not tolerate the presence of a divorced woman.

Although I believe he missed England, the Duke seemed comfortable with his nomadic life. I regard him as one of the first Jet Setters. Even as the charming Prince of Wales, he spent the Roaring Twenties and early thirties traveling around attending parties throughout the globe, then sneaking out alone from Buckingham Palace to go to Mayfair nightclubs in the evening. He seemed to be a man of great convictions, and one had to respect the way he stuck to them despite the consequences.

The party was black tie, but this was 1966, and the newest craze was the Nehru jacket. For those who cannot recall this artifact, it was a plain high-collar jacket made popular by the president of India. I chose to wear a black one thinking it would be fashionable — the word at the time was 'mod.' Cristiana was livid with my choice, and to make matters worse, of the hundred guests present, every male wore a tuxedo with one exception. Alexandre, the famous Parisian hairdresser (need I say more?), was also wearing a Nehru jacket — but in gold. I was feeling pretty low when the hostess ushered me over to meet the Duke. 'Your Royal Highness, may I present Mr. Gargia?' she said as she curtsied elegantly.

He was getting old by this time and misunderstood my name to be Garcia, which seemed to cause him great joy. 'Ah, Señor Garcia, you are from Spain I take it,' he said more as a statement than a question. Not wishing to disappoint him, I agreed. Delighted, he immediately jumped into Spanish with a great deal of enthusiasm. Fortunately I spoke Spanish well enough to continue the illusion, but apologized for the rustiness of my native tongue after so many years in other countries. 'I quite understand,' said the gracious duke, 'but don't worry Señor Garcia, we can practice together. I take lessons twice a week you know.'

He was sincere in this offer and remained by my side until I noticed the worried look on the faces of the other guests and the angry look on the face of his wife. The Duchess of Windsor was a petite, but rather forceful woman whom one would be wise not to annoy. The other guests were careful not to anger her, and actually I believed that the gentlemanly duke lived in fear. Cristiana interrupted the Spanish lesson, and the duke went off to mingle with the other guests. She castigated me for monopolizing him to the point where people might misunderstand our mutual interest and that the duchess certainly was not pleased.

With these fond memories in mind, I prepared for the coming evening. I arrived in Paris in the afternoon, and this time chose a conservative tuxedo. I knew most of the people there and was talking to some friends when they suddenly fell silent and looked respectfully over my shoulder. Turning around I saw the gracious Duke. He did not look very well. Nevertheless, he managed a great smile and said in fluent Spanish, 'Why Señor Garcia, what a pleasant surprise!' And so we went through our routine of practicing Spanish together until the duke looking carefully around the room then lowering his voice as if we were co-conspirators whispered that he better move on as the Duchess might wish him to greet some other people.

Sadly, he was soon to become very ill and with the same courage that he faced his dismayed country and his domineering wife, the Duke of Windsor died in 1972. Although bedridden as well as laden with needles and tubes, he managed to rise to his feet and remain standing for the visit of Queen Elizabeth, who decided to make peace with her uncle, the former king, shortly before his death.

Two days after the party, I called Cécile to see how she was getting along without me to share the arduous duty of being Greta's walking companion. Cécile sounded quite upbeat and said, 'I will pass you to Miss. G.' When Greta came to the phone, I laughed and said, 'I am sure you must be happy that I am not there to push you to go out all the time.'

Instead of agreeing with me, she said, 'Oh Massimo . . . I miss you so much.' Garbo was proof that absense does make the heart grow fonder. Had she been routinely warm, I would have soon taken her affection for granted. Had she remained distant and cold, I would certainly have lost interest. But Garbo was a master of giving an occasional morsel of warmth that kept one bewitched and begging for more. It is still a mystery to me whether she was even aware of how effective this was or if she just did it intuitively. I had just gone through a troubling episode of perfunctory sex, followed by immediate eviction from the scene of the crime, and then was not even permitted to discuss it the next day. All that was washed away by the childlike enthusiasm I now heard in her voice. As if she were promising me that it would all be different now, that I had somehow broken through, that she might be an iceberg to the world, but she would always be warm to me. And when she was like that, the years and experiences separating us made no difference at all, and a future seemed possible. Then she said, 'Please come back soon, Massimo . . . '

The next day, I was back in Saint-Raphaël.

I was greeted with such enthusiasm on the evening of my arrival that I decided to extract an immediate promise from Greta. 'If you are really so happy to see me, then we must go tomorrow night to a St. Tropez nightclub,' I said. Now the sharp eyebrows raised in surprise like two question marks. 'Are you crazy??' she asked with the lyrical intonation of 'crazy' conveying wonder, fear, and the excitement of a child about to do something very naughty.

'Yes,' I answered to all the questions her simple phrase had eloquently posed. 'Tomorrow we go dancing.'

Her answer, small and gratefully submissive, was simply 'Yes.'

She really never needed to use long sentences. She was able to compress so much meaning into a single syllable and something much more, too. Greta could speak volumes with facial expressions and most particularly with the way she raised her eyebrows. I told her once that what other people try to convey with flowers and poems, she can express with her eyebrows. And the conversation that had played itself out on her face during this short exchange was truly eloquent.

Cécile was doing her best to contain her shock and muttered that she would prefer not to join us. She was clearly happy for both of us and did not want her presence to risk what she regarded as a miraculous turn of events. So it was decided that Greta and I would go dancing alone after dinner the following night. Because she was frightened to eat dinner at St. Tropez, we decided to dine at home.

As expected, I was confronted with the usual

problem of Greta's time schedule, as she wanted to go dancing at eight. It was one thing to pretend that a party was to start extra early on her account, but to persuade St. Tropez to commence its night life three hours earlier than normal was perhaps too much to expect even for the great Garbo. Nevertheless, she expected it. We compromised and arrived at St. Tropez at ten where, to my horror, the clubs were not yet open. At that early hour, the only club open was a gay club called Le Pigeonnier. Not quite sure what to do, I suggested that we start there. To my surprise, she was delighted. 'Massimo! Let's go there. I love gays!' she exclaimed. 'Maybe they will take me for a boy.'

This thought seemed to really cheer her up, so I added, 'Yes, maybe they will think you are a boy, and you can dance with some of the other boys, and maybe have a love story with one of the boys.'

She seemed to love this subject (considerably more than she enjoyed our more-conventional attempt at sex), therefore it was with relief and a little trepidation that I led Greta Garbo to the dark St. Tropez gay bar that was to serve as the venue for her reentrance to the world of night life.

It was still early, and consequentially the club was not very crowded. We sat at a table drinking until Greta got up her nerve, and then we danced alone on the dance floor. She slipped off her shoes as she preferred to dance barefoot. (Just for the record, her feet were certainly not too large!) As she drew closer to me, she whispered in an excited voice, 'Do you think they take us for two men dancing together?' In her androgynous, gray uniform and uni-sex straw hat, I suppose it was possible. As the dance floor began to fill, she became more and more excited as she watched the men kissing and embracing one another. She steered us around the floor giving me a standing commentary on the progress of our neighboring dancers. 'Look, did you see they are kissing' or 'Massimo, look . . . he put his hand on the other man's ass!'

I was glad she was having such a good time, but I was not attracted to gay men. I suggested that we go on to another club, but Greta was adamant. 'No, Massimo this is so amusing. I want to stay here. Oh look where he has grabbed the other one!' This was the happiest I had ever seen her. I should have been prepared for a turn of fate and a mood swing.

We danced only a little while longer before the first person recognized her. 'Gar-bo!' he shouted. His inflection made it sound almost like 'Tally-ho,' as if he were the master of hounds alerting the hunt that the fox had come out from ground. I led her hastily to our table, but within seconds, we were surrounded by baying bodies. There were people all around us grabbing at her, trying to touch her, trying to tear off pieces of her clothing. We could not move for the press of bodies against us, and from the street, passers-by began to descend into the club to get a view of Garbo.

There was neither bouncer nor bodyguard available, so I grabbed two waiters, and we pushed our way toward the door. At this moment, I felt ashamed for having written off her fears as purely paranoid. The whole time she kept moaning, 'Massimo, help me! Do something! They are going to kill me! They will torture me and kill me! Why can't they leave me in peace? I am nobody. I am old. I am an old woman. I don't work anymore. I don't make movies. Why do they want me?'

For the first time, in that crazy club as I tried to fight our way out, I broke her rule and answered, 'For your past.'

'They must forget my past,' she shrieked. 'I want to forget my past. I like you because you ignore my past. You don't know about my past.'

It was a strange time to finally broach this restricted subject, but by the time our exchange was finished, I had her safely in my car, and we were on our way back to the safety of her somewhat more understandable prison. We said almost nothing as I drove her home and even less as we entered her darkened room and joyless bed.

4

BETRAYAL

As I had done the first time we slept together, the next day I dutifully accompanied Greta on her morning walk. It occurred to me that perhaps the night before she had felt that she was simply performing an obligatory duty just as I did now. As if she knew that it was expected and did it as a sort of kindness. I do not believe that she was sleeping with Cécile, and for that matter, neither was I during this period. So I did not believe that Greta's lack of enthusiasm had anything to do with guilt or jealousy. Naturally I avoided this subject during the walk and concentrated on the type of seduction that thus far had yielded better results.

'Miss G., your old friend, Carol Lebworth [heiress to the Gimbel retail store empire], has invited us to a party at Castellaras,' I began. Even before she could utter her automatic refusal, I could see her tense up. We had been on three outings and two had ended in disaster. Yet, after each episode, I felt she was a little stronger and more willing to try again. For my part, I was dying to be seen with her and was amazed by the fact that not a single paparazzo had spotted us. It took the entire walk and most of the afternoon, but in the end I persuaded her to go.

Cécile accompanied us with her car and driver, and we set out for the long drive to Castellaras and to the magnificent home of Carol Gimbel Lebworth. Greta neither complained about the time nor insisted on rescheduling the party. Things seemed to be improving. When we arrived, Greta was delighted to find that Charles Boyer was among the twenty dinner guests. They had starred together in *Conquest* in 1937, in which Boyer played Napoleon and Garbo his Polish lover, Marie Walewska, and had not seen each other since.

They must have gotten on well judging by her reaction. She immediately pulled him off to a quiet table, and the two virtually leapt into the past. It was clear that they wanted to be alone. From what I could occasionally hear of their enthusiastic conversation, it sounded like a reunion of the MGM fan club. It was later that I learned that Charles Boyer had lost his son to suicide only four years earlier and perhaps was as estranged from the present as Greta was. But after a while, I actually began to feel jealous, and as their tête-à-tête reached one-and-a-half hours, I managed to complain to her that she had not said a word to me. She looked at me almost in a daze and said, 'Oh Massimo, it was my past all coming back to me.' I was shocked. She had said 'past' with tenderness and longing. Exhausted by the emotion and memories, she soon asked to be taken home.

The time had come to return to Paris, and Greta decided to relocate to Cécile's Paris home.

I returned to my own apartment, but continued to visit the two ladies. Greta refused to eat out or go to any parties in Paris where she was convinced that recognition was inevitable. This logic somehow did not extend itself to her daily walks totaling six hours of exposure to curious eyes. One of her friends once called her a 'hermit-about-town,' and I think this was pretty accurate. It was as if she were flaunting her militant form of urban privacy in the faces of millions as we paraded about the streets of Paris. Yet try to persuade her to go to a small party with four guests and you would be met with a look of horror. Since it was pretty clear from the start that I would have no success arguing this point, I contented myself with accompanying her on the walks.

We would follow the same route two times a day. Beginning at Cécile's house at St. Honoré, we would walk to the last bridge at St. Germain. This is a very respectable distance and would take more than three hours round trip. Quite often we would cross the Seine and walk to Les Invalides to visit Napoleon's Tomb. She had an enormous interest in the emperor, and I often speculated on why this might be and what it might reveal about her guarded psyche.

Napoleon's final resting place is an extraordinarily beautiful cathedral-like building in which his sarcophagus rests under a huge dome. When one enters the building, the floor is cut out in a huge circle so that one can look down at the tomb, which is one floor below.

As Garbo did not like being so exposed, we

would descend directly to the level of the sarcophagus, which is framed by twelve enormous white-marble statues of the Winged Victory that in caryatid-like fashion support the ceiling. She would stand silent and motionless alongside one of these somber classic beauties almost as if she were one of them. We would often remain there for close to an hour with Garbo holding silent vigil over the tomb of the emperor. Her emotions and any hope of discerning the reason for them remained hidden behind her dark glasses.

The circular wall of the chamber is ornately carved with marble friezes depicting Napoleon's most important accomplishments. At these she would never throw a glance. Instead we would proceed upstairs to the army museum and walk directly to the reconstruction of Napoleon's death chamber at St. Helena. In this stark room furnished with only two curtained campaign beds, Napoleon spent his final years in exile and physical agony. In the throes of his daily suffering, he would pace back and forth between the beds, first throwing himself on one then the other.

Did she equate this to her lonely Spartan bedroom in Manhattan where she sat on her empty bed staring at the East River — alone in her exile to ponder her past victories until the memories themselves became the worst torture? Perhaps the lost glory was itself worse than any physical pain and even worse than anonymity so that the mere mention of the past became the thing most to be feared.

Was not the string of victories more painful to recollect than the few defeats? It is quite possible that when Napoleon accepted his final exile, his torment was greater at the recollection of the joyful moment when he grabbed the imperial crown from the hands of the pope and crowned himself emperor than it was at the bitter memory of Waterloo. Was Garbo's absolute refusal to acknowledge her past not likewise understandable? Perhaps, I speculated, that is why she comes here so often to commiserate with something that would not be easy for Greta Garbo to find — an equal.

The walks themselves were physically demanding, and the visits to Les Invalides were a huge emotional drain. I was twenty-nine and fit, but I was exhausted at the end of these urban marathons. We locked ourselves into this daily routine until I found myself becoming quite bored. I decided that the time had come for a change. I invited her to visit my home in Rome.

Instead of refusing outright, Greta took in this invitation with a deeply thoughtful look. She realized that this trip was important to me for a number of reasons, but primarily because I felt most at home at the apartment I had bought with my inheritance. The apartment, at the Piazza del Colosseo, was directly across from the Roman Colosseum and had large windows overlooking the ruins from both of the sitting rooms as well as my bedroom. I had it decorated by Tommaso Buzzi, who at the time was the most popular interior designer in Europe and had decorated the palaces of the Countess Lilly

Volpi as well as the chic Corviglia Club in St. Moritz. He created a very classic look in my home that still managed to be both elegant and comfortable. He even catered to my humor and life-style by installing a secret doorway next to the toilet in the en-suite bathroom.

The passageway behind this door led to a private staircase so my special guests could exit my apartment without being seen by the servants. The walls and ceiling of the window box in my bedroom were covered in gray stone so that one felt at one with the arches of the Colosseum. Indeed at night when it is illuminated, it is difficult to know where my apartment ends and the Colosseum begins. But the most special thing about my apartment was I had bought it with the money my father had left me, and more than almost anything else I was ever to own, it felt like it really was mine.

Garbo understood a great deal of this and took the invitation very seriously. She considered it with her eyebrows knitted in concentration, but fortunately not ridged in a frown. Finally she said, 'Massimo, I am frightened to go to Rome. It is very dangerous for me . . . but I want to give you a huge proof of trust . . . ' And so it was decided that Garbo would travel to the land of the paparazzi as an act of trust and affection. Cécile could not come with us because she had a meeting in Florence with one of her many charitable foundations. We decided that Greta and I would fly from Paris to Rome where we would spend one night in my home, and then we would join Cécile in Florence where we would spend two days visiting their favorite churches.

We arrived in my apartment without incident, and I fixed up the guest room for Greta. At this time, we were in the third month of our relationship. Yet I had not been permitted to spend an entire night in her bed. I thought I'd best arrange things so that I had somewhere to go when I was asked to leave. I have subsequently heard that Garbo once claimed 'I never said 'I want to be alone.' I only said 'I want to be left alone.' There is all the difference in the world.' Let me say that from my perspective, Greta clearly was not thinking about our nocturnal habits when she made this statement.

That evening we went to a small bistro at the picturesque Piazza del Popolo, and someone must have spotted us. I had been in public with Garbo now in three cities, and sadly the press still had not seemed to notice. But just my luck, this time it was simply a snoop and not a photographer.

Nevertheless, the next morning I received a call from Matteo Spinola, who at the time was the leading PR man in Italy. 'Massimo, is it true?' he began. 'I want to see you . . . give me five minutes,' he added when I did not answer his question. Now this was not a good man to annoy. He could do some serious damage to a fellow's reputation, and I certainly did not wish to make an enemy out of him. 'Let me come to your apartment and talk to you about what I heard,' he insisted. This was a pretty ridiculous suggestion, I thought. Does he expect to simply drop in for a drink with his friend Massimo and say hello to his new girlfriend, Greta?

I compromised and agreed to meet him at his office where I quietly received his advice and castigation. 'Last night you were seen at the Piazza del Popolo with Greta Garbo,' he began. I simply nodded solemnly, to which he exploded, 'Are you crazy? Do you have any idea what this could do for you if you just confirmed that you are with her? I can make you famous the world over if you just give me the scoop.'

I thanked him and refused as politely as I could. He handed me his telephone number anyway, and I stuffed it hastily in my pocket, immediately forgetting it was there.

Cécile's plans had changed, and her trip to Florence was delayed. Greta and I decided to return to Saint-Raphaël and accompany Cécile to Florence a couple of days later. Our trip to Rome had been a success. Greta and I finally spent a period of time entirely alone, she seemed to draw even closer to me after visiting my home, and she was getting slightly more extroverted and braver each day.

I should have known that it was too good to last.

When we arrived at Saint-Raphaël, Cécile seemed happy to see us and announced that we were all going to a lunch party the following day at the home of Eliette von Karajan, wife of the charismatic philharmonic conductor, Herbert von Karajan. I considered it a personal triumph that Cécile now just assumed that Greta would accept. The lunch was at St. Tropez, and we were driven in Cécile's car. We arrived at noon, and the house was already very warm. I felt hot and uncomfortable and began to drink a little too much. Something was bothering me from the start. Could it be that I sensed that in this beautiful oceanfront house, I would meet disaster?

I began to get even more nervous. It seemed as if everyone were looking at Greta and me. Our relationship was getting more obvious, and the other guests kept looking inquisitively at the happy couple. I was by far the youngest one at the party, and I felt as if there was a reticence among the other guests to talk to me. Nobody else was swimming, and I longed to dive into the pool. Instead I kept to myself and continued to drink.

Despite the splendor of their home, the von Karajans were not especially generous people and chose to serve a buffet consisting solely of a fish salad. By the time it was served, in addition to feeling ignored, uncomfortable, and hot, I was also hungry. I grabbed a large piece of fish and quickly swallowed it. Then it happened. There are moments that seem to be captured like a snapshot in your memory for the rest of your life. The fish naturally was not boned, and the rigid spine lodged itself horizontally in my throat with such force that it brought tears to my eyes.

By nature I hate to make a scene, and in the company I found myself, I was extremely embarrassed to even make a rude noise. But I knew I was about to die and did not seem to be able to manage it in complete silence. No matter how deeply I gasped, I could get almost no breath, and I began to choke. By this time, my condition was so obvious that even the snootiest guests began to make suggestions. One elegant lady offered me a piece of bread, while her escort pounded me on the back. I looked around and could see that the party had stopped. The other guests stood transfixed in a circle around me watching me die. My mistake as it turned out was in not dying more discreetly.

In the commotion that followed, I was able to catch glimpses of what ensued. Someone called for an ambulance, and I was told that 'it would be over very soon.' I was grateful for the ambulance, but was convinced that it could not arrive in time. Then I saw Garbo. She was hysterical, but perhaps not for the reasons one might suppose. She was staring at me with a look of fear, disgust, and disappointment. 'Perhaps he will die,' she said with an almost-clinical, inquisitive voice. The next line was the one Garbo quote I will never forget. 'I want to go.' Then when she sensed that even Cécile was amazed, she cried out insistently, 'I want to go. I don't want to stay. They will say it was my fault.' And with that she appropriated Cécile's car and was gone.

A few minutes later, the ambulance arrived, and I was taken to the hospital. There a small operation was performed, and the fish skeleton was removed from my throat. Cécile remained at my side the whole time for which I shall always be grateful. Greta chose not to even visit me in the hospital. Later she claimed that she was afraid that she might be photographed. From that moment on, I never felt the same about Garbo. I accepted a lot of strange behavior and was as patient as I could be with all her fears, but this was something else. We were lovers in our own peculiar way, but she simply deserted me when she thought I was about to die. The similarity of this reaction to her behavior toward the death of Schlee was little consolation to me.

Two days later, the three of us decided to go to Florence anyway. Cécile sent her car in advance to meet us at Milan because in those days there were no direct flights from Paris to Florence. We went through the motions of looking at the many churches and museums, but the whole time I was getting more and more angry as I thought about the way Garbo had deserted me and the fact that she never offered even the slightest apology. We were staying at a very exclusive hotel named the Excelsior. It was both elegant and romantic, but I was too upset to even consider visiting her room at night.

By the end of our stay in Florence, I was so angry that I could hardly look at her. As I paced around my room fuming at her behavior, I noticed the phone number of Matteo Spinola, the PR man from Rome. All right, I thought, if I cannot have your loyalty, then I will use your fame. I called Matteo and told him the time we would be arriving at the airport in Milan.

The next day we were driven to Milan, and as we got out of Cécile's car, we were greeted by five photographers who immediately began snapping pictures. At first Garbo tried to cover herself up with a piece of luggage the way you might grab a towel if someone catches you coming out of the shower. Then realizing that it was hopeless, she simply stood still then turned slowly toward me. She looked me straight in the eye with a cold, angry, sharklike stare and said with icy calm the last words she would ever say to me. 'You got me once. You will never get me again.'

I said nothing, but Cécile jumped in and tried to argue my innocence. Garbo would not speak another word about it. On the plane, she never once looked at me. When we arrived in Paris, I had to take a taxi home because she would not ride with me in Cécile's car.

5

LIFE AFTER GARBO

It was clear from the first moment that it was hopeless. Nevertheless, I went through the motions of trying to apologize to Garbo. I phoned, but she would not take my calls. I even sent a letter, but she didn't respond. Even Cécile had to concede that the relationship was over.

To console me, she told me the story of a similar episode that she had witnessed in the life of Garbo. Cécile claimed that Greta had been living in New York with an attractive, young, aspiring actress. One day an important film producer visited the Fifty-second Street apartment for lunch. Greta, in true frugal form, was doing the cooking herself. She did most of her own cooking and cleaning because, as she told Cécile, she was afraid that servants might poison her. Her household staff was limited to one companion named Claire Koger, who did not even live in the apartment.

While she was occupied in the kitchen, the producer and Greta's girlfriend seemed to really hit it off. Before lunch was served, he had offered the young lady a screen test. As both were aware of Garbo's somewhat odd reactions, it was decided that the test would remain a secret. Several days later, the screen test took place. The young lady returned to Greta's apartment to find all her possessions packed in suitcases and stacked neatly at the concierge's desk. This was probably the poor concierge who some years earlier had to notify Garbo whenever the unspeakable Valentina was in the lobby. What Cécile was trying to say was simply you can't fool Greta Garbo, and she does not forgive. It was a point well taken.

Although I was never to see Garbo again, the publication of the offending photos created an international sensation that exceeded my wildest hopes. The next day photographers and reporters were camped outside of my Paris apartment, while others tracked down my mother in Naples for material about my youth. A more recent example of this phenomenon was the media obsession following the very analogous case of John Bryan (who plays a large role later on in this story) photographed in the south of France with the Duchess of York. Most people still remember the famous 'toe-sucking' photo in which Bryan is bent over apparently licking or sucking (a debate still rages over which it was) the toes of Fergie. Thirty years ago, the image of an angry Garbo with her young Italian boyfriend was perhaps as equally well known.

The incident was reported on television and radio, as well, throughout the world, and by the second day, the story took on a life of its own. The press decided that we were engaged and would soon marry. Apparently Garbo had discovered me while staying on Onassis's yacht. I had been the young boy who sailed the motor tender to bring the passengers to land. She spotted me and, dazzled by my beauty, had asked that I be immediately brought aboard.

The rest was (apparently) history. If one knew Garbo, this story would be laughable. I never once saw her look at a man with lust. She certainly was more interested in watching other females. Behind her ever-present dark glasses, her eyes would often follow beautiful women. It was not uncommon for her to comment on them, too. But never had I seen her react in this way to a man. It was simply silly. Nevertheless, the public liked the story, and it soon became generally accepted as the truth. The result of all of this was I had become famous.

For the past several years, I had been an accepted fixture at the various venues of the Jet Set world, now I had become a star.

Perhaps it seems ridiculous that a person can achieve a sort of stardom simply by being romantically linked to a famous woman. Yet look at the cases of James Hewitt and Dodi al Fayed's fame due to their association with Princess Diana, or Steve Wyatt and John Bryan with the Duchess of York. Look even closer — wasn't Diana's fame initially due to her marriage to Prince Charles, as Fergie's was to Prince Andrew? In 1969 Greta Garbo was nothing less than a reclusive empress, and the fact that I was linked to her guaranteed me an elevated status in my superficial world.

What did all of this do to Greta's life? Actually, the incident did very little more than support her cynicism and distrust of other people. She remained friends with Cécile for the rest of her life and continued their routine of joint vacations. Garbo even made a secret visit to Rome the next year for a screen test with Luchino Visconti. Ironically, Visconti, who was also a friend of mine, had persuaded me and my friend, Riccardo Olivieri, to take a screen test at about this time, as well. After reviewing the results, he reported sadly that a great hostility seemed to exist between the camera and me. Riccardo, who had studied dramatic arts, was able to land a role in a new avant-guarde play in Milan. The play ran for a short time before being closed down by the police for being too risqué, freeing the two of us to return to less artistic and more pragmatic practices. Garbo's test for a role in *Remembrance of Things Past* also came to nothing.

Cécile, as usual, intervened in Garbo's life and tried to find a replacement for me. About eighteen months after the end of our romance, Cécile introduced Garbo to a New York art dealer named Sam Greene. Like me, Sam was thirty years old and equally uninterested in Garbo's movies and past. It seems that Mr. Greene was more patient and tolerant and despite a number of setbacks spent the next fifteen years as Garbo's friend and travel companion. He even accompanied Garbo and Cécile on their trips as I had done.

Perhaps not so surprisingly, his relationship ended in a way very similar to mine. In 1985, an article appeared in the *Globe*, a tabloid known for sensational articles, announcing that Garbo was to marry Greene. Although it seems likely that Greene was more innocent of this leak than I had been, he, nevertheless, received exactly the same drop-dead treatment. Garbo never spoke to him again.

For the remaining five years of her life, she only communicated with Cécile over the telephone and became more and more a prisoner of her fears. She finally stopped traveling and except for her walks remained, until her death in 1990, in her New York apartment. It is located on the most easterly portion of Fifty-second Street where the street actually forms a dead end against the East River. It is very quiet because there is no through traffic. I am sure she was happy there.

My social life had been quite extensive in the past, but a new era now began for me where all doors seemed open. I was invited to the best parties, and women threw themselves at me so they could say they had been with Garbo's ex-lover. I returned to the typical Jet Set circuit, which I had neglected during my time with Greta. There was one subtle, but significant difference. Since my ill-gotten celebrity, I found that I no longer needed a sponsor. I had earned my wings, and up among the stars in the rarified atmosphere of the Jet Set, I was now allowed to solo.

I suppose that the relationship with Garbo was the catalyst for this change, but it alone was not the reason. In the very social world of the Jet Set, one is ranked and invited based on one's current social portfolio. The group as a whole is intimately aware of the social connections of each member. The truly valuable connections are precious commodities and are subtly flaunted within the limits of minimalism. The natural quid-pro-quo implication is that in return for invitations, these valuable social treasures will be shared with the host at some point.

Everyone knew that I was no longer able to share Garbo, but they also were aware that my relationship with Garbo had exposed me to many valuable people, as well as winning me the approval of the group as a whole. This fact combined with the impressive array of connections I had accumulated during my time with the Agnellis and the Rothschilds seemed to place me in a new and slightly more secure category. Later as I took stock of the process in which I had been involved, I realized that a Jet Setter goes through a series of processes in the development of his social career. I had gone through the first two, namely, the apprentice period in which I was educated and launched by a sponsor. This is like being a squire to a powerful knight. The second stage comes after you win your social spurs. Then you become an independent knight-errant of the social world. That is where I found myself. It would take me several years and a lot of adventures before I was to even realize that I had reached the next stage.

As I pointed out earlier, the collective life of the Jet Set was played out in a series of prescribed locations each year. This circuit with some minor alterations remains a virtual tradition. I chose to throw myself into a complete program for the next year. I decided upon Christmas at St. Moritz, January in Acapulco, February in Gstaad, March in the Caribbean, April in Seville, May in Rome, June in Paris, July in St. Tropez, early August in Monte Carlo, late August in Sardinia, September in Capri, October in London, and November in New York.

Although the locations may rotate, the faces remain somewhat static and surprisingly limited. It is a world of wonderful illusion in which the ability to maintain the illusion is key to continued survival. To do so is expensive. Associated with each of these locations are the 'in' restaurants and the appropriate hotels. During my months with Garbo, I had drained a large amount of my inheritance, and now to maintain the image I had so carefully nurtured, it was necessary for me to continue spending more than I could afford.

I began to spend a lot more time with a woman whom I had loved for many years. Françoise Sagan had shocked the world with her first novel, *Bonjour Tristesse*, which she wrote when she was only eighteen years old. It was an international sensation and defined a new direction in the evolution of the novel and rendered her the symbol of a cynical and rebellious youth. She was a kind of literary rebel without a cause, except she had many causes. Hollywood made a film of *Bonjour Tristesse*, starring David Niven and Deborah Kerr. Deborah Kerr had incidentally married the son of Garbo's oldest love, Salka Viertel. Greta would frequently visit them in Switzerland.

David Niven played the perfect irresponsible Jet Set playboy in the film and a later role in this story due to his private friendship with Grace of Monaco. If you ever watch the film, you will note a young man who falls in love with Niven's daughter. It is perhaps not a real surprise that he looks quite a lot as I did then.

Unlike many geniuses who achieve early renown, Françoise continued to produce fantastic novels. *Aimez vous Brahms?* (*Do You Like Brahms?*) was turned into a very successful film in which a young Anthony Perkins gets romantically involved with the much older Ingrid Bergman. Was art imitating life?

Our first meeting took place several years before and was memorable in that it corresponded with a historic event. We met on that fateful day in 1963 in which Madame Nhu, the 'Iron Lady of Saigon,' fled to Paris after the death of her brother-in-law, the dictator Ngho Dinh Diem of Vietnam. I had just completed my law studies, and as a sort of reward, my father had sent me to study English at Oxford.

I decided to stop in Paris on the way over. Being a poor student, I had very little money, but knew that I would be unable to accept invitations were I to stay in an unacceptable hotel. At this time, the finer hotels had tiny single rooms for the servants. I was able to rent a cubicle that was used to house chauffeurs in the best Parisian hotel. It was just large enough to accommodate a small bed and two towels. As long as I did not bring anyone to the room, I had as good an address as any visiting royalty. Now strategically situated, I was able to accept prestigious invitations and began immediately.

I attended a dinner party the first night thrown by the prominent socialite Betty Estevez. She was the wife of the American fashion designer, Luis Estevez. It was one of those civilized, urbane marriages frequent among the Jet Set, in which both parties were allowed to pursue their individual sexuality. Bisexuality is so prevalent in the Jet Set that I would define it as the norm. I didn't know any of the other guests. Then I saw Sagan for the first time. She was a slender, short-haired blonde with a face of great strength, intelligence, and a tantalizing eroticism.

It was clear from the first moment that the chemistry was strong between us. Actually, I believe it was a true case of love at first sight. Before trying to strike up a conversation, I discreetly asked another guest if he knew the name of the woman at whom I was staring. He seemed shocked and amused by the question. 'Why, that's Sagan,' he breathed with a reverence that bordered on awe. Naturally, I had heard of her, but my companion was eager to fill in more detail to my incomplete awareness of her fame. 'She is the leader,' he went on, 'of la bande Sagan.' This, he was quick to point out, was not a rock band, but an intellectually militant group, which included many famous nonsocialites.

Although invited to the most elite parties, Sagan herself detested the Jet Set. In addition to simply enjoying each other's company, la bande

Sagan served some obtuse symbolic function that nobody was quite clever enough to figure out. The mere fact that la bande chose to cryptically spend its evenings outside of Regine's trendy club, 'Jimmy's,' was enigmatic and open to much interpretation. Such intellectual mystery was naturally very appealing to the Parisian intelligentsia and could not be ignored by the Jet Set. And so it seems that I had been love struck by one of the most dangerous women in Europe.

The eye contact bespoke a reciprocal feeling, and I finally approached and introduced myself. I was terribly disappointed to learn that my friendly informant had failed to mention that she was married. Although her American husband was present, I felt that I had to see her again. She accepted my invitation to lunch the next day and afterward the invitation to visit my apartment (as I described the cubicle). When she saw the look of delighted surprise in my eyes, she smiled and said, 'Treason is the only way to keep a marriage alive.'

As the taxi pulled up to the hotel, we saw that the area was swarming with photographers. The moment she saw them, she slapped me across the face, thinking I had set her up (foreshadowing my fateful experience four years later with Garbo). I protested saying, 'Believe me, Françoise, I had nothing to do with this.' Grabbing the concierge, I demanded to know the cause of the disturbance. We were informed that Madame Nhu had just arrived, and the journalists were hungry for an interview and photos. Sagan was contrite. Before going up to my room, she left a note for Madame Nhu introducing herself and saying she would like to have an interview. Always clever, this was not only a smart career move, it also established an alibi for her presence in the hotel.

Proceeding to my tiny cubicle, we used the only piece of furniture present. Françoise seemed genuinely shocked at the modesty of my accommodations, but after a moment's hesitation, shrugged her shoulders and laughed. Our mutual attraction was enormous, and Françoise had a sensual imagination that perhaps surpassed even her literary creativity. We were quite far along when someone knocked on the door.

Sagan wrapped herself in a towel as I answered to find a well-dressed, very polite man waiting outside. He asked discreetly if I had perhaps seen Madame Sagan. It appeared that the 'Iron Lady of Saigon' was a great fan and wondered if madame could visit her in half an hour. This rather ill-timed interruption resulted in an exclusive interview, which was very successful for Françoise.

Although not obsessed with wealth, Sagan regarded money as a necessary evil. One of her most-often quoted lines is 'it is better to cry in a Rolls-Royce than in a tram.' Whenever I hear someone parroting this line, I always laugh to myself as I recall how impatiently I lay naked and very aroused awaiting her return, she came back very soon, cutting the interview short because of me. As a result of the success achieved in our first meeting, Sagan has always felt that I bring her luck.

Despite the all-around success of our tryst, Françoise was evasive when I called her the next day. 'Can I see you today?' I asked.

'No' was her bored and distant response.

You are by now aware of my belief in persistence. Yet nothing I said seemed to grab her attention. She explained without overt sentimentality that she was about to leave Paris, and that was that. I was to learn and appreciate that Françoise was one of the only people I was ever to know who expected and allowed absolute freedom without any signs of possessiveness. It was not disinterest that she was showing, but the highest form of respect. My relationships before and since have invariably been undermined by an expectation that I must demonstrate a degree of total devotion, which I have never been able to achieve. Sagan neither expected nor granted this, telling me once, 'I am not jealous if you make love to another woman. I am only jealous if you laugh with another woman.'

She was so unpredictable that sometimes it was an adventure just to spend time alone with her in Paris. Sagan is truly unique and something of a creature of the night — irresistibly attracted to the dark. Like me, she slept late into the afternoon and really awakened at night. Together we would explore Paris in the dead of night. Unimpressed by famous restaurants, Sagan was fascinated with the darker side of the city. One of our late-night adventures took us to a Parisian hotel frequented by prostitutes. We found it stimulating to occupy a room illuminated by a naked, red light bulb and make

95

love in a bed still warm from the lovemaking of others. We were an unusual couple cemented together by our complicity and disregard for bourgeois rules. As a result, we have been able to be intermittent lovers, but constant friends for thirty-five years. The press periodically announced our marriage, and to increase their interest, I even acknowledged that I would like to marry her so that she could produce an intellectual offspring for me.

It was always enjoyable to travel with her and particularly to witness the manner in which people react to a famous intellectual. It is quite similar to the typical reaction to royalty or great wealth — an obsequious overcompensation that ultimately makes both parties uncomfortable. This reaction often came from unexpected quarters. Once while we were in New York, Françoise was bored and called Jackie Onassis, who promptly invited us to her apartment for lunch.

I had not seen Jackie since her days as First Lady when I had been invited to the Kennedy compound in Cape Cod. So I was curious to see how she might have changed. This was just two years after her marriage to Onassis, and the world was still recovering from its shock. We have now had thirty years to get used to the idea, but at the time, most people were very critical. The only modern equivalent I can imagine is if Princess Diana had married Dodi's father.

Jackie was an international idol who represented the glory of Camelot. Marrying a man so much older, and worse, so much richer than she, was a scandal. But it also underscored the general problem experienced by first-generation tycoons and Onassis in particular. They simply were not considered fit for high society.

Jackie's sister married a Polish prince, becoming Princess Radziwill. Everyone was pleased. When Lee later became Onassis's girlfriend, her mother was furious. It is hard to fathom the logic behind such a reaction, but that is how it was. In a way Onassis's marriage to Jackie, unpopular and otherwise unsuccessful as it was, represented the final stage of his victory over society. So it was with great curiosity that I accompanied Sagan to the lunch.

The couple was still in their salad years, but Jackie wisely kept her apartment on Fifth Avenue, which is where we were invited. It was a large, airy, well-decorated apartment in an attractive gray-granite building featuring a private elevator just for her. Jackie met Sagan with open arms and fluent French. Throughout the meal, Jackie tried to discuss literature with Françoise in a manner that Sagan found tediously pseudo-intellectual. When I had met Jackie with President Kennedy several years before, I found him to be a great host. He was a charming, friendly, somewhat self-effacing man while Jackie did her best not to notice me. Jackie claimed to remember the meeting, but I doubted it.

She ignored me then with exactly the same quiet contempt with which she discounted me on this occasion. What I found so humorous is despite Françoise's genuine affection and respect for Jackie, she hated to be forced to discuss her work with someone she did not regard as a fellow intellectual. Perhaps this was unfair, but I was glad to see Jackie receiving treatment similar to what she offered me.

As the lunch progressed, Françoise became increasingly bored and irritated. She finally said, 'Jackie, we know you have to catch a plane to Detroit and do not wish to detain you.'

To this Jackie responded nonplussed, 'You don't think I fly commercially, do you? The plane will wait.'

And so continued the well-intentioned torture of my intellectual friend.

After lunch with Jackie, I was curious about the odd turn of events that had prompted a wise man like Onassis to discard his ten-year-long romance with Maria Callas for her. I decided to play Sherlock Holmes to determine how they really were dealing with their separation. I admired Callas and was somewhat in awe of Onassis, who had begun his career as a penniless immigrant to Argentina. Through nothing but his own intelligence, he was able to become one of the richest men in the world.

His first wife, Tina, was the daughter of the great Greek shipping magnate Stavros Livanos. Yet, he neither married her for her wealth, nor did he ever use the strength of the father-in-law's empire. It was, indeed, the relationship with Callas that ended his marriage to Tina, who later married Onassis's rival, Stavros Niarchos. The Callas-Onassis romance was somehow bigger than life as was everything else about the man.

Although Prince Rainier was the Prince of Monaco, we would call Onassis the King of Monte Carlo. Maria, although never his wife, was his queen. It was inconceivable to picture Monte Carlo harbor without the image of the hulk of the *Christina* lit up like a Christmas tree and dwarfing all around it, somehow giving us all a feeling of safety and security. And it was equally impossible to imagine the *Christina* without hearing the endless arpeggios and scales of Maria Callas practicing in the salon.

I had the good fortune to meet Onassis and Callas for the first time very early in their relationship and watched with interest the evolution of their love story. When I was twenty-one, I spent time with a Neapolitan duchess named Sveva Caracciolo. She was twenty-four at the time, and for some atypical reason, our relationship remained platonic. Nevertheless, I was often a guest at her palace near Naples. Her father, the duke, was an interesting and cultured man who prided himself on his collection of artists and intellectuals. In fact, it was at his palace that I first met the director Roberto Rossellini recovering from his recent divorce from Ingrid Bergman.

Rossellini had just married a very traditional Indian woman named Sonali das Gupta, and the duke offered his palace for their honeymoon. I had long admired the cold, but vulnerable Nordic beauty of Bergman and found it hard to imagine how Rossellini could have changed gears so drastically. His new wife wore a sari and even her caste mark, spoke very little, and seemed to negotiate the honeymoon in a trance.

The duke took a liking to me and would often invite me to parties. In the summer of 1961, he took me to the most extraordinary party I had to date ever witnessed. It was located on an island on the coast of Naples called La Gaiola. One referred to it as an 'island' strictly out of politeness. In actuality, it was a rock — a stone escarpment that protruded out of the gulf perhaps fifty yards from shore. Nevertheless it could only be reached by boat. On top of the escarpment stood a lone villa, carved out of the stone. It made you think that you were about to visit the Count of Monte Cristo.

But the most extraordinary thing about this residence was that it was the home of the eccentric Baron Langheim, famed for flamboyance. His home reflected his extreme tastes as well as his almost-obsessive homosexuality.

On this particular night, as we glided noiselessly through the calm waters of the gulf, our first view of the small island was astonishing. The villa stood high on top of the escarpment, its windows glowing with light like a jack-o-lantern on Halloween. To reach the residence, about forty massive steps had been hewn into the local granite. Upon every other step stood one of the baron's twenty matched male-servants. They stood erect, at attention — as if they were standing for some strange midnight inspection. They were clad in skintight, black sailor pants, with wide red satin sashes about their narrow waists. Their torsos were completely naked, and each held a flaming torch in his right hand.

They remained silently in this strange formation until all the guests had arrived, at which point they would march into the villa to serve their master and his guests. The villa itself was a museum dedicated to the naked male form. Yet, oddly, it was done in exquisite good taste. The walls were covered with old-master paintings — even the bathroom had a Michelangelo of two naked men embracing. The great hall was decorated in large stone replicas either directly depicting or subtly suggesting the erect male organ.

There were not many guests — actually speaking, I would estimate that between the male servants and the artwork, the host's collection of penises outnumbered those of the guests by a ratio of ten to one. And it was in these unlikely circumstances that I first saw Onassis. I had been double-dating his daughter and niece occasionally, but this was the first time that I actually met Ari.

He was a short man with thick hair and a hypnotic smile. He emanated energy, enthusiasm, and a sense of fun. Maria Callas stood by his side. Her full dark hair and beautiful features were breathtaking. The duke introduced me to them, and we made small talk about our surroundings. I remarked how tasteful the room was — expecting either a laugh or contradiction from the macho Onassis. They both nodded their heads. Then Maria said, 'Ari, why don't you buy the island so we can retire here?' I am convinced that she meant this sincerely. Ari laughed that infectious laugh of his and said, 'I don't ever want to retire.' I guess that was a prophetic answer because he never did.

The baron was one of the most attentive and generous hosts I have ever encountered. The service, food, and sheer magnificence of the party and many others that were to follow sadly forced the baron to sell his home. It was bought unfortunately not by the equally generous Ari, but by J. Paul Getty, a man noted for his cheapness. It is an ironic end to a house owned by a man whose generosity bankrupted him that his successor, despite the largest fortune in the world, would install pay telephones in his homes so that his guests would be forced to pay for their own calls.

At any rate, my mind was filled with reminiscences of my subsequent meetings with Ari and Maria, and I was determined to get to the bottom of his current romantic choice and the obvious effect it was having on Callas. I decided to attend a number of parties in Paris where I knew Onassis would be a guest. I found him to be his normal, jovial, joking self. Maybe he was happy, but he was not a man to easily reveal his private feelings. Taking another approach I gave a dinner party in Rome to which I invited Maria Callas. My guests met at my apartment in Rome, which holds such diverse memories, including Garbo's visit. We had cocktails and chatted for a while before going to dinner.

Maria was a wreck. She had just been

performing in a new opera, and she looked exhausted. The reviews had not been positive, and she was heard by a friend to say, 'I lost my voice, and now I lost Onassis.' I was convinced that her fatigue was not a result of her operatic stress, but of being heartbroken. No one dared bring up the name of Onassis, but her longing for him was so great that it was as if he haunted the room.

Maria was perhaps the greatest opera star of the time and had a great deal of personal wealth. The reason she had spent ten years of her life with Onassis was simply because she loved him. We went off in two groups to a small restaurant called Taverna Flavia that had always been Liz Taylor's favorite bistro in Rome. When we arrived, Maria was in an absolute frenzy. She had lost a precious brooch that Onassis had given her. It had some unmentionably poignant sentimental value, and it had to be found. We retraced our steps and believe it or not, found it in the least likely place — the elevator cab of my apartment.

The fatigue of Maria Callas must have been so great that she needed an elevator to negotiate a ten-foot distance. She never really recovered from Onassis's marriage to Jackie and died in 1977, only two years after his death. He died a lonely man, left to die alone by a wife who was five thousand miles away.

I believe that the Onassis-Callas affair was one of the greatest love stories of our time. A lot of people consider the marriage of the Duke and Duchess of Windsor to be our century's greatest romance. I am not sure I agree. Perhaps the duke enjoyed the bullying that his duchess gave him in public, but I am not the only one who found it sad and quite embarrassing. In the case of Onassis and Callas, I believe their temperaments were well matched in their passion for arguing as well as laughing, and most of all, I am sure what she loved in him was simply the man.

At exactly the same time that I was trying to fathom the great love that Callas had for Ari, I was smitten with a degree of passion that I had not yet encountered. It is funny how an event or an unexpected meeting can change one's life. For me the Patiño Ball in Portugal was to have a profound impact on my future. It was there that I first met Cécile Rothschild and were it not for her, I might have become a boring lawyer with a stuffy office in Rome.

While still in Portugal two days after having met Cécile, I was invited to a party outside Lisbon thrown by Pierre and Sao Schlumberger. Pierre's grandfather had invented the pump associated with oil rigs, and as a result, the Schlumberger family received a 5-percent commission on all the oil pumped with their device. Their wealth is fantastic. One has only to follow the stock market to measure the size of their empire. The Schlumberger homes quite vividly expressed the wealth of their owner. Sao — unlike Garbo — was no disciple of minimalism. From the voluptuousness of her cleavage to the jewels that adorned it, there was nothing minimal about the blonde beauty that the oil magnate chose as his queen. Our attraction, as in the case of Sagan, was immediate and mutually obvious — but we did nothing to pursue it that night nor over the ensuing years during our subsequent meetings at Parisian parties.

I was free now of Garbo, unfettered by what Sagan would regard as antiquated bonds of sexual fidelity, and quite free to finally give it a try. I knew that Sao's best friend was the famed Princess Ira von Furstenberg. Ira's life is so astonishing and so representative of all the strange machinations of life within the Jet Set and would play such a large part in my own life later on that I would like to take this opportunity to tell you a little about her.

Daughter of Prince Tassilo von Furstenberg and Clara Agnelli — the older sister of Gianni Agnelli of the Fiat empire — she was married at the age of fourteen to Prince Alfonso Hohenlohe. Imagine that in this century arranged marriages still took place and at the age of fourteen. Yet, as I pointed out earlier, the great industrial families were still interested in linking their names to the great, old, titled families. This marriage was such an example, and the ceremony in Venice was a media and society extravaganza.

Ira and Alfonso had two children in the three years that they were together. Then a mother and wife at the ripe old age of seventeen, Ira met the Brazilian playboy Baby Pignatari at a party in the Italian winter resort Cortina. Baby's wealth and good looks were legendary. He came from one of the prominent South American families that

105

appear to own most of the resources of an entire country. The morning after their first meeting, Ira flew back with him to Brazil without even packing or bringing her children.

Such extraordinary events happen every decade or so within the Jet Set. Almost the exact situation occurred to Susan Barrantes, the mother of Sarah Ferguson, Duchess of York. Susan left her stuffy English husband shortly after meeting the dashing Argentinean polo champion, Hector Barrantes.

There must be something irresistible about wealthy, South American playboys.

Alfonso was naturally saddened by his wife's decision to leave him for an acquaintance she had known for less than twenty-four hours and decided to keep custody of the children. Seemingly unperturbed by this decision, Baby sent a team of kidnappers to Europe, and they surreptitiously brought the children to Rio in Baby's private plane. With almost unlimited resources at his disposal, Baby then entered into a legal duel with Alfonso and was able to ensure that the children would remain with their mother.

And so the happy family remained for the next eight years based in Rio. Ira could not conceive a child from Baby as he had decided to get himself sterilized after his son was born to his ex-wife. Apparently, each time he went out on a date, he would receive a suit for impregnating his date as soon as practicable after her first missed cycle. It simply became too time consuming to fight these false paternity suits, and so he nipped the problem at the bud, so to speak. This did not sit well with Ira, and in addition, she became bored with Rio and the constant necessity for high security, around-the-clock bodyguards, and Baby's incessant jealousy. So, taking only her jewels — and this time the children — she left Baby and returned to Europe.

Ira is an incredibly stunning woman, and in a short period of time, she found herself the lover of a major industrialist named Paolo Marinotti, the owner of SNIA-Viscosa. He showered her with gifts, giving her homes in Paris, Rome, Sardinia, and St. Moritz. He even gave her his mother's famous diamond, one of the largest in the world. That relationship was to have a rather strange end, but at this point, Ira was spending a great deal of time at her new home in Paris. When I say a great deal of time, I speak in the relative Jet-Set terms. Ira, like all the Agnellis, was a true Jet Setter and apparently never stayed in one location for more than three or four days. When I repeat that she was spending a lot of time in Paris that should be taken to mean seventy-two-hour visits usually booked solid with parties and shopping. For like most Jet Setters, Ira was never comfortable for more than a short time at any one place.

Ira was as great a shopper as Elizabeth Taylor. I have had the good fortune to witness both ladies on their respective expeditions and must say that I was certainly glad on each occasion that it was not my name that appeared on their credit cards.

If I had to decide which of the ladies was the

greatest shopper on earth, I would select Liz due to her all-time great performance on a visit with Malcolm Forbes. Malcolm had decided to throw a huge party for his sixtieth birthday in Tangiers, and Sagan and I had been invited. Macolm sent his jet to pick up Liz. When the plane arrived, he met her at the small private airstrip in the middle of the desert on a scorching hot afternoon. The heat was so great that the other guests wondered if the party would be cancelled.

The plane landed, and a hot, tired, but determined Liz emerged from Forbes's plane and said, on greeting Malcolm, 'Let's go shopping.'

Despite the heat, fatigue, and the preparations for the party, Malcolm tried to accommodate Liz and took her directly to the nicest antique store where he linked her up with Sagan and me. Knowing Liz's shopping habits, we knew we were in for a long afternoon. After a while, Malcolm, perspiring and tired, said, 'Liz, I really must go.' 'Fine,' she responded, 'just leave me your credit card.' She continued her shopping expedition. It was this type of fortitude and disregard for personal discomfort that marked Liz as the greatest shopper I had ever seen. Ira was a close second.

It was indeed the prospect of visiting some of her favorite designers that drew Ira back to her Paris home on this occasion. It was a fabulous home on the rue Francois I, later to be bought by the actor Alain Delon. She was doing a lot of entertaining. I told her that I was not involved with anyone at the moment, and she suggested that I renew my acquaintance with Sao. In fact, she would be happy to ensure that we would both be invited to her next party.

It was early fall, and Paris was beautiful and busy with social events. Ira kept her word, and I received an invitation to her next party. Of course, Sao was there, looking as if she expected to see me.

'Sao, I have admired you for years and find you the most attractive woman I have ever seen,' I said the moment I walked over to her. Remember that in my post-Garbo period such a compliment was a direct comparison to 'the Divine.' Sao seemed to accept it as sincere and appeared genuinely flattered. I think she had wondered why it had taken me so long to approach her. She eagerly accepted my invitation to dinner.

Pierre was older than Sao and either was genuinely ill or a very convincing hypochondriac. Let me be the first to sympathize with this. Now as I approach the age that Pierre had been at the time, I find myself obsessed with my health, and when I think about it, I, too, might very well be a bit on the melodramatic side when it comes to illness. But at that time, I was feeling strong and healthy enough to voice disdain — even contempt — for Sao's sickly husband as she voiced her complaints and the natural effects they had on the more personal facets of their life together.

Sao is still a very beautiful woman today, but it is hard to describe just how gorgeous she was then. She was a blonde goddess. She is tall, statuesque, with a dimpled face that typifies seductiveness. Her full blonde hair was then worn parted on the left side and blown back. It shone with almost platinum highlights. Her eyebrows were slightly darker than her hair and arched upwards seductively at the corners. When she smiled, her face creased on both sides in wide adorable dimples. And she really knew how to dress, coordinating a flashy personal style with a museum collection of jewels. To me there is nothing quite so sexy as deep cleavage filled with enormous diamonds.

I had desired Sao for a considerable period of time, and when she took me home to her hotel immediately after we left Ira's party, I realized that my feelings were not unreciprocated. In fact, Sao was smitten, and so was I. It was mutual. The whole situation acted like an aphrodisiac. Sao was beautiful, enormously wealthy in a flashy but not cheap way, she was well known, a socialite, and with all that, she was a very sensual person.

We saw each other almost every day. In January, she invited me to accompany her and her husband to St. Moritz. St. Moritz might be the snootiest place in the world, but not when you are the guests of the Schlumbergers. Pierre was civilized enough to get separate rooms for himself and Sao.

For our week in St. Moritz, we developed a wonderful ritual. Sao and I would go for walks or I would ski in the morning. Then in the early afternoon, we would return to the Palace Hotel to get ready for the various parties. We visited the chalet of Rosemary Kanzler (Henry Ford's in-law), with her companion, the singer Tony Renis of 'Quando Quando' fame. Rosemary's chalet had an enormous sitting room, with one entire wall made of glass overlooking the mountain. It had a huge roaring fire in the middle of the room — exactly like the opening scene from the *Pink Panther* movie.

We were naturally invited to the New Year's Eve party thrown by the Greek shipping magnate Stavros Niarchos at the Chesa Veglia Club. Niarchos was a man who, despite his enormous success, always seemed to follow in the footsteps and live beneath the shadow of Onassis.

Niarchos's fortune was similar in size and origin to that of Onassis. His personal conquests were almost as impressive as those of Onassis. He even married Onassis's ex-wife Tina after being cleared of the charge of killing his first wife. Sadly, Tina Niarchos was to die mysteriously of a drug overdose, foreshadowing the tragic death of her daughter, Christina, some short years later.

Despite the similarities and even interconnections, Niarchos was no match for Onassis. He was described by one associate as 'Onassis minus the personality,' but I believe that his most interesting epitaph came from his former girlfriend, the beautiful Princess Maria Pia Ruspoli. When asked what she felt of Niarchos after the end of their relationship, she paused for a second, then said, 'He is a small man in a big boat.'

Having said all that, the Niarchos's New Year's

Eve party was a very big deal. As the highlight of the St. Moritz social season, it was packed with personalities who either had or soon would play important roles in my life. On this occasion, the greatest benefit of attending the party was befriending one of the legends of the Jet Set.

Prince Johannes von Thurn und Taxis and Gunter Sachs were the reigning German Jet Setters. Gunter was famous for his conquests while Johannes was admired and feared for his strange wit. The enormous wealth and power of the Thurn und Taxis family dates back to the fifteenth century when the emperor had given them the privilege of running the mail service throughout Europe. Until the last century, it was coaches owned by the Thurn und Taxis that transported all the mail and even passengers. They had bought land along all their routes and owned an enormous empire of hostels and inns. Johannes lived in an enormous castle in Regensburg, but spent the year cavorting with us.

I say that he was feared because his wealth and fame allowed him license to act out whatever odd pranks his witty mind would devise. Several years earlier, he had been a guest at Niarchos's party, and to this day, the guests still whispered about 'the incident.' I have told you that some social events can suddenly change a man's life, and for me, the invitation to the Patiño Ball in Lisbon resulted in my relationship with Cécile Rothschild and even my first introduction to Sao. What I learned that night is that Johannes's humor had a very large effect on the life and reputation of Señor Antenor Patiño.

As it turns out, Johannes regarded Patiño as nouveau riche and was unimpressed by his newly bought social status. On that memorable New Year's Eve, Patiño, still married to Princesse Bourbon, had brought his girlfriend and future wife, Countess Beatrice Rovasenda, to Niarchos's party.

The countess was young and very attractive, and this seemed to antagonize Johannes even more. For although a powerful man, Patiño himself was rather diminutive. Under five feet tall and slender, by this point in his life, he was rather old and a little hunched over. He had taken to dyeing his hair a rather unconvincing jet-black and even applying makeup to darken his bushy eyebrows. Johannes eyed him suspiciously, then approaching the countess, asked innocently, 'Who is the pansy?'

The countess was scandalized. She thought that everyone knew that she was his mistress and soon might well be his wife. 'I promise you that he is no pansy,' she responded with obvious anger. 'I would like you to know that I am his woman, and I assure you, he makes love to me several times each day. He, sir, is no pansy!' Johannes looked stunned at the mistake, then said, 'I am sorry, Madame. I did not mean to say that he was a pansy. I meant chimpanzee.'

This exchange not only provided the leading gossip for that season at St. Moritz, but remains a legend today. So it was with some trepidation that I was introduced to the famous prince. For some odd reason, he took to me and instead of using me as a target, regarded me as some sort of ally in his hobby of playing mind and verbal games with the other guests. Our paths would often cross again, and I would witness some of the strangest pranks I have ever seen. But on this occasion, I was happy to be on good terms with the nemesis of the nouveau riche and truly enjoyed his company throughout the party. Afterward we all went to the Kings nightclub and danced ourselves into a frenzy.

Two weeks later, the Schlumbergers invited me along with a conveniently unattached young lady to go with them on safari to Angola. The young girl, Grazia Maria Ianari, was to be presented as my date. Everyone knew she had just been jilted by her lover who ironically was the brother of my old girlfriend Dindina — two of the grandchildren of Mussolini. So the alibi seemed plausible.

I was about to get myself involved in an almost Hemingwayesque situation. Remember *The Snows of Kilamanjaro* where the protagonist gets an infection in some remote African location and slowly dies in the arms of his lover? Well I had the privilege of experiencing this in reverse. Friends of the Schlumbergers had flown us to some semi-remote area where we were promised the usual assortment of animals that one is supposed to slaughter needlessly on these macho expeditions. I did not participate in the slaughter, but learned some hunting lore that would one day save my life.

Despite the rustic setting, the food was, naturally, catered, and one night we were given shellfish. Sao's dish must have been tainted, and she became ill — really ill. She was immediately hospitalized, but the prognosis was not good. In fact, it seemed almost certain she would die. This is when a very startling thing occurred that was perhaps the strangest part of the trip. I began to weep. I mean with sincerity! I kneeled at her bedside and cried like a baby, with periodic prayers and, as I recall, promises of reform should she survive. She was unconscious, but I kissed her repeatedly and held her hand. At that moment I realized something — I was truly in love. This revelation came as a surprise — not only to me, but also to Pierre who stared aghast in disbelief. I guess he figured that it was all right for his wife to have her share of pleasure, but not for a moment did he believe that any feelings existed. He looked at me with shock and I think anger — as if I was intruding, as if I had no right to love her enough to feel such fear and grief. Then he left the room.

Well, Jet Setters never die, they just fade away. Sao not only recovered, but was well enough for us to fly to Seville for the Feria ten days later. Now, that is a hard-core Jet Setter, when one does not even allow near-death to interfere with full participation in the circuit. Naturally we stayed at the Alfonso XIII. Remember, it's either the Alfonso or a yacht, and we had lost some time in Angola. We had to settle for staying in a hotel. Pierre and Sao had separate rooms. But something had changed. Pierre was distant to me and watchful. I think he felt threatened.

Count and Countess d' Odiel, the cousin to

the King of Spain, invited us to their castle outside Seville. We wore traditional Spanish dress (the Duke of Windsor would have loved it), drank enormous amounts of sangría, and danced the flamenco till the wee hours. By the time we got back to the hotel, we were extremely drunk and very aroused.

I decided to take Sao to Rome. It was early March, but Rome has always been a cooperative city for me, and it did me the favor of snowing heavily for the duration of her stay, giving us the excuse to remain indoors.

It would have been nice if I could have stopped time at that moment — if eternity could have been spent staring at the snow accumulating along the arches of the Colosseum and feeling warm, safe, and in love. But, of course, things move on and change.

I do not believe that Sao and I exchanged a word of criticism or censure until the day that we spoke of a life together. From that time onward, our life lost the innocent joy that comes from uncritical acceptance. Soon after our joyous days in Rome, Sao took me with her to New York. She was intimate with the New York social scene, and we were booked up solidly every night with several parties. We visited Alexander Lieberman, Mary Lasker, and Rosemary Kanzler. These people had difficulty with my presence in their homes. First, they simply did not know what my function was supposed to be in public. Remember, they were friends of Pierre, too. Secondly, at that time my English was very poor. Sao was unaware of that fact, and when she realized it, she was appalled. She looked at it as low class, as if it were entirely my fault, inexcusable, and totally unacceptable.

The trip was going rather poorly when I was at least afforded a small, but costly moment of comic relief. Sao found out that Prince Johannes von Thurn und Taxis was also in town and although she was unable to see him, allowed me the opportunity of attending a party to which he was invited. The party was to be hosted by an old New York society woman in her magnificent Park Avenue apartment.

Johannes and I agreed to meet for a drink ahead of time, then go over to the party together. When I arrived at his hotel, he was carrying a strange object in his hand. It was a little, glass, goldfish bowl with a small, rather unattractive fish inside it.

'What is that, Johannes?' I asked.

'A small gift for our hostess, Minimum,' he responded.

He had taken to calling me Minimum as the opposite of Massimo, I guess. Johannes was a great lover of nicknames, and generally the names he chose carried a greater sting than the harmless one he had given me. For example, we had a mutual friend who seemed perpetually aroused and ever in pursuit of young women. Sadly, as a youth, he had contracted polio, and as a result, his right leg was in a brace. When he walked, the afflicted leg would remain straight, and he would be forced to swing it in a circular motion from the hip.

To Johannes's strange mind, the movement

117

resembled the way the metal rod of a streetcar swings along the cable as it turns a corner. As a result, he called our unfortunate friend 'A Streetcar Named Desire.' As you can see, I counted my blessings to have gotten away with a nickname as innocuous as Minimum. In fact I even preferred it to the nickname I had unfortunately had to bear since my early days in the Jet Set. Gianni Agnelli is an unusual Jet Setter in that he is somehow able to run his Fiat empire, several other large enterprises, and still partake in the entire Jet Set scene. This comes from his indefatigable reserves of energy — as well as virtually no need to sleep. Even as a much younger man, I could not keep up with him. Because of this, he christened me 'Mozzarella,' after the soft, white, Neapolitan cheese. Sadly, this name has stuck with me to this day.

Johannes stared at the little bowl and giving a smile to his fish, continued. 'You will see that the old woman is a great collector of fish.' And as it turned out, indeed she was. When we arrived, I was amazed to see that the entrance foyer of her apartment contained a wall that housed an enormous aquarium filled with exotic, colorful fish. Apparently her obsession with this hobby made her somewhat suspicious to Johannes's sense of proportion.

'Hello,' he said as he embraced our hostess. 'I have brought you a small gift,' and he handed her the little glass bowl. She looked at the unattractive fish and unsure how to react, finally smiled and thanked the prince. 'It's nothing, really,' he said with his charming smile, 'but please, put him with his brothers so he can have friends.' Not wishing to appear ungrateful, the hostess instructed her butler to pour the little fish into the lavish aquarium where he seemed to disappear into the lush underwater foliage.

We went off to dinner where Johannes amused the table with his stories and assorted insults. It was a truly enjoyable evening, and without the feeling of linguistic inadequacy that Sao had instilled in me, I was able to relax and enjoy myself. After dinner, the hostess rose from table first to instruct her staff to serve us our drinks in the sitting room. We were about to follow her when we heard a terrible scream, then a dull thud. The guests uniformly jumped up to find the source of this disturbance.

There on the floor, by the foyer, we found our hostess lying unconscious at the foot of her aquarium, which was filled with fish skeletons and one rather smug, content, if somewhat bloated piranha. Johannes had had his little joke. It ended (as most of Johannes's jokes) in a costly lawsuit. But for him it seemed worth it, for yet another of his deeds became a legend among the Jet Set.

I returned to see if Sao, too, had enjoyed her evening. I was feeling a bit run down, but hopeful that the trip was still salvageable. However, as the evening progressed, disaster struck. I got sick. It was not too serious — just a case of bronchitis — but I am a poor patient. In all fairness, I must say that I showed a great deal of support when Sao was ill. Sao had little tolerance for another sickly consort. 'I already have a sick husband. I don't need a sick companion,' she screamed.

We were staying out very late at these society parties, and I simply was getting more run down, and my health wasn't improving. One evening, I had almost completely lost my voice. As we were driven to yet another party, I asked her chauffeur if he could stop at a pharmacy. Sao rolled her eyes and looked at me with unconcealed disgust.

I hurried into the drugstore and bought some cough drops. We were running a little late, and I guess she grew impatient because when I came out of the store, her limousine was gone, and it was raining pretty hard.

I returned to the Carlyle where we were staying and decided to place my breakfast order then go to sleep. When I awoke, I found her lying in bed finishing the last morsel of the breakfast I had ordered. That was the last straw. Remembering how Garbo had abandoned me to die when I swallowed the fish bone, I now felt exactly the same way. It seems that a good night's sleep had restored my voice for I certainly used it. We began by screaming at each other, and the confrontation ended with my decision to leave. I packed my bags and flew directly back to Paris.

I guess the moral of the story is let a friendship run its course, but don't spoil it by trying to turn it into something that you know is not possible.

Maybe there is even another moral — but it frightens me to think of it.

6

IL N'YA PAS D'AMOUR, SEULEMENT LES PREUVES D'AMOUR

(There is no love, only the proofs of love)
— Cocteau

For a little more than a year, I had continued at this frantic pace with great success, but growing terror. It was now 1971, and I was thirty-one years old, but had never worked. The typical solution to such a problem in my circles would simply have been to marry an heiress, but this I would not do. I have always refused out of purely pragmatic reasons. A great number of the aristocratic friends of my youth had succumbed to this method of support and found it uniformly unsuccessful. They generally were dependent not only on the whims of their wives, but also on the attitudes of their fathers-in-law, whose deaths they impatiently awaited.

In fact, there are primarily two types of wealthy debutantes — those with vacant and those with full family crypts. Unless you can stumble upon the first type, you will inevitably spend your life waiting for the second event to occur. On top of this sad state of affairs, men who marry solely for money, socially play second fiddle to their rich wives in a way I often found demeaning. Also, to a great extent, it was hard work and often did not even improve one's life-style.

So my bank account shrunk, and my fears grew. It was now the beginning of August. If it's August, it must be Monte Carlo. I was staying at the Hermitage when I received an invitation for a ball to be thrown by Lady Lydia Deterding at the Hotel de Paris. I had never met the hostess, but, of course, I was very familiar with the name. She was the widow of Sir Henri Deterding and therefore one of the richest women in the world.

In the film *Some Like It Hot*, there is a funny scene on the beach where Tony Curtis pretends he is a millionaire to impress Marilyn Monroe. When she asks him what business he is in, he tells her that it is oil and lifts up a seashell to indicate the logo of the company. This is not far removed from the story of my hostess's husband. At the turn of the century, Sir Henri Deterding was running the Royal Dutch Petroleum Company and with the financial help of the ever-present Paris Rothschilds, was able to achieve his goal of merging with his chief competitor. The other company had been named after the owner's original business of importing and collecting seashells. Thus was the Royal Dutch-Shell Group established with Deterding at the helm. Deterding was to live the fairy-tale life of a rags-to-immense-riches industrialist. He became the pioneer and leader of the world oil industry, merging hundreds of companies into a global conglomerate. By initiating the first international price regulations, he became one of the most important men in the world. There have been a number of books written about Deterding, but I was soon to learn the shocking truth of his secret life.

Lady Deterding's party was an elaborate black-tie affair in the lavish Empire ballroom of the Hotel de Paris, Monte Carlo's chic hotel. The center stage of Monte Carlo social life, the hotel had recently undergone massive improvements at the hands of Aristotle Onassis. It suggested a degree of suave elegance that made one sure that if James Bond appeared at any time, he would be completely comfortable. Indeed, it was not uncommon to discover Roger Moore in the dining room.

Lady Deterding was born in Russia, and to remind her guests of this fact, the theme for the evening was Russian. Two bands took turns providing gypsy and Russian music. I knew most of the people and was enjoying mingling with friends when an extraordinary event transpired. The band began to play a passionate Cossack tune, and suddenly an attractive, but very old lady, dressed in an exquisite Dior gown of fine black lace, began to dance.

She was a little more than eighty years old at this time. As she danced, the room became quiet and still — all eyes trained on this bizarre spectacle. Her grace and energy were impressive for an octogenarian. Yet, this behavior was slightly eccentric, even for Monte Carlo in August.

She swayed over to a young man and snatched

a white, silk scarf from his neck and then to my horror — dancing as sensuously as her withered legs allowed — approached me teasingly. She lashed out with the scarf, catching me around the neck, and pulled me toward her. The protocol in such situations is never clear, but I decided to accept her invitation and began to dance. The other guests (perhaps relieved not to have been so chosen) formed a ring around us, not unlike my last performance at the von Karajan house. They began to clap along with the vibrant Russian music. I had never danced such a thing before, but I began to relax and do my best impersonation of a wild Cossack. It was apparently convincing enough to send Lady Deterding into a new series of contortions. Finally the music stopped, and I was able to gratefully rejoin my friends. The evening was thereafter uneventful, and I returned to my room at the Hermitage.

The next morning, I was wakened by the porter bringing in a small, nicely wrapped package. Inside was a gold Cartier watch and a thank-you note from Lady Deterding. This was a rather extravagant way to say thank you for one dance, but it was her way of setting the stage for what was to come. I was about to experience the most extravagant and well-planned seduction I have ever witnessed.

Naturally, I called to thank her for the gift and immediately was invited to lunch. From this moment on, she began the chase in earnest. During lunch, she showered me with compliments and then launched what I was later to regard as the brainwashing campaign.

Lady Deterding was a very clever woman and knew how to manipulate people. She sensed my financial fears almost immediately. Perhaps she even had some research done on my position. However she may have become privy to my concerns about the future, she realized that playing up to these fears were her only chance of winning me over. From that first lunch, she began to intimate that a man like me was not suitable or even capable of ever holding a real job.

'Massimo,' she began, 'you are so beautiful and so charming, it would be a waste for you to work.' Naturally, I was forced to agree with this assessment. Our early conversations were almost exclusively dominated by this theme.

I was planning on leaving Monte Carlo the next day, but Lady Deterding begged me to remain while calling me persistently every couple of hours and filling the interim periods with flowers. I had never been so aggressively pursued before. In fact, her behavior was very masculine. It was essentially the traditional pattern of behavior one would expect an older man to use when trying to obtain the favors of a younger woman.

Again returning to the Marilyn Monroe comparison, Monroe pointed out that although it might be true that she was interested in men's money, was it not also true that they were initially attracted to her for her beauty, and was this not the same thing? In such a manner, I began to rationalize what was occurring and even agreed to remain in Monte Carlo where I saw a lot of Lady Deterding.

Our meetings were never boring. She was a great conversationalist and seemed thoroughly obsessed with helping me find a solution to my future. The message grew clearer after each date that she regarded herself as that solution. She was considerably more talkative about her past than Garbo had been, and this came as a relief. It was no longer necessary to watch my every word and live in fear of accidentally conjugating a verb in the past tense.

Like Garbo, Lady Deterding's life had also been theatrical. She was born Lydia Pavlovna, daughter of the White Russian general, Paul Koudayaroff, a staunch supporter of the czar. After the czar was executed, she left Russia and entered the theater. Although her acting career might have lacked the magic of Garbo's, she nevertheless landed the role of wife to two fabulously wealthy men. Her second husband, Sir Henri Deterding, was certainly one of the richest and most powerful men in the world. He was virtually running the international oil industry.

They lived a privileged and influential life. Possessing a number of fabulous homes throughout the world, the couple spent the majority of their time either at their London mansion on Park Lane or in their enormous country estate near Windsor Castle where Sir Henri liked to hunt and breed horses. It seems that their marital bliss and sterling reputation were mysteriously tainted just prior to Sir

Henri's death in 1939. Some undefined rumors had surfaced and then quickly disappeared, the source of which remained a mystery. This was to be the only subject Lady Deterding did not wish to discuss. How different my life would have been if only she had never revealed this secret.

Finally I had to return to Sardinia because a group of my friends had organized a party for my birthday on August 20. The Costa Smeralda in Sardinia was rapidly becoming the 'in' place for the end of August and was filled with avant-garde luminaries. The rugged and majestic landscape of this undisturbed paradise had been recently discovered by Karim Aga Khan, and clever industrialists such as Karl Hahn, the chairman of Volkswagen, had begun building summer palaces there. In Hahn's case, he blasted a building site into the stone cliffs overlooking the sea and using the local granite, built a medieval fortress into the rock.

It has been used as the setting of a number of films, including *Bloodline* and a James Bond movie. In a Jet-Set version of 'keeping up with the Joneses,' architects competed for the privilege of designing increasingly dramatic masterpieces. The trick was trying to subtly integrate massive homes into the hilly landscape. Minimalism demanded that these enormous summer palaces blend inconspicuously into the natural scenery. The result was magnificent. Homes were often carved into stone valleys or perched on sheer cliffs above the sea. The harbors were becoming filled with the large boats of the super-rich where the constraints of minimalism seem to have been relaxed. Days were spent with lunch parties on the yachts and dinner parties at the various mansions.

It was here that I befriended Crown Prince Carl Gustav of Sweden. We were the guests on board the yacht of a famous industrialist who produced toilet accessories. Despite possessing the romantic name of Annibale Scotti Casanova, he had irreverently been dubbed 'the Bidet King,' and to his dismay, this name had such appeal to the snobby Jet Setters that it stuck.

The prince and I were happily joined by two sisters who were beautiful, young French countesses. We kept them virtually without interruption in our cabins for a number of days. The Bidet King was enormously attracted to these girls, who unfortunately remained unimpressed with the physically unattractive industrialist who bore no resemblance to his notorious namesake.

Despite the Bidet King's source of riches, surprisingly his yacht was equipped with very few toilets. As a result, in between intimate sessions, the sisters would have to leave either Prince Gustav's or my cabin and pass the frustrated Bidet King's door in order to freshen up. This seemed to infuriate and frustrate him to the point that he finally departed, telling us we could remain without him on the yacht for the next week.

I gladly accepted this offer and remained with the urbane crown prince and our charming guests. After this manly bonding experience, I was not to see my royal friend again until many years later. I had the honor of selecting him as the top recipient of *The Best* Award in 1992. For his part, King Carl XVI Gustav chose to honor my old flame Greta Garbo in 1983 when he made her a commander of the Swedish Order of the North Star. The Jet Set is a very self-congratulatory society, and we are constantly recognizing one another for something.

It was also here in the Costa Smeralda that I came to know Princess Margaret, the sister of the Queen of England. With the exception of the Duke of Windsor, of all the members of the British royal family, only Princess Margaret was a member of the Jet Set. There are good reasons for this. Although Prince Charles plays polo, hunts, skis, and is fun at parties, he is loaded down with a schedule of official duties and is mantled with a cloak of propriety that precludes his participation in our group.

Prince Andrew is a wonderful man whose interests are restricted to his naval career, golf, and watching television. Princess Anne is busy with horses, charities, and turning around her formerly negative public image. Prince Edward is active with his theatrical interests and the precarious détente he enjoys with the press regarding the nature of his sexuality, which has been somewhat assuaged by his marriage. The Duchess of York was far too busy negotiating her divorce, trying to control her ever-mounting debts, and raising her two children to do more than ski twice a year at Klosters. Princess Diana was busy with her charities and never really was cut out for the superficialities of the Jet Set, although she certainly spent a good deal of time with members of our group. And so we were left with an aging Duke of Windsor and a vivacious, but somewhat odd Princess Margaret.

By the time I met her, she was well into her marriage with Armstrong-Jones. Their wedding in 1960 was to continue the trend set by Grace Kelly three years prior. It was a media event. In fact, it broke the record for television viewers that was set by the Grimaldis. In addition, the public was able to follow the bizarre details of this spectacle. For example, the press was allowed to report on the drawn-out and apparently difficult struggle to find a straight best man for Armstrong-Jones, ultimately settling for a gentleman who hardly knew him. Interviews of palace employees were eagerly published with fantastic stories ranging from Armstrong-Jones' sometimes-erratic behavior to stories of the newly-weds enjoying cross-dressing.

These might not be typical goings-on for the British royals, but they were excellent credentials for the Jet Set. In fact, the sexual antics of the royal couple provided us with many interesting party anecdotes. For example, while vacationing on the yacht of Karim Aga Khan, the enamored couple would adjourn to their cabin immediately after each lunch for somewhat lengthy afternoon sex sessions. Sadly, the overworked bed in their stateroom was unable to survive the cruise.

I met Princess Margaret at a party, and she seemed quite attracted to me. Throughout the evening, the rather attractive, but diminutive princess smoked and drank and flirted with abandon. She was so flirtatious, in fact, that I got quite encouraged, and by the end of the party, she made sure that I was invited to an intimate lunch the next day. I found her charming and was very glad to learn that I was to be seated next to her at the table. She had two distinct ways of treating people. If they attracted and interested her, she was talkative and charming. For those people who failed to capture her attention, she was very aloof and perhaps a little rude. The fact that she flirted with me during the party and then asked to sit next to me the next day indicated that I had fortunately fallen in the first category.

Unfortunately I was staying overnight on board ship and forgot to tell the captain to wake me up the next morning before setting sail. By the time I woke up, I was way out to sea with no hope of returning in time for the lunch and unable to even send my regrets. Naturally such a faux pas is not easily excused, and I was met with coldness during the few times I was to meet the stood-up princess at parties.

I arrived back on shore to console myself with the company of the famous banker, Baron Leon Lambert. His reputation for great wealth was only exceeded by that of both his flagrant homosexuality and excessive stinginess. I have often been found attractive by homosexuals and have developed a certain approach of allowing the development of strong, but noninvasive friendships to occur. As a result, I have often found myself courted more aggressively by men than by hopeful women. Lydia certainly was an exception to this. But on this particular day, the obsequiously interested Baron Lambert sent me a hastily wrapped birthday gift. It turned out to be a generic lithograph of the type found at framing stores and gift shops. It came with a card on which the words 'for your home in Rome' were scribbled. I rewrapped it and sent it back with a note saying, 'I am very sorry, but I only have real paintings in my home in Rome.'

This was not a mercenary act performed with the expectation of shaming him into a more lavish gift. It was an act of disgust for the cheapness of such a wealthy man. The next day, I received a package that contained an original Baruchello painting. Baruchello was famous and greatly valued even then. It was an extravagant, but eccentric gift, for the subject matter related to an almost-cartoon-like depiction of various erections and their respective contingents of sperm. Is it any wonder that I have never placed my money in the hands of investment bankers?

During the period of our separation, Lady Deterding continued to call three or four times a day, and I found myself calling her, too. As my birthday approached, she phoned to say that she wanted to see me soon to give me my present. We agreed that we would meet in Paris for dinner two days after my party.

I met her at the Grand Vefour, a dark, mirrored, and romantic restaurant built at the turn of the century. She had put great effort into her appearance and looked quite elegant. Instead of the black lace she had worn the night we met, she was wearing a cheerful Dior dress in red and white. Her hair was a light blonde, and I noticed perhaps for the first time just how piercing her deep blue eyes appeared.

'What an attractive dress,' I remarked, trying to be polite, although I thought the dress was really intended for a much younger woman.

'I will never wear black again as long as we are together' was her answer and also her promise. In the time we were together, I was never again to see her in black.

After we finished our meal, she took out an official-looking document from her purse. 'This is your birthday present, Massimo,' she announced quietly and handed me the paper. It was the deed of ownership for a large apartment in the rue de la Faisanderie. The deed recorded the sale and the fact that she as purchaser had guaranteed payment. The price was discreetly covered with a piece of ribbon so I would not be allowed to know the cost, although I was later to learn that its value was the equivalent of about one million dollars. The name of the owner was left blank, and next to it was a place for the stamp of a notary. The message was very clear.

If this were simply a present, my name would have already been filled in. I suppose some people might have been offended, but actually I found it rather touching. It is not every day that one is offered such an extravagant birthday present or the compliment that the expected form of gratitude should be so highly prized.

I decided to give it a try. My reluctance was not solely out of distaste for the situation. I tend to be much more pragmatic than that. I had a real fear that I would not be able to pull it off physically. There is a big difference between a woman in her early sixties (Garbo and Cécile for example) and a lady in her eighties. I would have described Garbo as regal and chiseled, Cécile as statuesque and elegant, but Lady Deterding seemed simply old. I have prided myself on my ability to get aroused in unlikely circumstances, but could I do it now? And how would she react if I failed?

In preparation for the event, we remained a little longer in the restaurant so I could fortify myself with an adequate amount of champagne.

We were then driven to her magnificent apartment on the Avenue Foch, which, incidentally, was extremely close to the address that had appeared on my birthday present. Her apartment constituted the entire second floor of the building, and as we entered the elevator and the door shut, I was confronted with the reality of what I had chosen to do. She sensed my growing panic and tried to lighten the air.

'Aristotle Onassis bought the fifth floor for Christina,' she began. 'It used to be the servants' floor, but he rebuilt it. Nevertheless, whenever I see him or Christina in the elevator, I like to tease them about how they like living in the servants' quarters.'

I just had time to giggle at the thought that the fabulous billionaire whose frequent marriage proposals were consistently rejected by Garbo was apparently also taunted by Lydia. Then I thought of Christina. As a very young man, my friend Alex Waldeck and I would double-date Christina and her cousin in St. Moritz. In those pre-drug days, our idea of a big thrill was to take the two girls to the mezzanine of the movie theaters where we would kiss and fondle them in the dark. It seems somehow naïve now in a more jaded time, but in those days, we considered ourselves quite daring. I wondered what she would think now if we ran into her in the elevator. Then the elevator door opened to Lydia's massive lobby, and it was time for romance.

I was still rather nervous when we entered her apartment. We went to her sitting room and had more champagne, and then she led me into the master bedroom. What was next to transpire had some similarities, but a world of differences to my first night with Garbo.

Lady Deterding also required absolute darkness, but for reasons I was to learn later. After adjusting the light to her satisfaction, she left the room and returned in a few minutes wearing a silk negligee. She climbed into bed and began kissing me with great tenderness, yet such passion that I responded sincerely to her. She undressed me slowly, her hands running lightly over my body the whole time. Her fingers were caressing me with a deliberate slowness and a seductive expertise that I had rarely experienced in a younger woman.

I was by now completely naked, yet she remained dressed. She began kissing me on my chest then slowly dropped down and began to perform what I must regard as the most fantastic oral experience I have ever known. I believe that her skill was probably always extraordinary, but she had developed her own technique in which she was able to use to her advantage the effect that age had wrought upon her mouth. My fears of responding were long past, and instead I concentrated on forcing myself not to let it end too soon.

Next she prompted me to enter her, and again I was amazed by her excitement and the skill of her movements. It was much the same as the Russian dance that first night. It was as if she was daring time to slow her down or steal one moment of her enjoyment of life. What I then had regarded as ridiculous, I now began to feel was courageous. The fact that I was in her bed and actually enjoying it was somehow a victory for her and a pleasant surprise for me.

I woke up in her bed late the next morning. She was an early riser and had already gotten up. I lay there thinking about what had happened. I did not feel disgusted with what I had done, but wondered how she would now react, having achieved what she wanted. I really did not expect that there would be any more talk about apartments, but again I was underestimating the unique Lydia Deterding. At about noon, she entered the bedroom dressed in an attractive negligee. I wondered if this meant that she wanted to have more sex, but instead she threw open the curtains, smiled, and said, 'Massimo, Massimo quick . . . we have an appointment with the notary!'

'What for?' I asked with studied nonchalance,

as if one is so frequently offered million-dollar properties that one cannot be expected to remember each promise.

'For your new apartment, of course,' she responded as if there could never have been any doubt at all. At this point, I could no longer restrain myself and jumping out of bed, embraced her and showered her with kisses. This seemed to embarrass her, and she simply said, 'I told you, yesterday,' meaning no doubt that she could not understand the fuss. We went to the notary and, by the end of the day, I was the owner of a fabulous apartment — a gift from a woman whom I had met three weeks before.

That night we had a quiet dinner together, and I must say, I started to take her more seriously. Perhaps it sounds like justifying a mercenary act, but I began to respect her pluck and integrity. She was a great manipulator and on this occasion showed true genius — she sent me home. Instead of sleeping with me again and risking the chance that it would cheapen her gift by the implication that she now owned my body, she simply told me she was tired and wished to be alone. In fact, she said that she would concentrate on having my new apartment furnished and decorated quickly so I would have an appropriate place to live.

'It would not look good for you to be seen staying over here too often. It would hurt your reputation,' she insisted.

The effect of this psychology was very poignant. Instead of feeling like a prisoner, I felt gratitude and some guilt. Naturally that drew me to her much more effectively than over-possessiveness would have. At the same time, her matter-of-fact statement about furnishing my apartment was also part of her masterful manipulation. It was like the story of Scheherazade who delayed her death by luring her would-be killer to listen to a new story each night for a thousand and one nights. With subtle promises of more marvels to come each day for quite literally a thousand and one days, Lydia would delay the fate we both knew awaited us.

7

SPRINGTIME FOR HITLER

On the very next day, in the guise of furnishing my apartment, Lydia began to execute her plan. In the early afternoon, she took me to see my new apartment for the first time. Let me say that it is one thing to be given a piece of paper that says you own a property and quite another to walk into a magnificent home that is now absolutely yours. The building was immaculate and new with a generous lobby clad in white marble and large glass doors opening onto a private garden.

My apartment was on the second floor and was an expansive, pristine space with a large sitting room, formal dining room, a large bedroom, and a terrace. But the first thing that struck me after that burst of exhilaration was the awareness of how empty it felt. This, of course, was part of the plan. Had Lydia chosen one of the many suitable old-world apartments with their intricate moldings, herringbone floors, and paneled walls, a minimal amount of furnishings would have been enough. But she cleverly chose a brand-new, postmodern building, and there is nothing quite so empty as an unfurnished postmodern apartment. It felt like a beautifully gift-wrapped box with nothing in it. This is where Lydia planned to step in.

First she contracted the finest interior decorators in Paris. They were given a carte blanche to convert this beautiful shell into a modern showpiece. They were not given a budget nor, of course, were they pushed to hurry the job. No, they had all the time in the world. Meanwhile, Lydia and I were to spend each afternoon shopping for artwork, furnishings, accessories, and my wardrobe. She would buy me anything I wanted, the only stipulation being that I try to keep the daily spending rhythm at one thousand dollars. This, in 1970, was a huge amount of money.

'Please, Massimo,' she begged, 'try to spend no more than a thousand dollars each day. I cannot afford any more than that,' she would often say. Lydia had a reputation of being frugal if not cheap, and my enormous budget was a great concession on her part. So this became the way we would spend our days together.

By creating this schedule from the first days of our relationship, she effectively trained me to expect to be with her in the afternoon. She knew that I slept through the mornings, and we were out at parties or alone together most nights. The afternoons were the most likely times for me to stray, and Lydia filled them in a manner that insured I would be with her.

We would browse the many Parisian antique stores and art galleries, and she took me to auctions, as well. I got so carried away with this spending orgy that sometimes she would hold my hand down to restrain me from bidding on yet another acquisition.

The excitement of buying kept me in a state of constant stimulation and actual physical arousal. Again, this suited Lydia's intentions admirably, and she increased the tempo and frequency of our sex life.

She would warn me one or two days in advance that we would be tête-à-tête on a particular evening. This was always understood to mean we would be sleeping together. In bed she became increasingly passionate, and the sessions lasted much longer. She always wore a negligee for, as I learned, in addition to her dentures, she wore a prosthesis where she had lost a breast. She was so skinny that I could feel her heart pounding furiously as the sessions got longer and more physical. I became convinced that I would kill her, but she refused to temper her enthusiasm. Whether out of pride or lust, Lydia refused to allow time to gain the upper hand in or out of bed.

At the end of the first four months, my apartment was outfitted to perfection, and my closets were overflowing with new suits. I even had five tuxedos. The walls of the apartment had been hand-painted and marbleized. Beautiful oils including an original Dali hung on the walls.

Aware that I was fond of my astrological sign, Lydia had begun a collection of antique lion statues for me. She bought me a pair of ancient, golden Buddha statues and a gorgeous seventeenth-century dining-room set. All the receipts were sent to her, which had a significance I was to learn later. In addition to this, I was given a very generous monthly allowance, and Lydia paid all my bills including the salaries of my servants and monthly cost of my apartment in Rome.

Lydia had also given our relationship a great deal of thought. 'You are not to feel as if you are a prisoner,' she would say. 'You can see other people. If you stay with me, you can have all the freedom you want.' She made it clear that her wish and expectation was that we would remain together for the rest of her life and felt that she had to be realistic about what not to expect from me in the way of exclusivity.

The first months went according to plan — and Lydia began to feel rather secure. Her generosity remained constant, but her concern for my reputation seemed to diminish. She began to brag. First she told her hairdresser, which is almost forgivable. Then she began to tell her old friends. When I say old friends, I mean other wealthy, bored octogenarians. I can only imagine with horror how she might have entertained a room full of conservative dowagers with her randy stories of our sexual exploits.

Maybe she enjoyed shocking them. If so, she certainly succeeded. The word was out and everywhere. Perhaps Lydia's circle of old friends predated the Jet Set, but they certainly were in direct contact with it. The word spread with the speed that only disasters and gossip seem to achieve. It had not gone unnoticed in the beginning that we were often together, but people generally assumed that I was simply her companion, or 'walker,' as the terminology of the time would have described it. This type of thing is not uncommon. Nobody really believed we were sleeping together, and no one was prepared for Lydia's claim that we were a couple with a future.

As our first Christmas together drew closer, I was torn. On one hand, I liked and admired Lydia. Perhaps I was in love with her already. It is sometimes hard to know where gratitude ends and love begins. Yet she simply could not prevent herself from becoming increasingly demonstrative in public.

My friends, who regarded me as their role model if such a thing is possible when dealing with playboys, now either avoided me altogether or admonished me for becoming a gigolo. In their eyes, I was a disgrace. I had violated the unwritten law that calls it macho and admirable to bed numerous young women, but unforgivable to love one old one. Of course, I was profiting from the relationship, but nobody could understand why I remained after receiving such a beautiful and valuable apartment.

Finally I confronted Lydia with this problem and was met with shock and denial. 'Surely nobody can be concerned about the tiny difference between our ages' was her response. If anything, she became even more open about our relationship. She would hold my hand in public and often kiss me. She took to calling me her 'boyfriend' and introducing me that way at parties. Think about the world's response to Anna Nicole Smith and her marriage to a man who was her senior by roughly the same number of years as Lydia was to me. In the 1990s, they were a laughingstock. Jay Leno devoted numerous monologues to describing how such a thing might be possible. 'When there's a will, there's a way' was his pithy answer. My relationship took place twenty-seven years ago in a far more conservative period, and I was the junior. Another major difference was my dependency on the approval of my friends. When I got to know Anna Nicole Smith many years later, I realized how much stronger and more independent she is than I was during my relationship with Lydia.

People began to have trouble concealing their amusement, for nobody dared laugh at Lydia to her face. At dinner parties when Lydia began talking about her future plans with her boyfriend, the women at our table would generally respond by pretending to search for their purses, while the men preferred to drop their napkins. This would allow time to giggle hurriedly under the table before excusing themselves for what seemed like hours to the rest rooms. Quite often we would be left alone at the table. Lydia would turn to me with a perplexed look on her face and ask, 'Where did they all go, Massimo?' oblivious of the embarrassing reality.

It got so extreme that at one point we were invited to a black-tie party thrown by the Count and Countess de Nora in the ballroom of the Hotel du Cap, in Antibes, where the guests are required to enter by walking down a long formal stairway. They would be announced at the bottom. As Lydia and I began to descend, she grasped my hand as one hundred and fifty faces turned slowly and gazed at us with open, speechless mouths. Maybe it was coincidence, but even the band stopped playing. I wanted to run back up the stairs and hide, but somehow we continued to walk into the open chasm of that silent, stunned dance floor.

To distract me from these unfortunate experiences, Lydia began to praise life in Monte Carlo. 'Paris is wonderful, but you must have a home in Monte Carlo, and you will need residency there, too,' she proclaimed. And so virtually on the day my home in Paris was complete, we started our search for a suitable apartment in Monte Carlo. This time it was not to be a surprise gift. Indeed, we both enjoyed the distraction of finding it together. Through late fall and early winter, we substituted our antique hunting for a tour of available Monte Carlo real estate.

At the end of February, we found a beautiful apartment, and Lydia bought it for me immediately. The apartment was on the twenty-ninth floor of a very modern building called Chateau Périgord. Similar in size and value to the Paris apartment, it featured a fantastic view of Monte Carlo bay, always filled with tastefully arranged yachts and sailboats.

Lydia then convinced the reigning interior designer of the day, Roland Terenzio, to decorate it. He did the walls in white-and-silver paper, the furniture was made of bamboo and designed by Valentino, and we filled it with a collection of oils by in-vogue modern painters.

At the same time, Lydia began to quietly pull

those invisible strings that very few people even know exist, but that seem to tie the elite together in an intricate spider's web. Naturally she knew Prince Rainier of Monaco, and by the time my apartment was complete, I was a legal resident of his exclusive country.

'It is important for tax reasons,' she explained.

My sole source of income was now Lydia, so I wondered what could she mean by this. Over the next year, I was to learn the amazing answer. For the present, I was content to shuttle between my apartment across from the Roman Colosseum, to my little modern palace on the rue de la Faisanderie, to my seaside residence in Monte Carlo. All mine, completely mine.

For me, life had become a tale of three cities, and like the Dickens novel, it was the best of times and it was the worst of times. I began to stop analyzing the source of my feelings for Lydia and accepted (or perhaps assumed) that I loved her and admired her control and intelligence. As soon as the Monte Carlo apartment was furnished, I cut down on spending her money.

The daily abuse I was receiving from society was getting worse. I was now a multimillionaire, and nobody could understand why I still remained with her. At this point, the cold shoulder turned to outright ostracism.

Invitations dried up for me, and those that Lydia received in abundance often made it clear that I was not welcome. One such painful experience was the ball thrown by the very same Antenor Patiño whose ball in Portugal had resulted in my first meeting with Cécile de Rothschild and even Sao Schlumberger. It was the same Patiño who had been disadvantageously compared to a chimpanzee by Johannes von Thurn und Taxis at that memorable Niarchos's New Year's Eve party.

By this time, Patiño was being referred to as the wealthy Peruvian 'Tin King.' In addition to forever seeking opportunities to honor one another, the Jet Set is quite fond of creating titles. For industrialists, 'King of . . . ' their chosen industry of domination is the generally accepted address, thus 'Bidet King' and now 'Tin King.' The ball was thrown to honor someone and, in this case, the accomplishment of his granddaughter Diane achieving the age of eighteen. Both Diane and her sister, Milly, were very close friends of mine, and we were all disturbed on learning that the King had no intention of inviting me, although Lydia had received an invitation.

I am not trying to defend my odd relationship with Lydia, but consider the double standard that Patiño was imposing on me. By this time, he had married the beautiful, young countess whom Johannes had so irritated by first insinuating that her betrothed was a pansy — then a member of the simian species. Despite a marriage with almost as large an age difference as that which existed between Lydia and me, it seemed perfectly acceptable to Patiño because he, as the male, was the elder. By reversing this time-honored tradition, I had become an abomination in his eyes.

His granddaughters cried, Lydia protested, and I sulked. In the end, Lydia declined the invitation and bought me a new Porsche for consolation. At this point, one would think that even Lydia would start to get the message. Instead, she began to talk of marriage.

As any hopeful young couple does at such times, Lydia expressed a desire to meet my mother. Perhaps she was traditional enough to ask for my hand. On the week prior to my mother's arrival in Paris, Lydia made it clear to our remaining friends that we could not accept any invitations for the coming week.

Her polite, but resolute response to all invitations was 'Oh no, Massimo's mother is coming next week to visit us, and she is very old.' My mother was fifteen years younger than Lydia. Oddly enough, the two women hit it off well. Lydia treated my mother with the deference and respect one would expect from a well-mannered, young fiancée, and my mother found her charming.

Now Lydia proudly regarded me as her fiancé, convinced that she had received the blessings of her future mother-in-law. She openly discussed our impending nuptials at every public opportunity. The disgust from our social world was reaching a crescendo that even Lydia no longer could ignore.

I am still not sure if it was in response to the insecurity that this might have created or whether she miscalculated my reaction, but suddenly Lydia did something rather astonishing. She made her first real mistake. Lydia chose to reveal a secret that was far better left buried in the deepest recess of her vault. I will never forget the moment of revelation and the effect it would have on our whole relationship, indeed, on the rest of my life.

It started when we received an invitation for a party in London. I was eager to accept. Since the beginning of our relationship fourteen months earlier, we had never been to England together. When I pressed Lydia to accept, she refused flatly. 'Your husband was knighted by the king,' I pointed out. 'What do you have against England? You don't even visit your daughters. If I didn't read the society papers, I wouldn't even know what they look like!'

Actually I knew considerably more than what they looked like. Olga Deterding was quite a colorful figure in London society. She had been born with her mother's spunk, but chose other ways to express it. A frequent diner at Langham's Restaurant, she was banned from returning after getting sick on the owner and insisting on peeing in the men's urinals. Enormously wealthy, she enjoyed making periodic bids to purchase one of the large British newspapers.

I would quite like to have met her for the flamboyant Olga Deterding was not fated to be with us for much longer. At exactly the stroke of midnight on New Year's Eve 1978, Olga tried to swallow an entire steak and died when it got lodged in her throat. Now this was something for which I had some compassion.

Lydia's response to my request that we go to

the London party wasn't quite what I expected. First she asked me to be seated and then regarded me somberly for a few moments with exactly that same deliberate, assessing glance one might expect a parent to levy before revealing the facts of life to a precocious child.

'There is something that you ought to know,' she said as she walked over to her massive wall safe. Opening the safe, she removed two framed photographs, glanced at them lovingly for a second, and then handed them to me. She sat down and watched me expectantly as I regarded the old photos.

It took me a few seconds to identify what I was seeing and considerably longer to accept that it was possible. Before me was a picture of a younger Lydia Deterding in a relaxed, intimate vacation pose. She was leaning against a stone balustrade constructed of arches supported by stout pillars. The pillars and arch framed her and the partner to whom she clung. Behind was an alpine panorama of mountains. A picturesque mountain scene, quite normal really, except that the man clutching her tenderly around the waist was Adolf Hitler. The second photo was similar to the first, almost like a family snapshot, with Lydia beaming from ear to ear sandwiched playfully between a grinning Hitler and Eva Braun.

I stared in disbelief for a few more seconds then looked up at Lydia. When our eyes met, I realized that she was excitedly waiting for my approval. If I had to describe that look, I can only compare it to the scene in *Casablanca* where Peter Lorre hands Rick the letters of transit after acknowledging that the German couriers, 'poor devils,' had been murdered. He looks at Rick with exactly the same pathetic hopefulness and says, 'I hope you have more respect for me now.'

The poor woman thought this would impress me. That was the most shocking thing about this incredible event. But worse was to come. She then began a monologue that sent shivers down my spine for it was a horror story told not from the perspective of the human victim, but of one of the monsters. I can try to paraphrase her words, but even more sinister than what she said was the almost joyful and proud delivery.

It appears that her late husband Sir Henri had very strong opinions. He had achieved success so easily that he was convinced that he knew best about a lot of things. Both he and Lydia despised the Bolsheviks, who hated Sir Henri, at least as much. He was convinced that Soviet agents were constantly trying to discredit him, and it was quite possibly true. Besides being a successful capitalist, Sir Henri spoke out against trading with the Soviet Union, and they hated him for that.

Their companies were in virtually every country, and they were always traveling and meeting with various heads of state. Sir Henri always formed strong opinions about them. He quickly sized up people and either liked or despised them. He could assess a man simply by looking into his eyes.

Sir Henri believed that a clear eye bespoke a

healthy liver. This led one to the only logical conclusion, namely, that the owner of such clear eyes and healthy liver would be an outdoor sports enthusiast. This showed character.

In the early thirties, Sir Henri started becoming political on a global scale. He spoke against the gold standard, lectured against communism, and was not very fond of democracy as it was currently practiced. He declared publicly, 'I doubt whether this so-called democracy stands for more than a lazy man's Elysium.'

Sir Henry loved order, discipline, and respect, and it was natural that he would be intrigued by the regimes that were successful in creating order out of chaos. The couple visited Mussolini first, and Sir Henri was quite fond of him. He felt that Mussolini had done an excellent job governing Italy. Sir Henri believed that Mussolini had 'shown a driving force almost unparalleled in running a country . . . one felt that if faced with difficulty he would get out his sledge-hammer and strike at its root.' He liked him as a person, too, despite their different temperaments.

At this point, I was already getting a little skeptical about where this story was leading as I had some firsthand dealings with the Mussolini family and had formed quite different feelings about the man. For many months, Mussolini's granddaughter, Dindina, had been my girlfriend. She was a warm, pretty, cuddly girl, and I enjoyed her company. After a while, I was introduced to her mother, Edda, and learned that her husband had been killed by Mussolini after an abortive attempt at assassinating Il Duce. Edda had begged her father to spare her husband, but Mussolini declined with the excuse that he would then have to spare the others who had been involved. Dindina lost her father at the hands of her own grandfather, and as a result, Lydia and Sir Henri's laudatory comments did not sit well with me.

The Deterdings made no secret of their visit to Mussolini and later to Pope Pius XI. Sir Henri said, 'Never had I met anyone more human or whose conversation was illuminated by more practical, sound sense' than the pope. Outspoken about these personalities, Sir Henri gave interviews to periodicals such as the *Saturday Evening Post*. Naturally, his opinions about the fascist leader began to bring some negative reactions. As a result, he was more cautious when they began their visits to Hitler.

According to Lydia, Sir Henri was captivated by Hitler. The Führer ran Germany with a discipline and economy that appealed to Deterding, and their shared hatred of bolshevism drew them even closer. Hitler appeared to be a symbol of order, which Sir Henri admired. Additionally, it cannot be disputed that Hitler possessed exceedingly clear eyes and as a nondrinker, doubtless a healthy liver. From their initial meeting, a friendship developed.

Hitler was certainly aware of how important an ally Deterding could be in helping him with his oil needs, as well as influencing public opinion. As he did with the popular Charles Lindbergh who won the love of America by making the first solo flight across the Atlantic, Hitler must certainly have realized the potential propaganda value in winning the support of a man like Deterding.

And so whether genuine or self-serving, a relationship began to grow. Lydia found Hitler to be charming. She too had strong anti-Soviet sentiments being the aristocratic daughter of a Russian general. She admired strong men, and Hitler concentrated on entertaining her more than many world leaders who targeted their charm only on impressing Sir Henri.

The visits to Germany started to become more social and relaxed. Hitler entertained them in Berchtesgaden, his mountain retreat. It was, indeed, here that the treasured photos were taken by Sir Henri himself (which is why he does not appear in them). Eva Braun was present during the visits to Berchtesgaden, and the four of them would go on walks together sharing their joint love of outdoor sports. They would then invariably dine together as two intimate couples.

Lydia was amazed at how indifferent Hitler was to food. His cook was not up to the Deterdings' standards, but Hitler seemed unaware of the unappetizing fare. On the other hand, the wines were fantastic. It appears Hitler was forever receiving valuable wine as gifts, and so rare vintages flowed in abundance. Hitler, a nondrinker since adolescence, was impervious to this.

Lydia began to fall under Hitler's strange spell. She found his eyes to be unlike those of any human being she had seen. They seemed somehow reptilian or perhaps metallic. They registered almost no emotion and yet had a hypnotic quality that made you stare at them.

Midway during their third visit, Hitler arranged it so that Sir Henri would be occupied after lunch. Throughout the meal, he regarded Lydia with those metallic eyes in a way that seemed to entrance her. After the departure of Sir Henri, she found herself alone with Hitler who silently led her to a bedroom. It was as if she were not in control of her own actions. There Hitler made love to her — or tried to.

The act was a terrible and embarrassing attempt to attain a state of arousal. Of course, there are many stories about Hitler's need for debasing fetishes to reach a state of excitement. Lydia was at least spared this added indignity. Instead she attempted through the more conventional means (in which she was certainly gifted) to induce a state of excitement. After considerable time, the talented Lydia was able to excite the Führer to the point where a tentative entry was at least possible, but sadly, climax was to prove beyond reach.

Not enormously well-endowed, the only partially excited Führer was unable to remain in the necessary position. After an unconvincing attempt to pretend that this was otherwise, they discontinued the act. Hitler dressed and quickly left an unsatisfied and very embarrassed Lydia. She had never been unfaithful to her jealous husband and was very upset. Yet the event seemed so unreal, so out of her control that it was hard to feel responsible. Hitler could not have initiated it for the negligible pleasure that it had achieved. Lydia felt convinced that he had another motive. He did it to ensure her backing. From their conversations, Hitler must have assumed that Sir Henri would never tolerate disloyalty. He now had a weapon he could use against Lydia were she to try to sabotage Sir Henri's support.

That was the last time that Lydia saw Hitler. It is hard to know what Sir Henri Deterding would have done — if anything — to help Hitler during the upcoming war. Despite a vigorous regimen of morning swims in an ice-cold outdoor pool, followed by a forty-five minute ride, Sir Henri Deterding died on February 4, 1939. He received magnificent obituaries throughout the world, particularly in Nazi Germany.

Imagine the thoughts that ran through my mind at the conclusion of this story and the months and years that were to follow. Actually, my first reactions were those of a person in shock. They ranged from denial, to physical disgust at the thought of having shared a woman with Hitler (him being first!), to attempts at humor.

I knew that Hitler had been greatly attracted to Garbo and until the beginning of the war, was in the habit of sending her love letters that invited her to visit him. It seemed we had the same taste in women, and I consoled myself that I was at least one up on him. But no degree of sardonic humor could change the fact that from that point on I felt differently toward Lydia.

One can accuse me of oversensitivity, but I

found it a turnoff to learn that my girlfriend had fucked the Führer. Perhaps even worse than imagining the perverse sex act (which I confess I often did) was the horrible realization that she liked and admired him. She even encouraged her husband to support his efforts. Sadly this placed a certain strain on our relationship.

Another lesson this story reinforced was my growing belief in the extraordinary interconnections that exist among the power elite. Certain names seem to constantly repeat themselves in a very frequent pattern that is often eerie. The Paris Rothschilds were responsible for financing Henri Deterding to achieve a status that ultimately made him potentially useful to the man who wished to exterminate the Jews. It is currently believed that Hitler's grandmother was at one time a maid for the Rothschilds. Hitler made love to the wife of Deterding, as I had, and wished to make love to Garbo, as I did. Garbo's best friend, and for three years mine, was a Rothschild. I offer no metaphysical or synchronal theories for such coincidences, but they are unnerving.

So in addition to trying to combat the negative sentiment that society showered upon us, Lydia also tried to compensate for the coolness I was showing since her proud confession. We decided that I should have a profession or a business. We hoped that this would somewhat minimize the notion that I was completely dependent on Lydia and only interested in her money. Lydia also hoped that such activity might stop my brooding over her questionable choice of former lovers.

We decided on an interior-decorating company that would provide designer furnishings and fabrics. The ground floor and basement were for sale in my apartment building in Rome, and I felt that they were ideal for such an enterprise. As ridiculous as the gesture may seem, I insisted on buying them myself with my remaining savings. For her part, Lydia financed the inventory.

We hired an architect named Gian Franco Farioli to run it and staged a large society opening party, attended by such luminaries as Ira von Furstenberg, ex-Empress Soraya, Sagan, and Rudi and Consuelo Crespi.

Rudi and Consuelo were an incredibly elegant couple, and Rudi was a genius. In fact, Rudi invented PR in Europe. He began life as a wealthy Brazilian count, but lost his money and had to come up with a clever scheme for supporting himself and his gorgeous wife. He moved into one of the most exquisite and famous palaces in Rome, Palazzo Colonna, which he shared with two rather unusual couples.

The first was Prince Aspreno Colonna and his beautiful wife, Milagros. The Pope traditionally has two assistants who stand on his right and left side at the highest official functions. This tradition has gone on for about one thousand years. The head of the Orsini family stands to his right and the Colonna to his left. Prince Aspreno was young for this honor, but filled the role well and used his remaining time to start a family and host parties in his palace.

The second couple was Count Brando Brandolini and his wife, Cristiana Brandolini-Agnelli (of the Fiat empire), my original sponsor, mentor, and companion. Rudi used this setup to create a brand-new market — the PR or introduction-to-society market. Designers, movie stars, and millionaires would pay Rudi to be invited to these lavish parties in the hope of beginning the slow acceptance process so they could someday get invited for free. Naturally business was informally conducted, and everyone profited from the arrangement. It was a revelation to me and put a seed in my mind that was to take root a decade later.

Lydia was staying in the small guest room of my apartment, and when I came home to prepare for the opening, found her flitting around the apartment excited, happy, and proud of me. She was putting the finishing touches on her appearance in anticipation of the party.

On her hand, she wore her treasure — L'étoile Polaire (the Polar Star), one of the biggest and most famous diamonds in the world. Like its owner, it was rich in history, as well as indestructible. Or so I thought. She reserved this gem for those events that to her were most important, and today she'd worn it for me.

'Are we ready, Massimo?' she asked, flushed with excitement.

'Look here, Lydia,' I began, 'the whole point of this business is to show that I am independent of you. What will people think if you are there?

They will assume that you are behind the whole thing.'

To this day, I will never forgive myself for that act of insensitive selfishness. It was as if I had struck her. The energy that animated her seemed to leave her frail little form and what remained was a sad old woman crying pitifully. She pleaded, but I was adamant.

The opening was a success, but the business was not. I lost my investment, but that matters much less than the memory that haunts me still of that proud, indestructible spirit brought to her knees not by time, but by my cruelty.

The next day, as we prepared to return to Paris, Lydia realized that she had lost the Polar Star. We searched vainly for the treasure then resigning ourselves to its loss, returned to France. Days later my trustworthy maid, Maria Teresa, was to call in a state of great excitement to tell us she had found it under the little bed in the guest room. It must have fallen off Lydia's finger as she cried herself to sleep that miserable night. I guess that she sensed that the cause of my behavior in Rome and the growing distance between us came from the same source. Her solution to obtaining what she wanted in the past had been achieved by generous applications of both checkbook and psychology. Perhaps she felt that this proven theorem would work now if applied in larger dosages.

Shortly after our return from Rome, Lydia offered to buy a third apartment for me, this one in Geneva. She explained that she had consulted some experts, and the best way to minimize the inheritance taxes I would have to pay upon her death was to have Swiss residency. Now Lydia was increasing the stakes. It was no longer simply a question of a new apartment, she was offering me a vast fortune of several hundred million. There is one thing that my experience in this relationship had shown and that was that Lydia kept her promises. There was no doubt in my mind that her offer was genuine. I thanked her, and we began a series of frequent trips to Geneva.

During the entire relationship, I had continued to see other women from time to time. Remember that Lydia had assured me I would not be a prisoner. Nevertheless, I was discreet. Preferring to avoid confrontation or unnecessary pain, I would invent excuses for my absence.

At around this time, I began to spend time again with my old flame, Françoise Sagan. I found her very attractive, sensitive, and I could discuss anything with her. We decided to spend a weekend together at St. Tropez. I told Lydia that I was flying to Naples to visit my mother. We arrived Friday night in St. Tropez and received an invitation to have dinner at the home of Brigitte Bardot. Outside our hotel was the usual contingent of generic photographers who endlessly snap photos that one never sees. On this occasion, I was mistaken. The photo of Françoise and me appeared the next day in the society pages of several newspapers. Lydia saw it and became irate.

It appears that Lydia had developed second thoughts about what constituted freedom now that we were engaged. But most of all, it was my choice of companions that offended her right-wing sensibilities. Françoise is very liberal and often defended the causes of communists. Can you imagine the combined insult of being unfaithful and with a communist sympathizer, no less?

It did not take too deep a scratch to reach the militant core of Lydia Deterding. Her response was immediate and extreme. The story and photo were released on Saturday afternoon. At the break of dawn the following Sunday morning, Lydia chose to march in. Taking a page from the book of her former lover (which in this case would be *Mein Kampf*), she initiated a blitzkrieg. With a column of trucks and an army of moving men, Lydia led a surprise assault on my Paris apartment. Although only one startled concierge was to witness this frightening spectacle, I have a picture of it in my mind's eye. I like to imagine Lydia clad in a black-leather jacket (possibly rush ordered from Dior the night before), standing upright in her open limousine followed by the column of her avenging army. In my imagination, Wagner's 'Ride of the Valkyries' is always playing in the background.

Although the apartment was irrevocably mine, as I pointed out earlier, she kept all the receipts for the furnishings. Lydia now exercised the right of ownership and repossessed everything. When I say everything, I mean down to the plants on the terrace, the wall-to-wall carpeting, the toilet paper from the bathrooms, even the last light

162

bulb. On the hand-painted walls, she painted large black crosses. The only thing that she left in that devastated shell was a copy of the newspaper lying on the bare floor open to the page with my picture. When I returned Sunday night, that was what I found.

As is often the case in such weird circumstances, there was a small amount of humor that came out of all this. I developed a close friendship with Roman Polanski, the controversial movie director whose wife, Sharon Tate, had been brutally murdered by Charles Manson and his deranged 'family' in the Helter Skelter murders. Many years after the breakup with Lydia, I had dinner with Roman and told him my sad tale. He was moved by the story, particularly the black crosses painted on the walls. To sum it up, I was engaged to the eighty-year-old ex-lover of Adolf Hitler who reminded Roman Polanski of Charlie Manson!

This needless act of brutality frightened and disturbed me. It was not possible to remain in that empty, gutted apartment, so I flew to Rome. After three days, I received a call from a sobbing, contrite Lydia.

'I am sorry,' she wailed through her tears, 'but Sagan . . . Massimo . . . SAGAN!'

I was still very angry and responded 'even though I was in the wrong, what you did was a terrible thing.'

'I know,' she cried. 'But I was so jealous . . . Please come back. I can't live without you.'

'Not until everything is exactly as it was in my apartment' was my resolute response.

'All right, Massimo, only please come home . . .'

I was now to become the beneficiary of the Eleventh Wonder of the Modern World, the unsung wonder. It had taken four months to complete the interior decorating of my apartment, and the majority of this had been spent on the elaborate hand-painted wall finishes. Lydia succeeded in duplicating this work in a total of ten days!

I learned from the same speechless concierge who had witnessed the invasion that three shifts with forty men worked around the clock to restore things. I often laugh now when I am presented long, complex construction schedules. I know the real speed that can be achieved when the critical path is the satisfaction of a lonely, frustrated, and somewhat ferocious woman.

Shortly after our armistice, we decided to take an extended vacation to the U.S. After one month, I began to miss my friends and being around people my own age. I pressed Lydia for us to return to Europe, and she reluctantly agreed. She was annoyed at ending the trip sooner than planned and argued for the first half of our flight back, then took a sleeping pill. This released me to have a drink in the first-class lounge.

At the bar, I met an elegant gentleman who turned out to be Robert Caillé, the director of *Vogue*. We had a drink together, and I began to relax.

'Hey, who is that lady you were arguing with, your mother or aunt, or something?' he asked.

I was so used to the idea that without even thinking, I responded in a matter-of-fact tone, 'No, she's my girlfriend.' He laughed, and I guess I respected his honest reaction because I joined in, too.

'How do you manage it?' he asked, but out of genuine curiosity.

If he only knew the half of it, I thought. We had a friendly chat about my life, and he enjoyed my experiences and delivery enough to offer me a job writing for his magazine. I took his card, surprised and flattered by his reaction. I did not immediately accept the invitation, but gave it serious consideration.

Perhaps I could work and support myself? My perennial insecurities had been so reinforced by Lydia's psychological machinations that I had come to believe that I was incapable of ever holding any job. For the first time, I began to question this conclusion.

8

LOVE WALKED IN AND DROVE THE SHADOWS AWAY

There was another reason why I was eager to return to Europe. Something quite unexpected had happened. I had fallen in love. I would like to say that it was a reaction to learning about Lydia's past or that it was the impetuousness of youth asserting itself, but that wasn't it. I had simply, foolishly, and completely fallen in love with another woman who was not even available. As I sat back in the comfortable, first-class seat and looked over at Lydia sleeping soundly, I thought back on the recent events that were drawing me steadily away from this complicated woman who could be so vicious and so stingy, yet so generous to me.

It had all happened very quickly. As I was busy furnishing my lovely apartment in Monte Carlo, I spent as much time with old friends as I could. Keep in mind this was the absolute golden age of the Jet Set, and Monte Carlo offered an extensive social playground. It hurt to miss a second of it.

Lydia, for all her social connections, was a member of the old guard. She was an old-world socialite. Her world was an elegant, highly orchestrated series of parties for the

166

staunch aristocratic-industrialist members of international high-society. They were wealthy, sophisticated, powerful people, but they were not in the 'in' group. Their world was stagnant, both physically and socially. Perhaps it was better this way. It might have been awkward if Lydia felt obliged to go topless in St. Tropez. But I missed my own world and took as many opportunities as I could to visit it.

Princess Ismene Chigi invited me to a party she was throwing at the Hotel de Paris. It was the sporty Ismene who goaded me into taking Garbo on our first outing on board Ismene's boat. Neither of us had ever forgotten that day with its bittersweet memories of Garbo. As a result, eager to see her and glad for the diversion, I readily accepted.

Here, in the same room that I had met Lydia just eighteen months before, I spotted one of the most beautiful and elegant women I had ever seen.

She was a stunning blonde with a chiseled face that radiated an almost icy arrogance that I found sexually stimulating. Her whole haughty demeanor seemed like a challenge that said, 'Admire me, but no one will ever have me.' I was intrigued and tried to speak to her. She responded with such a deliberate coolness that my interest was even more aroused.

Later I asked Ismene who she was. 'She is Baroness Donina Toeplitz Di Grand Ry,' she answered. This was an ancient family from Trieste that for generations had lived in a castle built on a rocky island in the middle of an ice-cold lake. The image of such a place was itself a metaphoric description as well as an explanation for the personality of the aloof woman whose inaccessibility so captivated me.

The secluded nature of this tiny realm caused the baronial family to feel quite regal. They even flew their own flag on the tallest tower as if they were an independent state. Donina was a definite product of this proud family. This was really a challenge.

'Please set up another meeting,' I pleaded with Ismene.

'It is a complete waste of time. She is living with Count Cesare 'Coco' Cicogna.'

This was bad news. Coco was rich, powerful, and worse of all, the best friend of the Fiat tycoon, Gianni Agnelli. It was Gianni and his sister, Cristiana, after all, who had been among the first to discover me. They had tutored and then introduced me to society. Yet, even with this complication, I was not willing to give up.

I was as insistent with Ismene as I had been with Cécile when I begged for the Garbo introduction, and it finally worked.

'All right, Massimo, I will take you to lunch at her house, but it is a great waste of time.'

The next day, I found myself at Donina's beautiful villa in Beaulieu. She was slightly less haughty toward me at lunch, which I was prepared to regard as virtual flirtatiousness. I waited for the other guests to leave and then sat next to her on a sofa, trying to make small talk. Her hands were placed one upon the other and rested on the knee closest to me. I stared into her eyes and slowly placed my hands over hers, pressing them together. She did not even blink, but met my gaze with a slightly amused look. Her hands remained perfectly still, and I knew she would be mine.

Instead of pressing my advantage, I simply stood up and asked her to come to my hotel the next day. My Monte Carlo apartment was still not completely furnished. And after the incident in my Paris home, I was concerned that the concierge might turn out to be a Lydia informer. So I was staying at my old room in the Hermitage. It was here that I had received the Cartier watch, my first gift from Lydia, after our wild Russian dance.

The last thing I wanted to do was ruin Donina's future for the sake of an afternoon of pleasure. Here was a woman who seemed to have everything and was, nevertheless, about to receive more. In a few months, Coco's divorce would be finalized. I met him ten years before when his daughter, Countess Marina Cicogna, had thrown an enormous masked ball in Venice. I was invited to escort my girlfriend, Countess Manuela Castelbarco, the granddaughter of the great Toscanini. I will never forget the opulence of that evening. We were slowly rowed in a gondola through the dark canals. The dock of the palazzo was illuminated with hundreds of candles, and the footmen, in brocaded uniforms, stood ready to help the gondolier tie his boat to the striped docking posts that carried the colors of the princely coat of arms.

We were led to an enormous ballroom whose gilded ceiling was supported by thinly fluted marble columns. Each of the hundred guests wore a different elaborate mask. Liz Taylor was there with her hair done in a series of points emanating from the top of the mask like rays of light. Richard Burton, dancing almost nonstop with a beautiful young Brazilian actress named Florinda Bolkan, was definitely irritating the jealous Liz.

In addition to being the patriarch of such aristocratic splendor, Coco owned numerous other properties, such as an apartment in Lugano and a chalet in Gstaad. Gianni Agnelli, with the limitless resources of the Fiat empire behind him, was not only Coco's best friend, but his business partner as well. This insured continued affluence. Count Coco Cicogna, the man who had everything, was about to add Donina to his collection of treasures, and he was known to be a very possessive man. Nevertheless, at the appointed time, his fiancée arrived nervously at the door of my hotel room with something other than Coco's riches on her mind.

When she entered the room, we did not even exchange words. She knew Lydia and was aware of what I had at stake, and I knew Coco and realized the risk she was taking. Our mutual attraction was too strong to consider these points at that moment — or perhaps was even intensified by the dangers of the forbidden pleasure we were about to enjoy.

Before the door closed behind her, she was in

my arms. The icy cold that had tortured, yet intrigued me was replaced by an explosive passion. It was the acting out of the age-old ice queen fantasy. What man does not believe, or at least fantasize, that he alone holds the key to opening the furnace door that lies behind the frozen façade of the ice queen?

On that day, I held that key — and the pride and the egotistical ecstasy that this realization caused fanned my desires to an almost-unbearable heat. We never left the bed that afternoon. We never stopped to think of the danger in what we were doing. Not wanting to be confronted with what could happen, we never allowed our bodies to reach the point where our minds would be clear enough to consider the future. We lived in a sexual trance that was to typify our relationship from then on.

After we had satisfied an almost bottomless pit of desire, we lay intertwined in my bed. This, I would like to point out, was not my standard practice after a sexual encounter. Our feelings were more serious, and the realization frightened both of us.

As we talked, I learned that the frequent coincidences that plague the small community of the Jet Set were to make our relationship even more complex. To begin with, Donina had been in love with Count Brandolini who was the husband of Cristiana Brandolini. As I had just learned, Donina had a voracious sexual appetite and chose to supplement her needs with the attentions of her boyfriend's brother. Unfortunately, Count Brandolini caught them in bed together and, as one might suppose, ended the relationship. As a result, both Brandolini and Cristiana despised Donina. I had fallen in love with a woman whose enemies were my closest friends.

On top of these perfectly good reasons to never see this woman again was, of course, the problem of Lydia's jealousy. Laughing, I pointed this out to Donina saying, 'Lydia went wild when I was seen with Sagan. Can you imagine if she found out I had fallen in love with a Jew?' Donina did not laugh at this. Perhaps she was unaware that her old friend, Lydia Deterding, was not a friend of the Jews. Then her eyes filled with tears, and Donina told me a story that was to prove as traumatic in changing the direction of my life as the strange story I had been told by Lydia.

Donina lay next to me. She looked regal, yet for the first time she seemed vulnerable, almost fragile. She turned one of her hands upside down and placed her arm on my chest.

'It is gone now. I had all traces of it removed,' she said. At first I thought she meant that she had once slit her wrists and had the scar removed. No, that was not it. 'It was a small tattoo, you know, just some numbers, some little blue numbers.' Then in a very small, distant voice, she began a strange monologue.

It was as if she was speaking from far away or deep within herself and the story she told was frightening. Like my last experience with such confessions, this, too, was a horror story — but it was told this time from the perspective of one of the victims, not the monster. These were her words:

The Nazis came to our home. An ugly little man in a black trench coat told me to prepare for a journey. I was told I could bring one suitcase and the equivalent of fifty dollars. My papers were stamped with a 'J' for Jew. The next day, I was placed on a hideous, packed cargo train and taken far away. I had no idea where we were going, but it turned out to be Poland, to a place called Auschwitz. It was a grueling and horrible journey in that packed, filthy train, and we were exhausted and ill by the time we arrived. We were herded off the train by SS men in black uniforms with skull insignias on their collars. They held vicious dogs on leashes that barely restrained them from mauling us. Some carried whips and slashed them at us, screaming for us to move faster while the dogs barked and snarled. We were told to leave our luggage as emaciated men in blue-and-white striped uniforms boarded the train to remove them.

It was late at night, but the entire area was illuminated by rows of bright spotlights, giving it a horrible nightmare quality. The SS men, whips flailing, screamed wildly, 'Women to the left. Men to the right!' We were marched off or perhaps trucked off, I can't remember. Then another SS man stood in front of us, an officer, dividing us into yet another category. When he saw me, he stopped what he was doing and stared intently at me. He pointed

173

his thumb to the side and told me to wait.

Five other women, also young and pretty, were so selected. We were marched off to a wooden barracks where we were given a stack of forms. Even in Hell, the Germans loved forms. We were asked to write the names and addresses of ourselves and of our parents. Date of birth, occupation, and other endless, pieces of information were required. Then we were told to sit on a rough wooden bench where another prisoner, dressed in those hideous striped uniforms, directed us to roll up our sleeves. There, blue ink was injected into our arms tattooing us with identification numbers. It was excruciating.

By this time, our forms had been collected. Two SS men came over to have another look at me. They were grinning, and one said, 'It is this one, she is the baroness of the Jews.' He laughed hard as if this were the funniest thing in the world. The Rothschilds were barons, even in Germany, but titled Jewish families were not common, and the Nazis found it hilarious.

I was very young and quite pretty. Later I learned that is why I had been separated from the others and also why I was still alive. It seems I had arrived on a day when no slave labor was needed. As a result, everyone who emerged from the trains was immediately gassed. The SS officer's appreciation for my appearance was the only reason I was removed from the march to the gas chambers. We were asked to line up with the other camp prisoners in alphabetical order, then we were given a piece of coarse bread to eat. That was my first night at Auschwitz.

The next morning, roll call was taken again, and we stood freezing for hours. The two SS men who had enjoyed their joke the night before brought over a high-ranking officer wearing a long gray coat. He looked me up and down as if I were a horse or a prize cow. Then he nodded to the guards. A few minutes later, I was taken from the others and led to his quarters. It was a Spartan enough room, but it seemed luxurious compared to the barracks of the night before.

He returned a while later and asked about my family. I explained about my lineage and that I was actually half Jewish. Although this minor distinction was officially insignificant, to him it mattered. You see, he wanted me to be different from the others. Naturally he made me sleep with him. It was the first time I had been with a man, and it was not what I had expected. I was nothing but his sex slave, perhaps not even a human being to his sick mind.

The sex was brutal. He seemed to revel in degrading me. I am sure the combination of my appearance and my title increased the joy he took in the act of humiliation. He allowed me to stay with him in the officer's barracks, and I felt sure that he would soon tire of the pleasures he took with me. But I was wrong. Instead of tiring of me as a sex toy, he began trying to know me more as a person. Despite

175

his consuming hatred of Jews, he was otherwise a ridiculously pompous and very bourgeois man who was as impressed as he was threatened by my title.

As the weeks turned to months, he claimed to have fallen in love with me and began to fear that his protection alone would not be enough to guarantee my survival. Finally, he asked me for the names of people whom I could trust in Italy. I gave him the name of an old family friend from Florence who was very powerful with the Fascists. He contacted this man and then organized my escape, ensuring that I would be met and transported to safety.

At this point in her story, Donina seemed to collapse in silent sobs. I let her cry for a while. Then she continued with the more current, mundane portion of her story. All the while as she told her horrible tale, I kept thinking of the night Lydia had spoken to me about her affection for Hitler. I recalled the pride with which she handed me the two photos of Hitler and her together. I felt sick and deeply ashamed. But Lydia had known Hitler before the war, I tried to justify. Perhaps she never anticipated he was capable of such atrocities. But I knew I was deluding myself. I knew that Hitler's hatred of the Jews was evident from the beginning, and I knew something else, too. The seeds of discontent that had been planted the night of Lydia's confession took root this afternoon. It was now just a matter of time.

After the war, Donina tried to return to the

life of a typical socialite. She married and subsequently divorced a wealthy Italian industrialist with whom she had two children, Isabella and Ludovico. I had met her children at various parties in the past. Both were attractive and famous in different ways. Isabella was a prominent and successful playgirl, while Ludovico was reputably the lover of the infamous 'Bubbles' Rothermere.

There are a couple of things about the infamous Bubbles that deserve special note. Bubbles was the wife of the powerful press baron, Lord Rothermere, owner of England's *Daily Mail* and *Evening Standard* newspapers. She was nicknamed Bubbles because of her eccentric way of always being escorted by two butlers. One constantly carried an ice-filled cooler with a bottle of her favorite champagne — thus, the name Bubbles. Ironically, I had just had the pleasure of being hosted by Bubbles at her new home in the south of France. It was a home I had previously only seen from the outside. The villa oddly enough was le Roc. Exactly. Greta Garbo's old house, the one I used as bait to lure her on our boat trip with Ismene. In a sense, the current relationship tied together many facets of my former loves. Donina, persecuted by the ex-lover of my current girlfriend, was engaged to the business partner of the family that introduced me to the Jet Set, while her son was living in Garbo's old house.

All things considered, it was a complicated set of circumstances. But of all the things that I heard and felt that afternoon, only two images really stuck with me. I could not forget the unbridled passion we had shared nor could I stop thinking of that sweet vulnerability I had seen as the regal, cold Donina told me of her troubled past. So despite all the other factors that spoke so eloquently about not getting more involved, we did. As I learned more about Donina, it seemed evident that she was mistaken about how young she had been when incarcerated and perhaps exaggerated the state of her virginity — but I found no other reasons to doubt her horrible story.

The plane landed, and my reverie was disturbed by Lydia's awakening. She smiled at me and said, 'Darling, don't forget to take the packages of complimentary cigarettes. We can use them for the guest rooms.'

The next several weeks were spent in Monte Carlo. I accepted as many invitations as I could to parties where I knew Donina would be present. Often Coco would be there, and as he already knew Lydia, we would sit down whenever possible as a foursome. Coco could detect that there was a sexual tension between his fiancée and me, and Lydia, too, began to notice that something was going on.

'Be careful we don't spend too much time with Donina,' she warned.

'Why is that Lydia? She and Coco are charming,' I would reply.

'She is a snake, Massimo!' Lydia would invariably say and occasionally, 'She is a Jew!'

I was searching for every free moment I could find to secretly drive to Beaulieu so I could visit

Donina after the parties that she attended alone. It was harder to be patient with Lydia and much harder to sleep with her. The situation was to reach an unexpectedly dramatic climax in a very unlikely place.

By some clever form of reckoning, the Shah of Iran came to the conclusion that Persia was about to become 2,500 years old. This happy event corresponded with the thirtieth year of his own reign. Such a coincidence could not be overlooked. A party was called for. If ever there were a Jet Set monarch, it was the Shah of Iran. Not only could he be seen in our circuit of events, he often flew the jet himself. He possessed a magnificent home in St. Moritz and would participate enthusiastically in the ski and aprés-ski events.

Although the composition of the Jet Set included many royal families, only the Grimaldis, the Shah, and perhaps the Aga Khan were actually governing anything. Yet, despite their busy professional schedules, these three men were instrumental in providing the fantastic surroundings and power behind a great portion of our social events. Having said this, I must quickly point out that no one was prepared for the party the Shah now had in mind. It was to be the mother of all parties and in a way would expedite his political fall.

In 1959, the Shah had married his third wife, Farah. For a number of reasons, he decided in 1967 to crown her empress and took the opportunity to crown himself, as well. The coronation was naturally spectacular, but more attention was paid to the lavish party he threw afterward. Perhaps encouraged by this success, the Shah decided to impress the world by the event he planned for October 1972. His stated intent was that on October 15, 1972, Iran and presumably his throne would be 'the center of gravity of the world.' He chose the level plain of the ancient city of Persepolis built by Emperor Darius and burned by Alexander the Great. There, he had a city of tents constructed to house the festivities and the guests he planned to invite. When I say a city of tents, I do not wish to give the impression of a camping site. 'Roughing it' was clearly not the intent.

The Shah summoned the famous Parisian designer Jansen, who had decorated the last Shah extravaganza. His list of satisfied clients included the Duke of Windsor, and he even had managed to earn the respect of Lydia Deterding. You see, it was Jansen whom Lydia had commissioned to decorate and then speed-restore my apartment in Paris. But coincidence is a constant part of our tiny world.

Jansen designed a city taken directly from *A Thousand and One Nights*. The tents in the encampment were made of striped Hermes silk. In the center of the plateau stood a huge tent, a silk 'Big Top,' that was used for the parties as well as the apartments for the Shah and empress. Around the big tent, rows of smaller tents stood like troops in formation. Each of these tents contained a suite consisting of a small sitting room, two bedrooms, and two marble bathrooms. The floors were either covered in wood or

180

paved in marble with Persian rugs over them. Crystal chandeliers hung from the peaked tent top, and the furniture was elegantly carved, sometimes with inlaid wood. It was as if someone had thrown up an Arabian tent in the middle of a suite at the Ritz.

Outside, the Shah had done his best to create a feeling of paradise. The roads were decorated with thousands of pots of flowers, dainty birdcages hung wistfully from the lampposts, the servants were dressed in Persian costumes, and the shopkeepers in spotless blue robes.

This wonderland was to be used only for the Shah's most favored guests. Heads of state, presidents, and members of the Jet Set were to be given the honor of feasting under the Big Top at the moment in which it would become the center of gravity of the world. A geological event of this magnitude was, alas, only to be witnessed by a relatively select few. The final guest list included Emperor Haile Selassie of Ethiopia as the senior guest, the King and Queen of Denmark, King Hussein of Jordan, King Constantine of Greece, Prince Philip and Princess Anne of Great Britain, Prince Bernhard of the Netherlands, Spiro Agnew (remember him?), and an assortment of socialites and industrialists.

Iran is a large oil-producing country, and in 1953, an international oil consortium had been formed to exploit Iranian oil. A fifty-fifty profit split had been agreed between the consortium and the Shah. Perhaps not surprisingly, the consortium was led by Royal Dutch-Shell. It

181

was, therefore, not unexpected when Lydia (Mrs. Shell) received her invitation. What I had not counted on was that Count Coco Cicogna and Donina were also invited. Worse still, we were all to be given the special honor of living in tent city next to each other. Less august guests were housed in a hotel about thirty miles away and bused in. What apparently had happened was that in my desire to see Donina as often as possible, I had given our tiny world the idea that the four of us were great friends. As a result, the Shah's staff, wishing to make the trip as enjoyable as possible, placed the four of us in the same group. What this meant was that we would be attending the same parties, visiting the same Persian ruins at exactly the same time, and living in adjacent tents. This was very bad. By the third day, I could not bear to look at Coco, and I am sure he felt the same about me. Lydia walked about shaking her head and muttering, 'A snake! A Jewish snake!' while Donina looked frustrated.

The Shah did all he could to assure his guests a good time. He had forbidden his soldiers to shave for the preceding month, so they all sported ancient Persian beards. Then he had them outfitted in ancient uniforms with armor, spears, and swords. He would parade them for us during the day. Legions of ancient Persian troops marched by or rode in their gilded chariots. All that was lacking was Cecil B. DeMille.

At night, the Persian ruins would be illuminated with different colors, and we would be presented a fabulous sound-and-light show. Then we would retire to the Big Top for our feast and entertainment.

The dining room was sheathed in red velvet, and the furniture was Louis XIV, gilded in gold. Naturally the food was not local fare. The Shah had everything catered by Maxim's. Our wine list was the finest I have ever encountered and even featured a vintage to which Cécile had introduced me, the almost-extinct Chateau Lafite-Rothschild 1945.

The highlight of our visit was an elaborate formal party for several hundred of the Shah's guests. The Shah looked regal in his uniform, replete with jeweled orders and decorations. Empress Farah looked like a storybook princess. She had been a young architectural student in Paris when he met her in 1958, but after fourteen years of imperial life, the transformation to royalty was complete. Her career mirrored that of Grace Kelly, really. They were both beautiful and decent commoners who were magically elevated to royalty, yet still cared about common people. Tonight she was every inch the queen in a fabulous Dior dress, wearing the crown the Shah had commissioned from Arpel's of Paris, with an emerald slightly larger than an egg in the center. We were given more gifts — by now a daily occurrence. On this occasion, Lydia was presented with a bottle of perfume that Elizabeth Arden had created just for this event and had named 'Farah.' I remember that gift because Lydia berated me for forgetting it. 'Massimo, it would have been good to leave in the guest bathroom.'

Naturally, the staff of the ever-gracious Shah

seated the four of us at the same table. As the evening began, I leaned toward Donina and said something that Coco apparently could not hear. Turning to Lydia, he asked, 'What did your gigolo say?'

Before I could react, Lydia grabbed her glass of red wine and poured it in Coco's face. I jumped up to come to Lydia's aid and was drawing back my arm to punch Coco when Donina decided to defuse the situation. She pretended to swoon and cascaded down to the floor. This naturally broke the tension, and we tended to her. The Shah in his regal way either was impervious to the scene or never was notified about it. But the other guests were scandalized. Our problem was now in the public domain of the Jet Set.

On the whole, the party was a failure. The next two days were awkward for Lydia and me. The biggest disaster, however, was the public reaction to the party. Reports were that the Shah spent more than $300 million on the event. To put this in perspective, this was a sum equal to about half the Onassis fortune when he died two years earlier. Poor Ari was forever criticized for his extravagance, yet his enormous empire could have afforded only two such parties.

The Iranian public, with an average annual income of $500, was not pleased with their leader's dinner bill. To make matters worse, by celebrating ancient Persia, the Shah overlooked the fact that his people were even more proud of their Muslim heritage. Khomeini viciously condemned this event cursing anyone who

Left, at 21 years old.

Below, as a youth in Capri, 1962, when I was befriended by Pierre Cardin.

With Christina Onassis and her cousin at the Corviglia Club, St. Moritz, 1964.

With one of my first girlfriends, Dindina Ciano—the granddaughter of Mussolini.

The photo of me that Cecile always carried.

Baroness Cecile de Rothschild bagging a large beast on safari.

A night out with
Françoise Sagan, 1974.

Escorting ex-Empress
Soraya in 1971.

Dinner with Lady
Lydia Deterding, 1971.

Dancing
with Lady
Lydia
Deterding
in Paris,
1972.

The opening
of my gallery
in Rome with
Princess Irene
Galitzine.

My thirty-sixth birthday party in Monte Carlo with Prince Albert enjoying the company of Diane Segard, 1976.

Princess Grace and David Niven enjoying my thirty-sixth birthday party.

Lynn Wyatt, mother of former Fergie lover Steve Wyatt, Donina and me.

Count Coco
Cicogna and
Donina with
Omar Sharif
at a party in
the Cicogna
villa at
Beaulieu,
1972.

Above,
with Jerry
Hall in
Rome,
1979.

Christopher
Reeve accepting
my award in
1985 with artist
Fernando
Botera and
Tiziana Rocca.

With Brigette Nielsen the
night she was to receive a
horse in her hotel lobby.

Introducing Matt Dillon to ex-Empress Soraya.

Marina Castlenuovo with
Roger Clinton, 1996.

With Joan Collins at the
Great Gatsby costume
party in Cannes, 1987.

At the 1990 Best Awards with old friend Roger Vadim.

With Gianni Versace in Sardinia in 1982.

The photo of me that Andy Warhol shot and signed in Venice in 1972.

The 1977 Best Awards in Rome. L to R: Karl Lagerfeld, Kenzo, Gina Lollobrigida, Francine Cresent (the director and chief of French Vogue who would become my wife), Carlo Palazzi, and Hebe Dorsey.

With Dewi Sukarno at Studio 54, early 1980's.

Filmmaker Roman Polanski and his wife
Emmanuelle Seigner in Paris, 1993.

Gunther Sachs and his wife, Mirja de Savoy in Paris, 1992.

On Elizabeth Taylor's yacht, the Kalizma, with John Bryan and Allan Starkie.

With Allan Starkie and Dewi Sukarno in Ivana Trump's town house, 1998.

With author Alberto Moravia, the man who coined the term "Jet Set".

Hosting an engagement party for Ivana Trump and her second husband Riccardo Mazzucchelli.

On a European trip with LaToya Jackson and ex-husband Jack Gordon.

Relaxing at a party in the South of France with Ivana Trump.

After my introduction to Ivana's new friend Count Roffredo Gactani, 1997.

Three loyal friends: Gina, Sagan, and Ursula, 1998.

With Francine and Versace.

With my wife Francine.

In Moscow with Prince Umar and Shirley Maclaine, 1999.

With Allan at the New Year's Party of Prince Victor Emmanuel (exiled King of Italy) in Gstaad, 1998.

participated. Overall, the party was not a success.

We returned to Paris to lick our wounds. I was in a state of great confusion, living a double life and unsure how to move forward. I decided that I needed a distraction. The social scene in the South of France is dominated by aquatic-oriented parties. Lydia did not care to own a yacht, and Donina had converted what was essentially a houseboat into a floating formal dining room. She decorated it with crystal, sterling flatware, and gold-trimmed porcelain with the family crest displayed everywhere, including the formal livery uniforms of the footmen and servants. I found this a bit over the top.

A shipbuilder in Miami had developed a speedboat called the Magnum that could cruise at 50 mph. He had made three prototypes, and two of them had promptly been bought by King Juan Carlos of Spain and Warren Avis. I decided to purchase the third and have it shipped to the South of France. This decision enraged Lydia, who found it upsetting that I would buy a boat whose speed would prevent her from using it. It annoyed Donina, who found it inappropriate compared to her floating dining room. I loved that boat, and it made quite a splash. It was fast, loud, and cast a huge wake.

As I was trying to lose myself in the joy of speedboating, I received an invitation from Countess Lily Volpi inviting me to a ball at her palace in Venice. On the same evening, there would be a dinner party at the Brandolini Palace, also in Venice. I could not resist — perhaps some of Johannes's weird humor was rubbing off on me. I had the speedboat transported to Venice, and on the night of the party — dressed in black tie — cruised it down those solemn, quiet, ancient canals to the Palazzo Brandolini. At this time, no one had attempted such an eccentric thing, and so there were no laws regulating anything but speed. I maintained a speed at exactly the specified limit and therefore was technically in conformance with the law. But a speedboat is constructed a little differently from a gondola. For one thing, its two massive engines throw off a lot more noise than the gently rowed gondola — even with the additional sound of the singing gondoliers. And if the truth be known, dual Chrysler engines are louder than even the most robust gondolier's heartiest rendition of 'Santa Lucia.'

Venice is one of the few cities in the world in which cars are forbidden. As a result, there is tranquility in that ancient city that one finds nowhere else. Finally, Venice has been sinking for centuries, making the water level very high relative to the streets and the buildings. A speedboat (even when driven slowly) creates a huge wake. The combination of the mere spectacle of this incongruous vehicle, combined with the noise of its engines, and its not insignificant wake resulted in creating a state of hysteria along the canals.

At the Bridge of Sighs, I was applauded. As I cruised along the Grand Canal, I was the center point of hundreds of amazed eyes, but it was as I turned into the narrow dark canals that the screams of the terrified gondoliers began. The next morning, all the Venetian papers would carry as their headlines 'Playboy Massimo Brings Venice to Ruin.' But as I approached the Palazzo Brandolini, I was feeling pretty good.

The startled footman helped me to secure my boat as the other guests came pouring out of the palace to locate the source of the disturbance. Andy Warhol came running out, his odd gray wig sitting a little off center. Clapping his hands, he immediately jumped on board and said, 'Massimo, you are so beautiful on your beautiful boat.'

Snapping a photo of me with his inevitable Polaroid camera, he made me promise that after dinner I would let him ride with me to Countess Volpi's party. At dinner, Yves Saint Laurent and Christina Onassis made me give them the same promise, and I am afraid ten other people as well. Speedboats are not built for a platoon of passengers, and it was with some trepidation that my small boat accommodated the fifteen people whom I ferried to the stately palace of the Volpi family that midnight in Venice.

Now I do not doubt that this entire adventure seems childish and even pointless. The press claimed it was destructive. But I think I needed to do it for my ego. You see my reputation as a wild playboy had really been damaged by living with Lydia. It was a miracle that I was even invited to these parties, and it was clear that the invitation did not include Lady Deterding.

I wanted to make a statement, and that is how

I chose to do it. Naturally, it changed absolutely nothing — not even the way I was feeling about myself. When the party was over, I returned to Monte Carlo and tried to decide what my next move should be.

Between the trip to Persepolis and the speedboating through the Venetian canals, I was tired and sleeping late. I was awakened when I heard my butler trying to prevent someone from entering my room. I was lying naked in bed and was afraid that I was about to be attacked by an angry husband when the door flew open, and Donina came running in with an overflowing box of jewelry in her hands. 'I am sick of it. It is disgusting. You want money? You want wealth? Here, take my jewels and leave that old woman.'

With that, she emptied the box on my chest and ran out of the room. Her impressive collection of diamonds and assorted gems featured a number of particularly sharp mountings and pins that pierced my skin in a number of places. When I looked at my chest, it seemed like a treasure chest had been poured on a mortally wounded pirate. War had been declared.

I went to Donina's villa to discuss her outburst and found her pacing around chain-smoking. 'What do you want me to do?' I asked.

'Leave that disgusting old woman, of course' was her reply.

'And Coco?' I asked.

'Anytime you want, I will leave him. Why stay with her? If you need money, I have plenty of it, but don't waste your life with an eighty-year-old woman when you can have me.'

What could I do? I was truly in love. At this point, Lydia was in the process of buying me an apartment in Geneva and organizing Swiss residency to minimize the inheritance taxes I would have to pay on the half-a-billion dollars I was one day to inherit. Despite the recent strains, Lydia had been generous and kind to me, and I had strong feelings for her. But I simply could not give up Donina and she was no longer willing to share me with Lydia. 'All right,' I said.

I put off the confrontation for as long as possible. Finally, I returned to Paris and took the elevator up to the palatial apartment on the Avenue Foch to see the woman who had everything to tell her that as of that night, she would no longer have the one thing she really wanted.

It did not go well. Lydia was generally a gracious woman. Tonight the grief was too great to maintain that front. The depth of her despair was too vast to describe. As I left her lying on the floor sobbing piteously, the last words I heard were 'you are making a mistake, Massimo.'

Although I never saw her again, I learned that Lydia kept her promise from the beginning of our relationship. She had said as long as we were together, she would never again wear black. From the moment I left her until her death several years later, Lydia Deterding, on those rare occasions when she emerged from her quiet, empty apartment, was seen only in black.

9

FATAL ATTRACTION

Although I would never see Lydia again, I learned that she died five years later in 1978. By default, her fortune was inherited by her surviving daughter. It was a very great fortune. In addition to the enormous holdings in Royal Dutch Petroleum, the extensive real estate, and art collections, Lydia left more than $200 million in liquid assets. I believe that Lydia would have been true to her word, and had I married her, that fortune would have been mine.

As I look back at the various extremes my life might have taken, these range widely. They include being a stuffy lawyer to perhaps an eccentric billionaire. I guess that the possibilities are what have made my life so wonderful and exciting. It has been a great adventure and many times a great gamble, too — but it has not been boring.

After the initial guilt I felt at my cruelty toward Lydia, I must admit that I was filled with a sense of great relief. It was as if I had broken a magic spell that she had over me. Now I could again face my peers without their constant taunting and ridicule. Also, I guess I felt that I had chosen love over wealth. Of course, I mean this in somewhat relative terms. I had chosen a little less wealth and a younger, more beautiful woman. Nevertheless, I was able to convince myself of the self-sacrificing nobility of such a deed. I fully expected that now I could love Donina completely and exclusively.

Naturally, things never work out exactly as one expects.

Donina's initial satisfaction at my decision in no way dissuaded her from her plan to marry Coco, whose divorce from the powerful Countess Anna Maria Volpi was imminent. In an attempt to act nonchalant and supportive, I did nothing to discourage her from this course of action. After all, Coco had much more to offer than I, at least materialistically. Donina and I saw each other as frequently as we could. Yet all the while she was preparing to quietly slip away to Lugano for a simple wedding accompanied only by Coco, Robert de Balkany, husband of Princess Maria Gabriella of Savoy, and his best man, Gianni Agnelli.

It was a rather bleak situation.

To console myself, and also, I suppose, to make Donina jealous, I started to date other women. In 1962, I had met Tyrone Power and his gorgeous wife, Linda Christian. Now, ten years later, Linda was a widow. Despite Power's incredible good looks, she had apparently lacked a certain degree of fulfillment in her married life. I did my best to fill this void, and she spent several months with me in Rome. Linda is a remarkable woman, and her life has featured the obligatory number of odd coincidences endemic within the world of the Jet Set.

The night that Linda met and fell in love with Tyrone Power was one of those magical evenings that we sometimes experience. It was a warm night in Cannes, and after a party thrown in honor of Maurice Chevalier, a group of adventurous socialites decided to visit the villa of one of the strongmen of Argentina's Juan Peron.

The party was filled with the usual faces and a smattering of movie stars. This predated the great influx of movie stars precipitated by Grace Kelly, but it was not strange to see some Hollywood greats as casual visitors to the scene. On this night, three such faces were present — Tyrone Power, Linda Christian, and the virtual goddess of sexuality, Rita Hayworth.

Ali Khan, son of the Aga Khan, was also there. That night at almost precisely the same moment, Ali Khan spotted Rita, and Tyrone Power caught a glimpse of Linda. The two couples were to begin romances that ended in marriage shortly afterward.

Linda and Tyrone choose to marry in Rome at the church next to my apartment. The wedding was organized by the PR genius, Rudi Crespi. Unfortunately the marriage did not fare as well as that of Ali Khan and Rita Hayworth.

Rita left Hollywood just as Grace Kelly would later have to do and embarked on a life of royalty and social obligation. She filled the role with great elegance and grace and lived a golden life even after her unfortunate divorce many years later. We all were to mourn her tragic loss to Alzheimer's disease.

Linda's marriage was not as successful.

Although she has continually insisted that the rumors that Power was gay were fabricated, she was not very happy with their life together and became involved with a good friend of mine, Fon Marquis of Portago. He was a very wealthy, handsome young man who had a passion for racing. Linda would accompany him as often as she could to watch him race. At the Mille Miglia, Fon made a quick pit stop long enough for the enamored Linda to run to his car and kiss him for good luck. That particular kiss has unkindly been labeled 'the kiss of death,' for before he could finish the next full lap, he lost control of his car and was killed in the crash.

Linda was shattered by her loss and by the added insult of being denied an invitation to Fon's funeral. Fon was still married at the time of his death, and his widow felt that Linda's presence would be inappropriate. Almost hysterical with grief, Linda burst into the funeral chamber clad in black mourning cloth. She ran to the open casket and threw herself upon the corpse of Fon. She embraced and kissed him as her body shook with sobs.

The other mourners were shocked at this almost sexual display of intense grief, and the widow asked that Linda be removed. Later Fon's somewhat less-distraught widow married Milton Petrie, the American millionaire.

It is safe to say that Linda was in a vulnerable mood when I began spending time with her, and I guess I was as well. I was worried about my future, and Linda was mourning her past. We spent a lot of time in Rome drinking and staying out late almost every night. She was a wild companion, and it distracted me from missing Donina so much. The courtship also succeeded in keeping my picture in the gossip press often enough to remind Donina that she had better not let me stray too far.

I also spent time with ex-Empress Soraya. She was considered one of the most beautiful women in the world and was also lots of fun to be with. So, not lacking female companionship, I managed to get along without the constant presence of Donina that I'd hoped for.

Soraya had attended the ill-fated opening of my interior-design studio in Rome, and since that time, we saw each other frequently. She was able to live comfortably with the settlement made by the Shah. In fact, in addition to the trust fund that he established for her, she was permitted to keep all the jewels that had been given to the couple as wedding gifts. This was no small collection of jewels, for the Shah was actually 'the Shah of Shahs.' This means that he was the ranking shah of an entire group or council of lesser shahs.

When the Shah of Shahs marries, the lesser shahs go absolutely crazy competing with one another with the most lavish wedding presents.

Soraya's collection was world class. She purchased her villa in Rome with the sale of a single necklace, for example. She had the required degree of freedom, affluence, influence, and beauty to be a perfect member of the Jet Set.

These charms made Soraya one of the most hotly pursued women, and she was constantly receiving marriage proposals from the world's playboys. Ironically, as with Linda Christian, she had recently lost the love of her life. Soraya only really loved one man, other than the Shah, and he was the respected Italian film director, Franco Indovina. In addition to being her lover, he coaxed her into beginning a film career and cast her in a movie called *The Three Faces*, with Alberto Sordi. (Many years later, Sordi selected me to star in his movie, *Paranormal Phenomena*, despite Visconti's previous assurances that the camera and I had a hostility toward one another.) Shortly after the release of the film, Franco was killed in a plane crash ending their love affair and her fledgling film career.

She never really recovered from this loss and would remain aloof to a growing number of celebrity conquests. Among her suitors were the prominent playboy Gunter Sachs, film star Maximilian Schell, and even Prince Johannes von Thurn und Taxis.

This was really a coup considering that Johannes preferred young men. Nevertheless, Johannes was crazy about Soraya. One of the competitors for her hand was Prince Raimondo Orsini, whose family was one of the two important, ancient Italian families that are given the special honor of assisting the pope at official functions. In addition to their papal privileges, the Orsinis conducted many business ventures throughout Europe, and their family was accorded a great deal of respect.

This, of course, in no way would deter the witty wrath of Johannes. Not a good man for rejection, Johannes decided that the Orsinis could use a small lesson. He photographed a naked prostitute in a very vulgar pose and replaced her face with a photo of Prince Orsini. Above this creative collage, Johannes had the crown and coat of arms of the ancient Orsini family engraved. Under the photo, he wrote, 'Many greetings from Raimondo Orsini.' He had several hundred of these prints made and sent them out as Christmas cards to friends and associates of the prince.

I am not sure whether the Papal Father received such a greeting nor how he might have reacted, but the other recipients were shocked, and the Orsinis scandalized. As with many of Johannes's practical jokes, this one found itself in the courtroom.

Soraya did not seem more inclined to favor Johannes's proposal even after this odd act of love. It is a shame really for Johannes finally married Princess Gloria, a woman of even more eccentric wit than he. She so intimidated him with her own practical jokes that poor Johannes ended his life as a quiet and subdued man, never really sure what his wife might do next. The last time I saw them together was at his sixtieth birthday party at their castle in Regensburg. Gloria brought out the cake, and instead of sixty candles, it had sixty life-size, pink penises, as sort of a tribute to a life of sleeping with young men. At any rate, although I never felt the urge to become a suitor of the ex-empress, I enjoyed her company and, of course, the publicity it gave me.

This type of treatment worked wonders in

driving Donina crazy. She became more and more jealous and projected her anger and frustration on her poor husband, whose only fault seems to have been that he married her. She compensated by spending as much time alone with me as she could, often scheduling rendezvous in hotels. She was never a very generous person, but she took to giving me extravagant gifts. That Easter, she presented me with a solid gold, life-size Easter egg with the inscription 'I love you so badly because I love you so much.' An odd choice of gifts I thought as I had thrown away the goose that laid golden eggs on Donina's account. Donina began to speak of leaving Coco and hinted at the magnitude of her own wealth and the independence it would bring us. Yet as she continued with this theme, it became apparent that a great deal of her wealth was tied to Coco. Divorce, therefore, was not really what she had meant by leaving him. No, Donina had a slightly less conventional solution in mind.

'Massimo, we can't go on any longer like this,' she began. I certainly agreed, but I asked, 'What can we do? You condemned me for selling myself to Lydia, but are you not doing exactly the same thing?'

She looked deeply into my eyes with a look I had never seen there before. 'Yes,' she breathed. 'Yes and I am sick of it.' Then her lips curled almost into a snarl, and her beautiful, ice-cold face seemed to be contorted in a look of pure evil. Not evil as a form of ugliness, but evil in the way that a shark stalks its prey without thought or remorse. 'There is a way Massimo . . . we could kill him.'

Let me put this into context. Within the odd mores of the Jet Set, violent death, suicide, and murder are not really that uncommon. Donina's own stepson had killed himself in Rio after being jilted by Britt Ekland and going bankrupt. I would later be privy to another plan of this type — but with more gruesome results. That comes a little later in my tale.

At this point, I must say that I was as impatient with the current state of things as Donina seemed to be, and her suggestion did have some merit. Sometimes I think that her best friend, Grace Kelly, had unintentionally put the idea into her head.

Grace was discouraged from flaunting her Hollywood past. It was not a Garbo situation in which the subject was taboo, but it just did not sit well with Prince Rainier to discuss it. Several days before Donina's odd suggestion, she had been up at Roc Agel, the secluded mountain retreat where Grace and Rainier spent their solitary family weekends together. Apparently, the only trace of Grace's former career to be found either in Grimaldi Palace or in their weekend home was in her large Roc Agel bathroom, where there was a virtual temple dedicated to the former movie star. Even her Oscar stood proudly across from the bidet.

When Donina returned, we got to discussing some of Grace's films, and Donina seemed particularly interested in *Dial M for Murder* in which Ray Milland pays a hit man to take Grace

Kelly's life. Well, I guess this might have been another case of life imitating art because I really think that this particular film directed Donina's frustration into a plan of action. We never really got much further with the details though since something came up that made our strange discussion a moot point.

According to Donina, Coco was not an especially talented lover. Perhaps his problems resulted from an anatomical disorder. At any rate, several days after Donina's strange suggestion, Coco was scheduled for a routine prostate operation. He chose a fine Swiss hospital in Lausanne, and Donina stayed at his side during the procedure and remained for two additional days as he began his recovery. He was scheduled to remain in the hospital for several more days, and this, of course, offered Donina the opportunity to spend some time with me. She flew immediately to St. Tropez where I was engaged in my usual ritual of admiring the topless beauties during the day and dancing with them at night.

I do not exaggerate when I say that Donina and I enjoyed an extraordinary sex life, and from the moment that she arrived, it might have been Siberia in the winter for we never saw the sun nor the beach. Our reverie was interrupted by a frantic call from Lausanne. Coco had been struck with an embolism and died. As odd as the timing of his demise may have been, it was truly a coincidence. Remember I did say that life in the Jet Set is filled with coincidences.

Donina flew at once to Switzerland and made

the final arrangements for a man who a short time ago had everything life had to offer. Then a strange thing occurred. Donina had the combination to Coco's safe and naturally opened it to find his testament. The safe was filled with documents and a number of sealed dossiers. She opened them, and her shock almost rivaled that of mine when I was allowed to view the contents of Lydia's safe. The envelopes were filled with photos — not of Hitler and Eva Braun this time, but of Donina and me. Compromising photos, personal photos, and reams of back-up material that spoke for itself. There were copies of hotel registries, signatures that proved where and when we had been together. In short, Coco had done his homework well. But that was not all. No, Coco must have had a premonition.

Coco was a businessman, and he left little to chance. He had power of attorney over all of Donina's accounts, and three days before his death had transferred over one million dollars from her Swiss account to his. He had then drawn a will that left his possessions divided equally among his children and wife. Even the things that Donina had owned prior to the marriage were joint property to be divided among three people. Coco's death had actually diminished the wealth that Donina had prior to the marriage. She was left with some money and a great number of estates filled with expensive staffs of servants. Despite a dearth of liquidity, Donina now possessed a villa and apartment in Florence on the river, overlooking the Ponte Vecchio, the old covered bridge that is the center point of Florence; a chalet in Gstaad; a home in Lugano; a home in Milan; a villa in Beaulieu; seven cars (including a Rolls); and a yacht.

When one added to this my homes in Rome, Monte Carlo, and Paris, we had an impressive array of ten properties and a staff of more than twenty people. It took a while before Donina actually let me know how little cash she had. For now I realized just how close we had come to disaster. Had Coco lived, who knows how far Donina might have gone with her plan and had she not, her marriage would certainly have ended in an embarrassing and expensive divorce.

Donina kept the details of her financial concerns secret from me. What I did understand was that she was taking some extraordinary measures to retain her possessions. Shortly after Coco's death, she suggested that we buy an apartment in New York and that it be purchased under my name. This was no great act of generosity for although it was a large Park Avenue apartment, it cost only $25,000 as it was rather run down.

As soon as the title was mine, Donina sent the impressive collection of paintings that she and Coco had at Beaulieu to New York, registering the shipment under my name. The paintings included the famous Francis Bacon self-portrait in which he depicts himself as sort of a monster in the center of a circus. Donina had effectively avoided the issue of any disputes over the inheritance of this collection by simply relocating them to my new address. We then renovated the apartment at a cost of an additional $225,000 to make it representative of the entertaining we planned to do as we increased our social circle.

10

PUTTING ON THE RITZ

After the compulsory period of mourning, which was short in both time and sincerity, Donina and I launched a life-style that to this day, remains the fondest memory of my life. In retrospect, I understand how pointless and superficial our life was, but at the time, it was one of the most glamorous life-styles anyone had seen.

Donina was sophisticated, beautiful, fluent in every European language, and came from an old and respected family. I was simply Massimo — charming, handsome, and flirtatious. We threw ourselves into the social world with a vengeance. All our homes were open to guests, and we threw parties virtually every night. I inherited Donina's society friends, and she allowed me to introduce a new group of younger, more attractive movie stars and fashion stars to her rarified world. What resulted was much like what Princess Grace was in the process of doing. We created a social group that was comprised of a vast network of non-aristocratic elements. But most of all, it was fun. We were not attempting a social experiment. We were not trying to reform an antiquated system. We were simply trying to have fun. And we succeeded.

In addition to Donina's impressive real-estate holdings, as a couple, we inherited her three best friends — the Duchess of Bedford, Estee Lauder, and Princess Grace of Monaco. I liked to think of them as the Three Graces. They were like that classic statue intertwined and self-supporting, able to inspire or to destroy. Let me tell you a little about these three ladies for they were to spend a great deal of the next seven years with us, and afterwards they were to play an even more significant role in my life.

Estee Lauder is a name synonymous with the cosmetic empire that she founded. Born in the humble surroundings of Corona, New York, Josephine Esther Mentzer began creating face creams in her home in the early 1940s. With the help of her husband, Joseph Lauder, she founded Estee Lauder in 1946. Through her own pluck and creativity over a fifty-year period, she grew her tiny enterprise into one of the largest family-owned businesses in the world with headquarters in the General Motors Building on Fifth Avenue.

Not satisfied with financial success, Estee Lauder became a powerhouse in the social world and was a force to be reckoned with in New York and Palm Beach society. Her alliance with Grace Kelly certainly added an enormously valuable ally to her social standing which, by this time, was international.

Next came the Duchess of Bedford, a small, plump, but witty lady. Like Grace Kelly, she began her career as an actress, but succeeded through marriage in upgrading her status to only that of a duchess (as opposed to Grace becoming Her Serene Highness).

Despite her marriage to a duke, the Duchess still enjoyed the stage and actually launched a television talk show on Monaco Television. She would host debates over touchy, controversial subjects and at one point had me on the show as a guest. I debated the issues of good and evil with a respected local priest. I was the devil's advocate. I guess in a way the Duchess of Bedford was a scaled down, less-violent Jet Set version of Jerry Springer.

But Donina's greatest and most powerful friend was Grace Kelly. I suppose that the world has been saturated with descriptions and stories of Grace Kelly. But from my perspective, she was one of the most unusual human beings I encountered. I'd already met her a number of times.

I will never forget our first meeting. In late 1971, Cécile called me at the last minute to take me to the palatial Rothschild estate outside Paris in Ferrières for one of the many parties that the press has reverently titled 'the party of the century.' Maybe they were right each time, too. In this case, it was a masquerade ball in the style of Marcel Proust. Although Cécile would often bring me to great events without even going through the formality of sending me one of the famous Rothschild engraved invitations, in this case, if one could reconstruct the guest list, it would read like the *Who's Who of Celebrity*, as well as the index of this book.

The home was crowded with people I had

known since Capri in the sixties and people with whom I would later become intimate. Richard Burton and Elizabeth Taylor were there arguing just as ferociously as when I had last seen them at the ball in Venice. The Duke and Duchess of Windsor were there with the Duchess sporting an enormous feather strapped around her head like an Indian on the warpath, which indeed she once again seemed to be with the Duke. But my attention was riveted immediately to Princess Grace as I saw her for the first time. She wore a dress from the turn of the century and looked every inch the storybook princess.

Plato believed that there was a world of ideas and a world of reality, and the perfect form of each creature dwelt in the world of ideas. That is why without ever seeing a perfect horse, we can identify the defects of any horse we see. We somehow compare reality to a perfection that lives only in the world of ideas. Princess Grace was the perfect image of a princess. If one were to imagine a fairy-tale princess who at once radiated a magnetic sensuality as well as a grace, charm, vitality, and attractive aloofness, you might be able to get a feel for what I was seeing. It is no wonder that she took Hollywood by storm and defined a new type of sex symbol. And even if her father began his career laying bricks, she was more a princess than any of the ancient blue bloods I had encountered all my life.

An interesting addendum to that evening is that the gentleman photographing the guests was Cecil Beaton. Cecil was court photographer to

Queen Elizabeth and also the only man to ever claim to have slept with Greta Garbo. The others who might have made a similar claim, such as Stowkowski or actor John Gilbert, remained silent on the issue. Actually, Gilbert was more than silent — he was militant. It was not the myth that Gilbert's voice cost him his stardom during the advent of talking pictures. In actuality, Gilbert's fall from grace came as a result of his decision to punch Louis B. Mayer in the mouth after Mayer insinuated that Gilbert was sleeping with Garbo.

At any rate, Beaton's posthumously published memoir left little opportunity to question him on the details, particularly in light of his homosexuality. I had just finished my relationship with Garbo at the time of the Rothschild party, and he undoubtedly recognized me from the press stories that had been widespread just weeks before. I had no idea at this time that he even knew Garbo and was surprised at the coldness with which he greeted me as I approached him for a photo.

'This is a Proust party,' he announced, glaring at me as if I had dressed for a toga party instead.

'Yes, Cecil, I am aware of that,' I responded. He looked me up and down with a slight sneer then finally said, 'I am afraid, young man, that your suit postdates Mr. Proust's death by at least ten years.' And with that, he turned his back and walked away.

I was later to learn that Cecil was an embittered man. He had high social hopes and had targeted not only my poor Greta, but also

Princess Margaret. As you may recall, I had accidentally stood up Princess Margaret in Sardinia that very summer. Like Adolf Hitler, it seems that Cecil Beaton and I shared the same taste in women (even if it were strictly for social conquest in his case), and like Hitler, I was one up on him. Apparently he never recovered when Princess Margaret married his professional and social rival, Lord Snowdon. Too bad really. I would have liked a photo of that evening.

Although Donina and I would divide our time among all of her estates, we made it a habit to spend three months a year in Monaco and Beaulieu. Grace's friendship with Donina was intimate, but casual, and she would often call unexpectedly just to chat with Donina. Ironically, the evolution of Grace's relationship with her husband and even its ultimate estrangement coincided with the development of my relationship with Donina, leading the women to develop a special bond. Additionally, Grace was going through a metamorphosis in which she was becoming more European. Her accent became more British, her manners more continental, and she began replacing her former group of close American friends with titled Europeans from old families. Donina was steadily becoming a substitute for Grace's distant friends, and although I never really can say that Grace confided in me, through Donina I became very involved in the lives of the Grimaldis.

In the early 1970s, Grace's relationship with Prince Rainier had lost some of its magic. Still, the couple spent a great deal of time together, and Grace was very occupied with raising the children. It was interesting watching them develop from adorable children into headstrong teenagers and finally tabloid legends. In those days, they were raised almost like American children and each year would be sent off to summer camp in the States. It is hard to look at them now and remember the cute, but precocious children I watched grow up for those seven magical years.

Well, that was the social world I had inherited. This time not as the taunted escort of an eighty-year-old woman, but as the lover and companion of a beautiful, sophisticated Jet Setter. I should have known it was too good to last.

I had gone through my apprentice stage in the evolutionary process that exists within this rarified world with Cécile Rothschild and the Agnellis. Garbo had earned me my wings, enabling me to solo. My Deterding experience was a bit of a distraction from the process of social acceptance, but now the relationship with Donina had restored my credibility. It allowed me to progress to the next step in which I was able to organize events. Instead of being always the guest, I transitioned into becoming the host.

The story of Daphne De Maurier's book *Rebecca* was similar to the scenario in which I found myself. The blue-blooded Mr. de Winter replaces his dead socialite wife with a young bride who is awed by the pomp and social protocols to which she is exposed. But there was a difference — I felt ready for the task. As you will see, in some respects, I was correct in this assessment, while in others, I had greatly overestimated my abilities. At any rate I had a plan.

I don't mean to say that Donina's social group represented Madame Tussaud's wax museum. The Duchess of Bedford had a great sense of humor, Estee Lauder was interesting, and Princess Grace was magnificent. But the remainder of Donina's friends were old titled socialites who bored even each other.

My strategy was simple. I felt that we needed to utilize our various estates to create what Hemingway would have described as a 'moveable feast.' To the old guard friends of Donina, we would add glamorous and avant-garde people. I guess the question is what was I trying to accomplish? The answer simply is that I wanted us to become the first family of the Jet Set and to create an elite subset (sort of like la bande Sagan) that included interesting people from various fields.

Today I might ask myself why anyone would regard that as a life objective. I did. And the odd thing is that I succeeded. It took a long time and a number of fortunes to realize the shallowness and the cost of this victory, but at the time, I threw myself into achieving it.

In the early years of my life with Donina, we traveled extensively and entertained constantly. With ten homes, seven cars, a yacht, and twenty servants; coordinating the events that we hosted required about the same effort as running a medium-sized business.

Our villa in Beaulieu had seven guest rooms, and the chalet in Gstaad had six. It is no exaggeration to say that these rooms were never empty. All our homes were open to our friends and always filled with guests. The two principal residences for our major entertaining were our villa in Beaulieu (ten minutes from Monte Carlo) and our chalet in Gstaad.

Donina was perfect for the role of hostess and would begin her typical day at 7:00 A.M. to develop a schedule for our guests. She would have an itinerary of the day's events printed and distributed to the rooms before the guests even awoke. These daily programs mapped out the day's events in detail. Most of our guests came from backgrounds where they had never encountered a great deal of regimentation and were often amazed at Donina's degree of preparation. One morning at breakfast in Beaulieu, I remember that Elsa Martinelli's ex-husband, Willy Rizzo, stared in disbelief at the program. It went something like this:

Breakfast in the dining room from 10:00 to 11:00
Lunch on the yacht at 2:00
Cocktails at 7:00 at the Hotel de Paris
Dinner at 9:00 at Rampoldi's

Elsa's husband looked at me and said, 'This is not a holiday. It is more like summer camp or dormitory life.'

At the end of each day, Donina taped to the wall of the butler's pantry a sheet of paper listing each and every error made by the servants in the past twenty-four hours.

Our summers would pass in a whirl of parties and entertaining. The typical routine would be that of entertaining during the day either on our yacht or on the boats of our friends. The harbor was filled with enormous yachts owned by such people as Academy Award-winning Hollywood producer Sam Spiegel, Darryl Zanuck, and millionaire Tony Murray. These men with their resources and power were surrounded by beautiful starlets and aspiring models. Tony Murray had a reputation for giving ten thousand dollars a month to every woman with whom he slept for the rest of their lives! Can you imagine the way this information would draw legions of gold diggers? The evenings began early and invariably involved a cocktail party at someone's villa and then dinner usually at the Hotel de Paris, then dancing until three or four in the morning.

Estee Lauder would rent a home nearby at Cap Ferrat, and she and her husband, Joseph, were always around Donina and me. Estee is a very interesting woman, but sadly it became obvious that she was not in any way interested in me. She was tirelessly and almost obsessively devoted to her career. She never relaxed. I cannot think of an example in which Estee appeared to be interested in anything, but expanding her empire. She did not seem to even notice attractive men.

At any rate, I occupied myself chatting with Joseph, her quiet and unpretentious husband. He reminded me of the Duke of Windsor — not in terms of appearance, charm or elegance, but in the way he was dominated and perhaps even frightened of his wife. In a way, he was my ally. He was kind and gentle and never critical about my relationship with Donina.

I later learned that his wife advised Donina to get rid of me from even the earliest days. 'You should end your life with an older, richer man, not a young Italian playboy' was how she put it.

Fortunately, in those days Donina was too much in love to heed this type of advice. Nevertheless, it irritated me and convinced me that I needed to create a younger, more fun collection of friends for our social group.

The Duke and Duchess of Bedford lived nearby, and we would spend time with them, as well. The Duchess was amusing, and the Duke had a style of sarcastic humor that only the British can pull off. Yet despite my best attempts to charm them, I met with almost exactly the same reception that I had experienced with Estee Lauder. They were not openly rude — not at first — but there was a certain restraint and aloofness that indicated clearly that they were willing to tolerate, but never really accept me.

In winter, we continued the same routine of daily entertaining a home full of houseguests, the only difference being that the venue was changed from the beach to the Swiss Alps. Some of my fondest memories from these years took place in the lovely village of Gstaad.

As mentioned earlier, the Jet Set divides its time between Acapulco and Switzerland in the winter. In Switzerland, there are only two possible destinations, St. Moritz and Gstaad. The question of which village deserves the title of the supreme snootiest in the field of winter sport locale is subject to debate. Each features its own respective infrastructure of Jet Set accommodations, which in both cases (and in general) remain invisible.

You see, I believe that the Jet Set itself for the most part is essentially invisible. At such places, they transport themselves silently, almost surreptitiously, from one elegant chalet to another. They are only exposed to curious eyes when they congregate in the late evening at their usual stomping grounds, which in both villages is their respective Palace Hotel. But even in such a public place, they are sheltered by obsequious attendants who keep them secluded from the public. In the case of the Palace in St. Moritz, for example, Gunter Sachs avoided unnecessary exposure to the hotel guests by purchasing the great tower of the hotel and converting it into his bachelor pad.

During my early years with Donina, the summers were exhausting, and I looked forward to the tranquility of Gstaad to recover and relax. I do not mean to say that social life in Gstaad was tranquil or quiet, not with our house always filled with guests. I mean simply that the alpine splendor and natural beauty of Gstaad rejuvenated me. Let me describe the village so you can get an idea why celebrities such as Richard Burton and Elizabeth Taylor chose it as the place where they could find peace.

When one speaks of Gstaad, one generally means Ober-Gstaad (upper Gstaad), so named for topographic not sociological reasons, although, oddly it serves both functions. To reach the idyllic winter wonderland of Gstaad, one is forced to leave the highway, which is about fifty miles from the village, and then negotiate a narrow, frozen road, full of hairpin turns, that slowly creeps up the Alps. Alongside the road one follows a bubbling river that is fed by the mountain's melting snows. As you drive upward, the countryside becomes sparse and less populated, and the terrain more rugged and beautiful. Finally the mountains appear through the mist, snowcapped but for the stony peak of the Matterhorn.

One passes through quaint little villages with a handful of antique homes perched upon the sides of the mountains. Then finally the terrain opens slightly, and the mountains seem to take a step back, allowing the mere suggestion of a valley flanked by rolling hills to accommodate Gstaad in its mild breast. These hills are peppered with lovely chalets that are generally only occupied three months a year. The consistency of the architecture and the mellow-aged way in which they conform to nature create a setting out of Grimm's fairy tales.

The chalets are constructed of unpainted, rough-hewn wood. They feature a mildly peaked roof supported by ornately carved, massive wooden brackets. The roof overhangs the front and sides, giving shelter to the inevitable expanse of balcony that runs from side to side. The

215

balconies have railings of wood carved into simple geometric patterns. The windows are generally shuttered with green wooden shutters. It is the only painted surface to be seen.

Sometimes large, rustic cowbells are hung from the eaves, and they clang together ringing slightly as they are swung by the icy wind. But the only real source of adornment is simply the natural aging process by which the wooden exterior becomes more and more weathered, blending itself each year a little bit more into the harsh, beautiful, yet somehow cozy environment.

In winter, white lights are attached along the entire eave of the roofs. They are illuminated all night, thus forming a series of inverted Vs randomly sprinkled along the hillsides, pointing upward toward the stars. And indeed, they are occupied by stars and millionaires who open their homes to accommodate the winter migration of the Jet Set. The chalets of people such as Elizabeth Washer, Edmonde Labbé, and Heidi Ekles shield the Jet Setters from the curious eyes of the tourists.

The chalets are not built in neat rows, but sit haphazardly scattered along the hills and valley. But if there were some pattern to be discerned, it would be that the homes become more dense as one approaches the village center. The village itself conforms exactly to the chalet architecture. The small village center allows only pedestrian traffic and horse-drawn sleighs. These clever coaches feature retractable wheels so they can still be used when sufficient ice is not available. The stout horses are adorned in weathered leather harnesses and bedecked with garlands of cowbells. The drivers wear traditional costume, and the passengers generally are clad in mink.

The village is built at the foot of the steepest of the valley's hills, and at its top is situated 'the Palace.' The name is not simply a pretentious name for a luxury hotel, but an actual architectural description of the edifice, which is built exactly like a medieval palace. Perhaps it is better to say that it resembles a slightly out-of-balance, almost Disney-like interpretation of a medieval palace.

The Palace is a large rectangular structure with massive towers on each of its four corners. It is placed a little askew so that only three towers are ever visible at one time. Of these three, one is considerably higher and covered with a pointed turret. This makes the building appear oddly asymmetrical, much like St. Stephan's Cathedral in Vienna where the city simply ran out of funds to complete the second tower, giving it the permanent appearance of being somehow unfinished.

In winter, the Palace is illuminated like a Christmas tree. It always gave me exactly the same warm feeling as when I would look out on Monte Carlo harbor and see the Onassis yacht strung from stem to stern with strands of light. The lights of the Palace can be seen from anywhere in Gstaad, but the oddly turreted tower seems particularly ablaze. It is covered with so many cascading streamers of white lights that the effect is almost aggressive, even accusatory. It is as if the Palace were both

217

inviting and taunting you or as if it might be the tower of a lighthouse throwing out a warning beacon to the isolated chalets floating in the night in a sea of snow.

And indeed the signal works. For each night after a round of parties at the various chalets, we inevitably meet at the Palace. Just as the Hotel de Paris serves the same function in Monte Carlo, the Palace is the center of our late-night dinners and dancing. Inside the lobby, there is a great hall deliberately made to resemble the great hall of a castle. The ceilings are very high and covered in carved wooden paneling supported by rectangular columns of roughly hewn stone. Upon the columns and walls are mounted gothic wrought-iron sconces.

On the left side is a bar with a built-in grand piano and on the right an enormous hearth with a roaring fire. The room is filled with small tables and large chairs upholstered in faded red velvet. To look at it, one would expect it to be an informal and relaxed après-ski hangout, which would, of course, be a mistake. Even here, there are subtle rules. One of the many unwritten rules that govern such places has dictated that chic people may only sit on the right side of the room. The left was for the tourists. The staff, fully aware of this law, cleverly places 'reserved' signs on all the tables so they are able to direct the Jet Setters to their little area and route everyone else to the shameful left side.

The restaurant and even the nightclub in the basement are governed by similar rules. So even in the public places, the society guests are segregated from everyone else. The guests are encouraged not to stare at the famous faces. In that way, for the most part, the Jet Set remains insulated even in a public hotel and restaurant.

In Monte Carlo, a bathing suit is strictly optional, and the same holds true for skis in Gstaad. The daily routine usually entails dinner at around 9:00 P.M. and dancing at Greengo's, the Palace's underground nightspot, until three or four in the morning. As a result, it is generally only the most enthusiastic skier who will brave the slopes in the early morning. I must add that in the early days with Donina, I was happy and relaxed in Gstaad.

Our chalet was strategically placed ten minutes from the Palace. Like all the chalets I described (and indeed it is even dictated by the local zoning laws), it was a traditional wood design. Inside it was quite luxurious. The walls and ceiling were made of unpainted wood with recessed lighting giving them an aged warmth. The fireplace was always roaring, and the walls were hung with beautiful art.

My only complaint was that Donina insisted on filling the shelves with her ancient collection of Ming china. Although beautiful and priceless, they hardly reflected the rustic Swiss look that the chalet and the entire village were trying to convey. One of my hobbies was to try to make each of our homes fit the ambiance of the country and region in which it was placed. My apartment in Rome across from the Colosseum is decorated with ancient Roman marble busts. My Parisian apartment is decorated with Empire furniture. I would have preferred the Swiss chalet to look a little less like the Forbidden City during the Ming Dynasty and a little more Swiss, but Donina was resolute in her tastes. I succeeded in replacing her floating dining room in Beaulieu with a more conventional yacht and so had to compromise with the furnishings in Gstaad.

It was in Gstaad that I began actively to alter the configuration of our social group. I invited new people whom I found exciting. The village was already the winter home for King Constantine of Greece, Elizabeth Taylor, Richard Burton, and Roger and Louise Moore. Donina and I started to spend time with this group and then to expand it with a younger crowd that included the designer Valentino and the beautiful American socialite, Lynn Wyatt. Lynn was married to the Texan oil tycoon, Oscar Wyatt, and was the mother of Steve Wyatt, later to become infamous as the first lover of the Duchess of York and the cousin to his successor, John Bryan. See how interconnected the whole thing is?

In that pivotal Patiño Ball in Portugal where I first met Cécile Rothschild and later Sao Schlumberger, I had been introduced to the exquisite Gina Lollobrigida. We had kept in touch, and now she was a frequent houseguest in Gstaad. Gina is perhaps one of the most fascinating people of our era and has been my most loyal friend and ally through virtually every crisis of my life. There are many beautiful actresses who simply are photogenic and seem larger than life on the screen. Marilyn Monroe was that way. If you saw her relaxed in her dressing room bleaching her hair while reading a book with large-rimmed glasses, you would probably not recognize her — and you most certainly would not have regarded her as a sizzling sex symbol. Gina, on the other hand, is just as beautiful off as on screen. She requires virtually no makeup and has a sensuality that seems to assault your senses. It is probably that fact that led Humphrey Bogart to say that 'Gina makes Marilyn Monroe look like Shirley Temple at Sunnybrook Farm.'

My personal opinion is that it is a sad thing that Gina was born so beautiful. She was an extraordinarily talented art student when she was finally persuaded to enter the film business. Her beauty and talent as an actress and her subsequent stardom obscured the fact that Gina is something that simply does not exist anymore — a Renaissance person. She paints and sculpts, writes, sings, is an excellent experimental photographer, explorer, and sociologist. Most of all, she is a true friend.

During the midseventies, as Donina and I expanded the social network of our ratified group, Gina was too busy to join the circuit full time. But her life was so full that her visits to our chalet were always fascinating. In fact, it is a strange irony that although the Jet Set is constantly globetrotting, we are so isolated from the world below the aircraft or outside the walls of our luxury hotels and palatial homes that we actually are quite out of touch.

Gina was a source of information about the

outside world. I don't mean the Hollywood world, but the world of current events. In addition to being an actress and artist, Gina had begun photographing world figures, interviewing them, and even making documentaries. In 1972, she published a book called *Italia Mia,* which illustrates the contrasts of life: humor and sadness, wealth and poverty. In 1974, she did a photojournalism project on Henry Kissinger and Neil Armstrong. Shortly after, she received an invitation from Fidel Castro and created an incisive hour-long documentary on him. A year later, she was trekking through uncharted wilderness to study a newly discovered tribe of Philippine natives that had never encountered civilization. We would sit for hours by the fireplace in Gstaad as she recounted her adventures and perspectives.

Another addition to the group we were forming was Dewi Sukarno, a most enigmatic woman. Born of Japanese parents, Dewi was discovered in Tokyo by the founder of Indonesia. Her legendary beauty, strong will, and intelligence won his heart, and in 1959, they married. She became the first lady of one of the most highly populated countries in the world at a time when Indonesia had enormous strategic importance to the West.

For eight years, the couple was inseparable until the 1967 coup at which point Dewi had to flee the country. It was shortly after her exile that we met at a cocktail party in my apartment in Rome. My first impression was of an exotic, more-perfect version of the actress, Merle

Oberon. Although it was a simple afternoon cocktail party, Dewi arrived in a formal gown. Her exquisite beauty had earned her a reputation as 'the pearl of the orient.' She was very polite and seemed genuinely interested and impressed with my apartment.

I was with Lydia at the time, and although I knew that Dewi shared the general amazement and humor about the relationship, she always treated Lydia with kindness and respect. She even found her charming because Lydia would always blush around Dewi as she described her feelings for our future. At that time, Dewi was involved with the Duke of Sabran, an aristocrat from one of the most ancient families in France. He looked a bit like Robert Redford and was quite a ladies' man. In fact, he was reputed to satisfy his prodigious appetite wherever he could. The apartment that Lydia gave me in Paris had a strange, mildly retarded concierge. She was somewhat attractive in an unkempt sort of way and loved to talk to my guests. I discovered that while waiting for me, Sabran had actually killed the time by seducing the poor, simple woman. Despite these odd proclivities, he and Dewi together made a striking couple. Gina was dating a very handsome German baron. The six of us would spend a great deal of time together until a certain friction developed among the ladies.

Besides assembling a group of stars and glamorous women, while living in Gstaad I had a chance to meet a man I had long admired — Prince Vittorio Emmanuel di Savoia, the son of the last king of Italy, Umberto II. The prince was living part-time in Iran and spending winters in his chalet in Gstaad with his friends and family. He was married to the beautiful world champion water skier Marina Doria.

The prince told me the fascinating story of his life. As is well known in Europe, an Italian constitutional law prohibits all male members in the succession to the throne from returning to Italy. Thus, as a boy of eight Prince Vittorio Emmanuel was banned from Italy. I believe the law banning him will be repealed and he will soon return to his country.

This man who was destined to rule a nation had been exiled from his country, so he decided to conceal his royal heritage, go out into the world, and prove himself from ground zero. After studying economics he went to the United States with Professor Jacques Piccard on a deep-sea submarine project in San Diego. He liked working anonymously with the American technicians under the guidance of Professor Piccard, and he learned a great deal about technology. An accident he suffered during an underwater operation precipitated his departure from California.

Victor Emmanuele decided to take a vacation. With his old Dodge, which he had previously fixed himself, he drove for several months all over the United States. When his identity finally became known, President Eisenhower brought him to Washington for an interview. He later met several times with President Nixon.

The prince worked on Wall Street until he could purchase a small plane in order to start a school of acrobatic flying. His friendship with the Shah of Iran, who shared with the prince a passion for aeronautics, enabled him to go into business selling helicopters to Iran. Victor Emmanuel developed an affinity for Israel, and during the Yom Kippur War he became the first foreigner to volunteer his services for the Israeli air force, though he ultimately was not needed.

It was during this time of personal prosperity that the prince felt financially stable enough to marry Marina, the love of his life who he had met seventeen years earlier.

These were the stories I would hear each night by our fireplace. Gina's globetrotting adventures, Victor Emmanuel's stories of intrigue, Dewi Sukarno's revelations of life as the First Lady of Indonesia. Countless celebrities and world leaders joined our small group. I loved it. I felt not only special, but also especially informed. It was as if we were at the pinnacle of the world elite where only a selected few really knew what was going on and who was controlling the events of the day.

Of course, it was not all great stories and intrigues. We had Donina's old socialites, and we had the guests who would not depart. In fact, Donina and I would often be forced to leave a house full of guests and a retinue of servants to care for them in order to meet our social commitments in other countries. This turned out to be a very costly form of entertaining, and Donina began to show signs of financial concern. She became nervous about money and tried to economize, often in small, but symbolic ways.

For example, one of our constant guests was my friend, Prince Carlo Giovanelli. Carlo spent his whole life simply enjoying being a prince and living on the endless invitations that his old family name ensured him. He was particular about his habits and seemed overly fond of honey. In fact, it bordered on an addiction. Not only would he consume an entire jar of honey with his tea each morning, but he also insisted on a particular brand produced near Gstaad and costing nearly $200 a jar. Ironically, one of the few other patrons of this exclusive honey is Her Majesty Queen Elizabeth of England. In her effort to economize, Donina instructed her staff to substitute a less-expensive brand of honey and explain to Carlo that the store in the village had run out. This seemed to shock and depress the addicted prince who immediately donned his fur-lined coat and proceeded posthaste to the village. There he learned from the proprietor that 'the Countess has requested the less-expensive honey.' Carlo was not to be that easily put off. He simply ordered a case to be delivered to our chalet. Returning, he greeted Donina with a big smile and announced, 'I have very good news. The store has received a new supply of my favorite honey.' And so even Donina's subtle attempts at economizing were thwarted.

Despite the growing financial concerns, we were rapidly becoming one of the best-known hosts within our group, and our reputation for being an elegant, generous couple with fascinating friends was spreading. In fact, it became so widely known that we were recruiting young talent that Prince Carlo Giovanelli (still unabashed by the honey episode) appeared at our villa in Beaulieu with an attractive young Romanian woman named Puia. He had found her as a virtual illegal vagrant in Rome and thought she was pretty and charming and just what we needed for the last unoccupied guest room in Beaulieu.

Donina despised her at sight, but I took pity on her and agreed with Carlo that she had potential. We designated her our pet project and after making her over, installed her in my vacant apartment in Monte Carlo. We brought her along to various parties, almost like an Eliza Doolittle experiment, and before long, we had her happily married to a rich industrialist named Jermi. Later, she was to show her gratitude in a rather odd way.

Not all my society launches required as much work as the revamping of the Romanian refugee. I was introduced to a gorgeous actress named Pia Giancaro. She was a true beauty and no stranger to the Jet Set. It was she who summed up Niarchos with the famous phrase, 'He is a little man in a big boat.' She preferred not to speak about her relationship with Niarchos. However, we were all aware of his eccentric tastes, particularly when it came to sex. He loved to watch his girlfriends go through the elaborate and time-consuming process of getting ready for a formal ball. This took hours, of course. After the hairdresser had left and the cosmetologist had applied the last bit of makeup, Niarchos would pounce upon his pristine beauty and generally standing up, would despoil and consequentially dishevel them.

He seemed to take particular pleasure in the fact that guests were waiting patiently below and also that his woman would require a makeover in record time before greeting them. Pia was gorgeous, sweet, and a decent person, and it was with pleasure that I introduced her to Prince Ruspoli, and with greater pleasure that I watched her go through the ceremony of becoming his princess.

Even with the addition of interesting, younger, and more diverse people, Donina's core of the three Graces and the old guard socialites seemed to haunt me. I still had my friendship with Sagan, but I had neglected the other intellectual friends I had known and admired before my relationship with Donina. I sought their friendship now, hoping that I could somehow draw them into our social world and by doing so, enrich it.

The man who coined the term Jet Set was the distinguished Italian writer and intellectual Alberto Moravia. His books have remained bestsellers for decades, and many films have been made from them. Some of his more than fifty classics include *Time of Indifference*, *Disobedience*, *The Conformist*, and *Two Women* in which Sophia Loren gave an Academy-Award-winning performance in the 1960 film. Alberto hated the Jet Set, and in his famous article in which he coined the term, he recommended that they all be annihilated with the exception of me. I always remembered this kindness and never really understood why he liked me. I decided to spend more time with him and his housemate, whom I also admired. I hoped that I could somehow incorporate them into our group. This proved to be a rather silly idea.

Alberto and his housemate could not have been more opposite to everything that Donina represented if they tried. Alberto shared a home with a very leftist author named Pier Paolo Pasolini. Like Moravia, Pasolini was a living legend. He was a poet, writer, and a filmmaker. Some of his classics included *The Gospel According to St. Matthew*, *The Witches*, and *Medea*, with Maria Callas. Imagine two such talents sharing a house. It was tantamount to Norman Mailer sharing an apartment with Ernest Hemingway.

The two men were very close friends, but were the original odd couple. Moravia adored women, and Pasolini loved men. The problem was that Pasolini's homosexuality was bizarre and dangerous. He was not attracted to gay men. His practice was to frequent dirty bars in terrible neighborhoods where he would offer money to truckdrivers for sex.

These men were often persuaded because Pasolini would lead them to believe that he simply wished to satisfy them orally. When he got them home, he would essentially force them to perform and receive acts that they had never anticipated. There would often be violence, and this seemed to stimulate Pasolini even more.

Notwithstanding this terrible habit, I was determined to introduce Donina to two real intellectuals and drove her to their home near Rome. What I found was astonishing. Alberto had had enough of Pasolini's behavior, but could not bear to lose his friend. His solution was to build a wall in the middle of the living room so he would not need see or hear the carryings-on. The house was still joined through the kitchen.

When I saw this, I had to laugh. Alberto shook his head and said, 'Massimo, every morning when I see Pasolini having breakfast, I think it is a miracle that he is still alive.'

Neither of the gentlemen was interested in my Italian countess. They despised everything she stood for, and she certainly reciprocated the feeling. She found their home filthy and spent the afternoon scrubbing the bathroom and kitchen. The visit naturally came to nothing, but I would make it a point to try to have dinner with them as often as I could. Perhaps not too surprisingly, this practice did not continue for long. One morning, Pasolini was found dead, murdered by a young man who meant it when he said no. But like the death of Kennedy, Marilyn Monroe, and even Princess Diana, a debate still rages over whether Pasolini was wantonly murdered or whether a conspiracy by some of the many groups he had alienated resulted in his brutal death.

Despite this abortive experiment in importing intellectuals into the Jet Set, I was pleased with the group we had developed and the reputation we had so far earned. Overall the first two years of this life-style were heady times.

Before long our excessively social life-style made quite a stir. By 1976, we had entrenched ourselves so inexorably into society as the perfect couple that when we celebrated my thirty-sixth birthday in the south of France, the party was considered the social event of the summer next, of course, to the Red Cross Ball. We hosted the party at Regine's tropical club the Maona, in Monte Carlo, and my guests included Princess Grace, Prince Albert, and David Niven (who had recently completed a film with Gina and had starred in the movie of Sagan's *Bonjour Tristesse*).

David Niven always impressed me as a true gentleman and fitted with ease in the snootiest circles. At one point many years before, David waited patiently with a feigned ignorance to the situation as the sexually insatiable John Kennedy entertained Mrs. Niven below deck during a yacht party.

Yes, we were one big, happy family. Although the famed poodle was by now deceased, even Grace Kelly's dog Oliver had been a gift from Cary Grant! During the party, I sat Prince Albert next to socialite Diane Segard. My hobby as matchmaker has resulted in several alliances. Many found romance through introductions that I made.

As I reflect on it, life within the Jet Set includes a constant undercurrent of sexual tension. Perhaps Freud was right that everything ultimately boils down to sex because our events often seemed like complicated mating rituals. The selection of the guest list, the seating arrangement, and even the risqué conversation seemed an elaborate form of foreplay.

As I became more proficient in my role as host and organizer, certain people regarded me as someone capable of launching them into the Jet Set or finding them an appropriate mate. I believe this to be the final stage of the development — that of patron. Before long, beautiful young people and wealthy older people approached me with hopes of being discovered, created, or well matched.

It was, of course, flattering and when one considers that a mere four years earlier it was difficult for Lydia and me to keep a table of guests from running off to the powder room to laugh at me, I guess this was just what my ego required. And it turned out that I had a bit of a flair for it, too.

11

BETTER TO REIGN IN HELL THAN TO SERVE IN PARADISE

But things began to change in paradise. Donina became increasingly concerned over money. One can imagine how expensive our life-style was, but I was unaware of how little cash she actually had. To maintain appearances and continue at the pace we had set, we sold off real estate. Each subsequent year after the first two lavish years, we sold off another property. In the remaining years we were together, we disposed of the homes in Milan, Lausanne, and the two in Florence. We spent our time in Beaulieu, Gstaad, my apartment in Rome, and an increasing amount of time in our Park Avenue apartment.

We had set a pace for entertaining that simply was not sustainable with our still-large, but limited resources. Yet, it seemed inconceivable that we could change or downscale our life-style. Any reduction in our lavishness would have immediately been noticed, and our egos simply could not accept the resulting admonishments.

Donina's failed attempts to economize and even our real estate sales were not enough. We began to secretly sell off our art collections, taking large losses to avoid the embarrassment of public auctions. Soon our prized Bacon found its way quietly into the hands of a New York art dealer who purchased it for a fraction of its value. As a symbolic gesture, I sold my beloved speedboat and even contributed the remaining savings I had from my years with Lydia to the household accounts. Yet our expenses still greatly surpassed our resources, and we found ourselves becoming frantic over where this negative cash flow would lead us.

Donina placed the blame squarely on my shoulders. 'You should have been working, Massimo, not depleting my fortune,' she snapped. 'The extravagance is something we both created,' I would respond. Nevertheless, I, too, felt my anxiety rising. My frustration that I had not done more to contribute combined with the memory of Lydia's claim that I was unfit for work gave me a feeling of guilt and even inadequacy. At the time, I thought the situation and Donina's behavior unfair. Yet, in retrospect, it was exactly what I needed.

I decided to find work.

I can still remember quite vividly the day that I made the conscious decision at long last to support myself. I was thirty-seven-years old, and I had never really held a job in the traditional sense of the word. No matter how independent I acted around the women of my life until now, I had really only been pretending. The reality was that I was dependent upon them for my subsistence. This financial dependency had always placed me in a vulnerable position, and my lack of confidence in my talents other than those of my charm and sexuality had effectively trapped me in relationships.

The act of receiving financial or material gain was so linked to my understanding of relationships that it had become an addictive part of my sexual awareness and even the stimulation from which my arousal was based. I was as addicted to profit from love as a drug addict would be to his daily fix. It forced me to accept situations that I never would have found desirable and to fool myself into mislabeling them as something else.

Constantly reminding myself of Cocteau's famous lines, 'There is no love, only proofs of love,' I made it my philosophy.

Words have always seemed cheap and illusionary to me. I have watched people's actions and drawn my conclusion almost exclusively not from their words, but from their behavior. Their words of love became sounds that might have been spoken in another language or in some code that I could not decipher. I regarded and evaluated the relationship totally by what was provided as tangible evidence of love.

It was a cold winter day in Gstaad when Donina finally said, 'Massimo, you must get a job now. The time has come.' The words stung me with anger, shame, and perhaps some self-loathing. To escape the unpleasantness of our confrontation and to distance myself from the perpetual social obligations I was under as host to a chalet full of friends, I took my skis and went to the mountain.

From the top of the Wassengrad run, the village of Gstaad looked like a tiny speck lost among the enormous mountains that surrounded it. Our chalet, our world of social responsibility, and the money shortage we faced seemed distant from the top of the mountain.

I skied for many hours that day, but at four the gondola was making its last run, and I had to go. I was not ready to return to that house filled with its precarious social microcosm that I had built like a house of cards. A house that would tumble down the moment our financial vulnerability was exposed.

I drove my car, not back home, but in the other direction until I reached the neighboring town of Gsteig. Although only fifteen miles away from Gstaad, it might have been another world. Unpretentious and small, Gsteig is simply a quaint Swiss village. Its one hotel, the Viktoria, is comfortable and cozy and has an old rustic pub with wooden walls and a paneled ceiling stained brown from the smoke of many fires and countless pipes.

I sat in that simple inn and looked at the other guests. They seemed like ordinary faceless people, but on second glance, I saw that they did indeed have faces. Not the faces I would recognize or read about in society magazines, but these anonymous faces were smiling at one another. I realized that they were just happy people. There were six of them, three couples probably married for a long time. Probably six hard-working people simply enjoying a moment of relaxation.

One of the men took out an accordion and began to play. His wife fixed her eyes on him adoringly as he went through his repertoire of old Swiss and German ballads. The other two couples began to sing. A few minutes later, the innkeeper returned. He was a jolly-looking man of Italian extraction with a bushy mustache and a floppy, white chef's hat over his cheerful, florid face. He, too, carried an accordion, and he joined in a duet while the others sang enthusiastically. They sang 'Über den Wolken,' a song that literally means 'above the clouds freedom must be endless, and the problems that seem so great down below here seem negligible and small.'

It was funny for that is how the world had seemed from the mountaintop that day. They shifted to a more upbeat Viennese waltz, and one of the couples jumped up and began to dance. They danced the way couples that have been together for a long time can dance. What I mean is no real steps, just a synchronization that comes with time and practice.

I was fifteen miles away from the beautiful people having their evening cocktails at the Palace, and I could have been on another planet. The innkeeper approached my table respectfully and quietly placed a glass of hot Glühwein on my table. He indicated that it was a gift from the other table. Raising the glass to toast them, I saw looks of concern on their faces. It was then that I realized I had been crying.

Feeling ashamed, I quickly took my leave and drove home. There I searched through my desk for the card I had been given several years earlier by Robert Caillé, the director of *Vogue*. He was the gentleman I met on my flight back from New York with Lydia.

I telephoned him the next day and was surprised that he remembered me. I asked if he was still interested in having me write for *Vogue*, and he said he would love to have me write profiles on the Italian fashion industry. He promised to call me to introduce me to the appropriate *Vogue* editor.

Next, I called my friend, Giorgio Pavone, who was a partner in the PR firm of Rudi Crespi. He quickly offered me a part-time job helping him organize PR events and parties. Both of these jobs were to yield many benefits above the small revenues they would generate. They both would channel my life in new directions.

In the PR office, I was able to work sporadically and still manage to fulfill the traveling and hosting responsibilities demanded by my role in the Jet Set. One day as I was checking the mail in Pavone's office, I came across a ballot sent by my friend, Eleanor Lambert, a widely known American society journalist. Eleanor had long ago developed a contest for the best-dressed people in the world. She nominated the people, and a list of her nominees was sent out internationally. Eleanor would compile the votes and then publish the winners in her syndicated column. There was no ceremony or award. It was like a mail-order beauty contest that served no real purpose. It generated very little press or media coverage, and the selection criterion seemed somewhat random.

In the 1970s, the fashion industry was primarily dominated by French and Italian designers. Yet, they were not involved in the selection process. I found Eleanor's idea to be intriguing, but the execution left something to be desired. I made a decision to expand upon this idea and to create a truly international award with more European involvement and lots of international fanfare.

This decision was to change my life and also cost me Eleanor's friendship. She never forgave me for tampering with her system.

I realized that the person who controlled selecting the most elegant people in the world would have a strategic position within the Jet Set not unlike the Oscars have over Hollywood. I felt that I had to be this person and immediately began to use the network of friends and contacts that I had assembled over the years.

I visited the presidents of the Italian and French fashion syndicates, and they enthusiastically accepted my plan to include them on an international selection committee. Then I assembled a group of famous designers such as Pierre Cardin, as well as celebrities such as Gina Lollobrigida. Together we formed the Committee of *The Best* and decided to begin that very year with our first selections.

The award would be given personally to the winners at a cocktail party at the Palazzo Pecci Blunt in Rome. In subsequent years, the award ceremony took place at a formal dinner. The press was invited, and the coverage added to the celebrity of the recipients. This would keep the glamorous world of the Jet Set in the limelight and guarantee me a position of importance in our social world.

We began in 1976, and the committee threw itself into the nomination and selection process. This yielded an impressive list of recipients that included HRH Prince Charles; designer Hubert de Givenchy (who claimed that in his whole life he never received so many press clippings), accompanied as he often was with my friend, the beautiful and charming Audrey Hepburn, whose careers really intertwined; actor George Hamilton; Indonesian ex-First Lady Dewi Sukarno; Ira von Furstenberg; and even Philippe Junot who by this time was clearly going to marry Princess Caroline of Monaco.

Philippe was a typical playboy with a good sense of humor. I enjoyed his company. But if the truth be known, his selection for my award was meant to please Princess Grace and allow the Grimaldis to feel less embarrassment about the choice their eldest daughter had made.

At any rate, I had created an institution that would continue unbroken (with one sad exception that you will learn about) until today. It has resulted in the development and sometimes the come-back of great careers, in a rebirth of media interest in the Jet Set, and in many love affairs. The stage on which I have given my award has changed location from Rome to Paris and then New York. But regardless of the venue, it has been a magical stage on which many romances have been forged, from Naomi Campbell to Christopher Reeve

The Best awards were a great success and would one day assist me in my future work in the PR industry, but for now they did nothing to generate the much-needed cash that Donina and I continued to spend at a very alarming rate. The PR contracts I made weren't overly lucrative, so I was delighted when Robert Caillé called to schedule a meeting with his editor-in-chief of Paris *Vogue*, Francine Crescent.

Francine is a statuesque blonde with a natural beauty that requires no makeup. Like Garbo, she chose to wear no jewelry and dressed in very simple, but elegant clothes. I found her aloof and a bit cold. It was clear that she was skeptical of my abilities and had granted the interview at Robert's insistence.

Hearing my Italian accent, she voiced concern that I would not even be able to write in French. Naturally I explained that it would be my responsibility to insure that the grammar would be perfect. She agreed to send me to Milan to do a word portrait on each of the new Italian designers. Among this group was Armani, Versace, and Ferré.

This opportunity was to result not only in my career in magazines, but in a lifetime relationship with fashion and the beginning of friendships with the top designers. I carefully arranged for a bilingual countess to translate the article into impeccable French. I made appointments with these new faces in fashion and scheduled meetings with each one in Milan. For some reason, the chemistry never clicked between Armani and me. I found him too taken with himself and very serious in an almost fanatical way. It seemed to me that he was more suited to the clergy than the fashion industry, and in my profile, I said that he might have been a great priest. This offended him, and we have remained cool to each other over the years.

The opposite was the case with Versace. Gianni was living in a small, unpretentious apartment with his companion of the time. He worked out of his own sitting room and was so preoccupied with his craft that his modest surroundings did not embarrass him in any way. Gianni came from a part of Italy just a little south of where I was born, and we Italians always have a regional affinity for one another. We hit it off. I praised him in my profile, and he regarded me with a mutual admiration. Gianni never had any time for the Jet Set life, and in those days, fashion stars were only just beginning to receive social acceptance. Gianni and I were to remain close for the rest of his life, and I would play a role in his career as it reached the next step.

Dutifully, and with some trepidation, I wrote my profiles, not at all sure that I would ever see them in print. I was surprised when the next issue of *Vogue* was released. Francine had not only published the portraits, but placed them in a key position in the magazine. I sent her a large bouquet of flowers with a note thanking her for her kindness. She called to say that no thanks were needed as the article was tremendous, and she wanted me to do additional portraits.

Do you remember the thrill that I experienced — actually a sexual charge — when I received those valuable gifts from Lydia? I felt the same when I was offered the gift of a magical life-style from Donina. I was addicted to the dependency of receiving and expecting support and affluence from other people. It was a bad addiction. When I saw my articles in *Vogue* — and then when I received a check for what I had written — I felt a real independent pride for my own words. It was the first time. I cannot describe how proud I was that I had written something of value. This was to be a turning point in my life.

Until now, I believed I was incapable of supporting myself. I was grateful to be born with the natural gifts that made other people eager to sponsor me. Now I felt that I could overcome the dependency syndrome. I was experiencing a form of freedom that every working person in the world has known, but I'd believed was unattainable for me. Suddenly, I saw something that should have seemed pitifully obvious my whole life — I could work!

Francine expanded the mandate to include socialites, and I wrote profiles of my friends and acquaintances. In the next issues, *Vogue* published my articles about the Duchess of Bedford and Jackie Onassis.

Francine invited me to Milan with her staff to write about the social life surrounding the showing of the next ready-to-wear selections. It was on this trip that I became aware of Francine as a woman. I found her distance and snobbery to be curiously appealing. The fact that she was unwilling to accept any social invitations from designers other than lunch meetings intrigued me. Unlike me, she disliked large parties and did not even own an evening dress. She wore conservative business clothes, gray or black suits.

She would invariably arrive late at any fashion show, confident that they would not begin without her. Surrounded by a minimum of three or four assistants, she would not even carry a briefcase or a pen.

She seemed completely indifferent to the angry expressions with which she was greeted after her typically late arrivals. This was how she treated the designers whom she admired. Those that did not meet with her approval were treated much worse. In the case of those designers who failed to capture her interest, she would place a crossword puzzle in the middle of the press release that she was given and occupy herself throughout the show with the puzzle. What seemed to be a deep interest in the various creations was actually Francine's concentration on choosing the right word to decipher the puzzle.

With the exception of a very limited number of true geniuses, Francine never really showed any enthusiasm at all. Saint Laurent, Lagerfeld, Versace, Krizia, and Gaultier were among the chosen few to elicit Francine's elusive approval. Francine seemed totally impervious and ice cold to everyone.

Her total lack of interest in all the superficialities of the world of fashion and even of the Jet Set was so extraordinary that I found myself attracted to her. She reminded me of Garbo's distaste for pretension and celebrity. On the third night in Milan, I escorted her back to her hotel room and attempted to kiss her at her door. She was appalled. It appears that I had misunderstood her regard and undercalculated her antipathy toward men involved in another relationship.

I was mortified, but I asked, 'Don't you like me?' Her angry answer was 'I do not even think of a man when he is involved with another woman.'

I didn't try again. In any case, she was even colder toward me thereafter. Again, similar to the Garbo situation, we continued our relationship without ever mentioning the incident, and I continued to enjoy writing for *Vogue* — even in light of the ice-water treatment I received from Francine.

Between my *Vogue* royalties and the small income from the PR firm, I was far from contributing a sum of money commensurate with the expenses of life with Donina. I considered what else I might do to earn money. Handicapped by my lack of work experience, the time expended on *Vogue*, the occasional PR assignments, the extensive travel schedule, and the obligations of being a host so taxed my time that an office job was not a practical possibility.

In Rome, there was a nightclub called Jackie O. The owner had a poor reputation. The majority of the clubs he operated were the type where the revenues were generated by cheaply dressed women coming to your table and asking you to buy them drinks. He decided that he needed to upscale his image, and he reasoned that if I were the host at Jackie O, my circle of friends would frequent the place.

He asked me to take care of his PR, which essentially meant hosting parties at his club fifteen nights a month for a year or so. His offer for these services was five thousand dollars a month, which I found to be almost insulting. When I refused, he doubled his offer. Donina said, 'Take it Massimo. We need the money.'

Actually, like the other sources of income I was generating, it was essentially symbolic. You see, the assignment began in early winter, and, of course, Donina and I were hosting *tout le monde* in our chalet in Gstaad. Donina never expected that I would simply relocate to Rome and leave her with the sole responsibility of caring for our guests. Instead I assisted her as I always had and then simply left a house full of guests and flew to Rome.

Donina either missed me or mistrusted me and would generally join me in Rome, as well. If you added up the airfares associated with commuting between Gstaad and Rome, it was very close to the salary I was generating. Nevertheless, the assignment paid for most of my personal expenses. I tried to concentrate on doing an imitation of Rick from Casablanca and being the perfect, but detached host, but I would often find the guests staring in shock at the doorway. For inevitably a striking blonde socialite clad in mink over a costly designer dress, glittering with what probably appeared to be the crown jewels, would enter and sit disdainfully at the bar waiting for me to finish for the night.

This odd ritual continued for several months, and it ended abruptly in a rather dramatic way. Drama has always played a large role in my life, but never so much as it did in the final years of my life with Donina. I personally found Donina's breasts to be ravishing. They were firm for a woman of her age and just the right size. But Jet Setters are perpetually dissatisfied with their appearance, and Donina was no exception. She decided that her breasts could use a lift and chose a specialist in Rio.

Jet Set plastic surgeons are themselves stars, and the virtuoso of this period was Dr. Ivo Pitanguy. The plan was that I would drive her to the airport for an early-morning flight after finishing my duties at the club. She would fly to a private clinic in Rio and after a few days of recuperation meet me at our Park Avenue apartment for a series of parties thrown by our New York society friends.

She decided to bring her favorite jewels to Rio since she wanted to have them for the formal parties in New York. Rio being a beautiful, but dangerous city, I discouraged her from taking her most valuable diamonds. So Donina packed a conservative case of jewels she had designed herself. At the early-morning appointed hour, Donina appeared at Jackie O ready for her excursion into the world of cosmetic surgery.

She dressed exquisitely for the flight and

looked every inch the socialite in our Mercedes as I drove her through the empty streets toward the airport. Suddenly I was lurched forward as a car smashed into us from behind. It was a strong collision, but we were late and in a hurry, so I drove on.

Donina shouted, 'Stop Massimo! We must get their papers.'

I was too tired to argue, so I stopped. Two emerged from the car. It was really not such a cold night that one would expect two adults to seek the warmth of those odd woolen ski masks that cover the entire face, but this pair, revolvers in hand, were clad in precisely such head wear. One of them got into the back of the car and told us to drive on. A revolver was pointed at my head.

As I drove, I glanced at Donina. Not intimidated, she was surreptitiously removing her rings and sliding them into her yet-unlifted cleavage. A cool cucumber. At such times, it was easy to believe her claims of having survived Auschwitz. Despite my advice to pack lightly and Donina's use of her cleavage as a secure vault, the robbers still managed to get away with about $200,000 worth of jewelry.

Perhaps I should have stuck to women with larger breasts.

We were left unharmed on the street and had to walk back to safety. Initially Donina was convinced that the nightclub was behind it. Later she suspected that I organized it. I won't list the reasons why such a plot would not have been possible. Instead I will say that I was getting the feeling that our relationship was drawing to a sad conclusion.

After the robbery, the tension between us intensified. Donina's behavior toward me turned increasingly accusatory. I began to avoid her company and that included sexually. A great component of our prior happiness and stability had been the frequency and fullness of our sex life. I shut myself down, and she became intolerable to be around.

I tried to distract myself by making the second annual *Best* Awards more comprehensive than the first. Instead of simply an award presentation and cocktail party, I expanded it to a formal dinner. Pleased that I had succeeded in upscaling Jackie O, I threw the award dinner in that club. Among those honored were Egypt's President Anwar Sadat whose bravery in trying to resolve the Middle East crisis would soon cost him his life. And ironically (considering the venue) the award was also given to Jackie Onassis. The press interest in the award was growing exponentially as was the interest in prospective recipients. From the very beginning, people sensed the rich value of an award that guaranteed widespread media coverage.

I resigned from my job at Jackie O that spring, having decided to spend more time with Donina to recover our lost intimacy. Instead I continued to find myself doing anything possible to avoid being around her. I found excuses to stay in New York when she was in Europe. Donina would fly to join me, but the effect was to continue our ongoing argument.

She was becoming increasingly violent and began to get physical when we argued. I think she was hoping I would hit her back. Perhaps she thought that by inciting a physical response, she could break through my coldness and elicit a sexual reaction.

Now Donina became convinced that I was sexually involved with someone else. She had me followed. One warm day in early May, she burst into our New York apartment in an absolute frenzy of jealousy. I was standing by the window looking at the elegant streetscape of Park Avenue. I did not even expect her to be in America and was unprepared for her surprise entrance and hysterical assault.

'I know you are sleeping with someone else,' she shouted as she looked about the room.

'Please Donina,' I pleaded, 'let's not start that again!'

'Admit it! Admit it! At least have the decency to tell me the truth,' she screamed, charging at me like a wild animal.

'Donina, I can't live with this paranoia anymore.'

My response set her into an absolute fit of total hysteria. I remember from my ill-fated safari to Africa with Sao that one only has a split second to shoot a charging rhinoceros, and you have to hit them exactly between the eyes, or you are finished.

It was this image that flashed across my mind when Donina began her charge. As she ran toward me, she drew back her right arm and swung it toward my face. I was able to sidestep, not realizing that the combination of the momentum of her charge and her loss of balance at not connecting her fist to my face would carry her past me and through the open window thirteen stories above the concrete Park Avenue pavement.

As she flew by me and began her death plunge, I instinctively grabbed her blouse with my left hand. Her momentum swung me around and allowed me to get a tentative grip with my other hand as she disappeared out the window. It all happened in an instant, but as is often the case with such disasters, everything seemed to take place in slow motion.

Even now, I recall the horror vividly. I clung to the fabric of her blouse as she flew past me and out the window.

The force of her charge carried me precariously toward being pulled out with her, but somehow I clung to the back of her blouse with all my might as my forearms smashed against the windowsill, and I could feel the skin being scraped from my arms.

For a moment, the frenzy of activity stopped, and I found myself in a ridiculous situation. Donina was hanging upside down over 150 feet above the pavement. My grasp on her life was held in two clumps of the fabric of her blouse.

Let me pause to point out that Donina, as a true socialite, seemed to intuitively dress correctly for every occasion. Always impeccable, always correct, Donina had chosen the ideal outfit even for this event. Her blouse was a creation by a Milanese designer named Raffaella

Curiel. In addition to boasting elegant creations, Curiel was known for the robust nature of her garments. Astonishingly, Donina's entire body weight was suspended by two handfuls of stitched fabric, her life hung literally by a thread. Yet the blouse did not rip at all. It had saved her life.

Turning my palms upward, I hoisted her slowly and dragged her back inside the window. Exhausted and shocked, we collapsed on the floor. We were both sobbing and shivering.

When she was able to speak, she cried frantically, 'Forgive me, Massimo! Forgive me!' And for the moment I did, and I even believed that the trauma of this drama had somehow cleansed us of our sins.

As is often the case, as the poignancy of the incident faded in our memories, the jealousies and arguments began again. Donina resumed her interrogations and accusations and took solace by complaining about me to the three Graces. Estee Lauder and the Duchess of Bedford fully supported Donina and reminded her that they had never trusted me.

Princess Grace tried to be less judgmental. After all, her marriage had its infidelities and misunderstandings, and in general, she was a fair person. By this time, Grace had taken an apartment in Paris and was almost as distant from Prince Rainier as I was from Donina. In the biography *Grace*, Robert Lacey relates a conversation between Grace and Donina during this period.

Countess Donina Cicogna told her [Grace]

one day in these years of a man whom she loved passionately, but who, she discovered was flagrantly unfaithful to her. ' 'But you did have love,' said Grace eagerly almost desperately. 'It's love that matters isn't it, not the pain?' '

Sadly, love was not enough. Donina insisted on creating, perpetuating, and concentrating on pain. I tried to compromise with her and suggested a trial separation for six months. 'No,' she said, 'we stay together, or we end it completely.'

It was early June, and the Jet Set was readying itself for the event of the year. Grace's oldest daughter, Princess Caroline, was about to get married. It was the first marriage of any of Grace's children, and the event created a media frenzy.

I had honored Junot as a recipient of my *Best* Award. He was a charming fellow, but nobody seemed to think he was appropriate. In those days, most people hoped Caroline would marry Prince Charles. Instead, she selected a typical playboy whose diverse business ventures had included an abortive attempt at introducing fast-food restaurants to the south of France. I considered that about as good an idea as trying to introduce haute-cuisine restaurants at truck stops along Route 66.

Despite everyone's reservations, Caroline's wedding and the inevitable reception was the social event. The ceremony itself would take place in the small private chapel of Grimaldi Palace, but the reception and follow-up parties promised to be fantastic. Attendance was not only mandatory, it was essential in assuring one's status among the Jet Set.

I never doubted that Donina and I would sit at a table appropriate to the closeness that she shared with the bride's mother. I was half right. As it turned out, Donina received an invitation, but it did not include me.

I was astonished. After all, we were a couple. Donina had begun flexing her muscles and chose to do it through her relationship with Grace.

I appealed to Grace through a mutual friend and learned that Donina had specifically requested that I not be invited. This was going too far! Instead of pressing the issue, I decided to use the event to make my escape.

On the day of the wedding, I flew to New York to the apartment that had been purchased in my name and paid for with my personal check. I changed the locks. As I had thought, I was being watched, for the news reached Donina before poor Junot could even say 'I do.' By the time the reception began, the news had spread. Terrible, faithless Massimo had deserted his loving Donina and had seized their home and art collection.

Scandal is always more interesting than sanctioned romance, and naturally the news of my atrocity usurped the attention of the guests at the reception. Princess Caroline's wedding ball became the scene of crowds of whispering Jet Setters passing on the news of my defection. And lost among all the gossip was a somewhat-ignored bride and groom.

12

FALLEN FROM GRACE

Donina now suffered not only a major rejection, but also the humiliation of creating a public scandal. She was not one to take a slight with good temper. Within twenty-four hours of Caroline's wedding, Donina had hired a team of lawyers to file suit against me. Although the New York apartment was in my name and the artwork that it housed had been shipped secretly in my name to avoid inheritance issues with Coco's family, Donina made the claim that it all was her property.

Her lawyers filed an injunction to prevent me from selling any of it and began proceedings to reclaim what Donina had given me. It appeared that not unlike Lydia, Donina kept books. She had a ledger in which she kept copies of invoices for everything she had ever given me.

I remained in New York and simply did not answer the door when the bailiff tried to serve me the injunction. Things went from bad to worse.

The last years with Donina were dramatic, but I was unprepared for what was to come. About three weeks after parting with Donina, I left the apartment only to feel that I was being followed. I felt extremely unsettled. It was late at night, and I turned into Seventy-eighth Street to see if I could shake the feeling. As I walked west on Seventy-eighth Street toward Madison Avenue, I heard footsteps behind me increasing in tempo.

Suddenly a man appeared to my left holding a container in his right hand. I tried to look at his face, but my attention was diverted to the motion of his right arm as it lifted to pour the contents of the container on me. Not unlike the reflexes that saved my life when Donina charged me, I sidestepped the rush of liquid that had been aimed at my face. It splattered against the brick wall behind me as the assailant ran away. I looked at the wall and watched the nasty liquid sizzling as it oozed down the brick. It had been hydrochloric acid meant for my face. My good luck did not leave me, for as the man ran away, a policeman who had witnessed the assault apprehended him at the corner. He was arrested and charged with the atrocious assault. The next day a five-thousand-dollar bond was anonymously placed and my would-be assassin disappeared.

Knowing that Donina was behind this, I wasted no time and booked a ticket on the Concorde. I had the doorman hail me a taxi, made a mad rush into the cab, and told the driver to take me to Kennedy Airport. As we drove, I again got the feeling that I was being followed. After the recent events, I supposed that it was just the jitters. Suddenly, I was lurched over to the left side of the taxi as a large, four-door car slammed into the side of my taxi. The driver panicked when it became obvious that this was no accident. Again and again, the car tried to push us into the lane of oncoming traffic.

My driver was screaming and took turns looking at our assailants then back to me with questioning, terrified eyes.

'Drive on!' I shouted.

'Are you crazy, man? I'm going to stop. I don't want anything to do with this shit,' responded the frantic driver as he began to slow down.

'Wait,' I tried again. 'I'll give you a thousand dollars in cash if you get me to Kennedy.' Greed scored a quick win over terror, and the now-fearless driver darted dexterously in and out of the expressway lanes until we reached the terminal at JFK.

We had managed to lose our attackers. They may have feared that the taxi driver would radio his dispatcher. At least that's what the police thought.

I made my flight and tried to locate Donina, but I was unable to find her. I related to a mutual friend the story of the attacks on my life. I was told 'Donina never meant to kill you, she only wanted you hospitalized so the bailiff could serve you with the injunction.' This did little to cheer me up. I hardly found a liter of hydrochloric acid in my face the standard method of serving injunctions. Nor did I reckon that the oncoming traffic would have collided with my taxi at a speed guaranteed to only hospitalize me. It seemed like a good time to get a lawyer.

I have always been too impressed by titles and

success. Whenever I have needed the services of a professional, I always tried to hire the person who carried the title of 'the best.' I was assured by my friends that the best lawyer in America was Roy Cohn. It was only later that several books, a play, and even the film *Citizen Cohn* (in which the actor James Woods plays a convincing Roy) were made. Nevertheless, Cohn had been famous for some time.

In 1950, when Senator Joseph McCarthy began the Red Scare by announcing that he had a list of 205 names of members of the Communist Party who were allegedly working in the Department of State, Roy was at his side. At the hearings, Roy was the number-two witch hunter. His handling of the Rosenberg atom bomb trial and his association with J. Edgar Hoover were to become legendary. He was known to be tough and ruthless. In fact, a recently produced play about his life was titled *Vain, Ruthless, and Driven.* After the treatment I had just been given, I felt I could use a little ruthlessness on my side. So, at considerable expense, I hired Roy.

A costly and bitter legal battle raged for one year. Donina wanted everything — from the toilet-paper holders to even the small silver saccharine dispensers. She wanted it all. We reached a stalemate in negotiating, and a trial was scheduled. Then a funny thing happened. Roy seemed to get scared. My ruthless, tough, communist-hunting, fear-nothing lawyer started hedging and recommending that I forgo my claims.

I was amazed, but I agreed to turn everything over to Donina for $250,000, which was the purchase price and renovation costs for the apartment.

Once she took the title, she liquidated it immediately for $450,000.

I learned later why Roy had his change of heart. It seems that Donina had given him $80,000. Roy, known to be unscrupulous, certainly did nothing to convince me that giving up my plans for a law career was a wrong choice. In a weird twist of fate, Roy, who had not limited his attacks on communists, but had vehemently pursued homosexuals although he was one himself, died of AIDS.

Now, for the first time in my adult life, I found myself completely alone. Generally juggling several women, I now had nobody. Usually surrounded by sycophants and friends, I was now ostracized by a social group that was terrified of displeasing the Grimaldis. When my residency in Monaco was rescinded, I decided to sell the apartment in Monte Carlo that Lydia had given me. Rumor had it that Grace told her family not to attend functions to which I was invited. This was tantamount to social isolation.

Most of my old 'friends' did their best to avoid me. One former regular houseguest even hid behind the large columns in the Hotel de Paris to avoid having to greet me. Others took to taunting and teasing me in the hope of pleasing Donina. For example, the Duchess of Bedford had a great talent for mimicry. She took to calling me, and pretending that she was the social secretary to various people, invited me to parties where she knew I would not be admitted.

One such party was a yacht luncheon thrown by Puia. Although I had launched Puia into society and even helped her find a rich husband, she took Donina's side. This was odd considering that Donina's dislike for Puia was so great that the poor woman had to sleep in my apartment because she was not welcome at our villa in Beaulieu.

The plot was that the Duchess of Bedford's fake invitation would lure me to the yacht where I could be publicly humiliated by being refused entry.

Even my livelihood was threatened. I received a call from *Vogue*'s Robert Caillé asking me to meet him for lunch. He seemed nervous during the meal and finally I asked, 'Robert, what is it? What is on your mind?'

'I am sorry,' he responded, 'but it simply is too risky to have you continue writing for *Vogue* right now.'

'What should I do, Robert?' I asked.

'Massimo . . . move to an island, maybe in the Caribbean, and just disappear until people forget.'

This seemed like good advice, but I wanted a second opinion. I made an appointment with Princess Ghislaine de Polignac, the reigning matriarch of Parisian society.

'Should I move to a deserted island, Ghislaine?' I asked.

'No, of course not, darling,' was her reply. 'Paris is a large and liberal city. If you just carry on, people will get over this.'

I took her advice and stayed. As it turned out, her advice was excellent.

In Paris, I threw myself into the two avenues still open to me, namely PR and my *Best* Awards. I was pleased to find that all my invitations had not dried up, and some people remained loyal. Foremost among my true friends were two people — Sagan and Gina Lollobrigida. Sagan took her intellectual approach and was never really concerned with the Jet Set. She barely noticed the change in my life.

Gina took a generally more militant approach and verbally assaulted anyone who disparaged me. At a large party in Monte Carlo, she attacked an entire table of my former friends reminding them of the generous way they had been treated at my home for so many years. Later, during an even-greater crisis, these two ladies would once again defend and shelter me from harm. But for now, I slowly recovered my faith in people and my stability.

Americans are the most fearless when it comes to braving social disfavor. With the exception of Estee Lauder, my American friends were unconcerned about the social risks they incurred by their associating with me. It occurred to me that although the Jet Set regarded it as a large concession when they allowed actors into their ranks, I wonder if the Hollywood greats really cared whether the old guard of high society welcomed them.

Among my fearless American friends, none showed a greater lack of concern for the wrath of the three Graces than my friend, Jack Nicholson. Since the late sixties, Jack and I had enjoyed some good times on the yacht of Sam Spiegel. After spending a somewhat bleak early summer in Paris, I heard that Jack was on board Sam's yacht in St. Tropez and decided that I could use a diversion from my woes.

I met a very attractive eighteen-year-old girl in Rome who aspired to be an actress and decided to bring her. She'd stay with me in a villa of one of my remaining friends, the beautiful Countess Eugenia de Serigny. When we arrived, I was surprised to find that the young lady insisted on separate rooms. I concluded she was young and doubtless did not want to give our hosts a poor impression.

In St. Tropez, it is unusual to see women wearing bikini tops, but when we went to the beach, my date had covered her body in the most concealing one-piece bathing suit I had ever seen outside of the Bible Belt. In addition to this, each time we encountered a naked breast, she would turn bright red. Finally I asked her if anything was wrong.

'Well, this is all so new to me,' she responded. 'I mean I have led a very sheltered life . . . I have no real experience . . . of any kind.'

It took a moment for her message to register. Regarding her with the curiosity a zoologist might reserve for the study of the last specimen of an extinct species, I asked, 'You mean . . . ?'

Instead of answering, she lowered her eyes shielded by luxuriant, long eyelashes and again proceeded to turn crimson. This was a surprise.

Indeed, this was exactly the sort of thing I needed to get over the doldrums, I mused. Well, one must respect this, I told myself. One must be patient. I decided then and there that I would wait until evening.

What better way to impress and inspire an aspiring actress than to introduce her to a great star? So, calling Sam Spiegel's yacht, I told Jack that I was in town.

'Great, we have a party tonight. Come on over,' he purred into the phone. My young virgin nervously prepared herself for the evening yacht party and emerged from her room wearing an outfit that might have been considered conservative in the Royal Enclosure at Ascot. Nevertheless, she looked stunning, fresh, and eager.

At nine, the tender picked us up and cruised us to the enormous yacht of the producer of such classics as *Bridge over the River Kwai*. There on deck stood Jack, beaming from ear to ear with that infamous, infectious smile of his. It was clear that he could care less about the intrigues of the Jet Set. It again occurred to me that in all those years of feeling virtuous by allowing movie stars to join our ranks, for the most part, this privilege meant very little to them. At least Jack gave the impression that pleasing the old guard of continental high society was not what he had in mind for the evening's program.

I introduced him to my date, and it was clear from the moment that they set eyes on one another that the chemistry was strong. I pulled

Jack aside and said, 'Leave her alone. She's very timid and without experience. I've tried several times, and she is a very determined virgin.'

This was precisely the worst button I could have pressed. Jack turned to her and very slowly his lips curled into a devilish smile as he looked her up and down. Instead of averting her angelic eyes or blushing, she stared back into his eyes and returned his smile. This was too much. I felt protective of the poor girl. If the fates had chosen tonight as the night that she was to lose her virginity, then I felt it was my responsibility.

After the party, the Turkish-born recording king Ahmed Ertegun, Jack, my inebriated virgin, and I made the rounds of the usual St. Tropez clubs. With each change of venue, the young lady found a way to sit ever closer to Jack, who by now was at the peak of his drunken charm. He was doing imitations of mutual friends (something at which he is truly quite talented) and in general stealing the show. Finally, as the last clubs were closing, I said 'Well, looks like it's time to go home.' My date responded by placing her arm around Jack's waist and announcing, 'Jack is going to take me home.'

Giving me one of his fiendish grins, Jack said, 'Don't worry, Massimo, she will be safe with me.' Then he laughed hysterically, and took her back to Spiegel's yacht.

At two the next afternoon, an unshaven and tired-looking Jack Nicholson delivered the young lady back to my villa. I answered the door myself and said angrily, 'Keep her, Jack. She is yours!'

'I don't want her anymore,' protested the

exhausted star. Without another word, he left. She stood on my doorstep. It seems that Jack discovered to his great disappointment that the girl was only pretending to be a virgin to avoid sleeping with me. After this revelation and the subsequent physical exertion, Jack lost interest. And for that matter, so had I.

Let me tell you a little story that might at first seem unrelated to that one. I once kept a horse in a stable that like many stables housed an old dog. In this case, it was a motley old German shepherd. I would pet it sometimes on the way to visit my horse, and it seemed friendly enough.

One day, I was riding three miles away from the stable deep in the forest, and I lost control of my horse. I had been under a lot of stress, and I think that my horse sensed he could get away with it. He bolted from the trail and tried to throw me. He succeeded.

Bruised and embarrassed, I limped back to the stable. At the gate, stood the dog. I reached over to stroke his head. The old shepherd pounced on me, biting my hand and then tried to take a chunk out of my leg. What do you suppose made him do that? I believe it is because he sensed vulnerability.

That is just what the incident in St. Tropez reminded me of. That girl sensed my lost confidence. Women had courted me, adored me, and even supported me, but suddenly a young girl pretended to be a virgin simply to avoid sleeping with me. I was thirty-nine years old and still attractive, but I was vulnerable and perhaps a little desperate. For some reason, this often elicits the worst reactions in other human beings.

For the next six months, I was feeling defeated, and it got me nowhere. I tried to bury myself in my PR work and the *Best* Awards. That winter, the third annual *Best* Awards ceremony was held in Rome. Among the recipients were King Juan Carlos of Spain and Paloma Picasso. Paloma wore a golden pagoda on her head that virtually doubled her size. Other winners included actor Omar Sharif, conductor Herbert von Karajan (in whose house I almost died on the offending fish bone while accompanying Garbo), and my loyal friend, Gianni Versace. Gianni took this kindness very seriously and would soon amply repay me with his friendship and patronage.

Several weeks after the ceremony, a strange set of circumstances unfolded that was to place my life on a different track. It started in Rio. Each year the city goes wild in mid-February with its famous Carnival. It is similar to Mardi Gras, but on a more massive and even-more decadent scale. Part of the ceremony is the selection of a Carnival queen. She is the woman that the Brazilians consider to be the most beautiful and sexy woman in the world.

That year, they selected the gorgeous actress, Ursula Andress. Ursula created her international mystique in that unforgettable scene when she walks out from the ocean to greet James Bond in *Dr. No.* She was the first and perhaps most memorable of the 'James Bond Girls.' Her long blonde hair, cascading over deeply tanned skin and a remarkably curvaceous body set the definition of sexuality in the sixties.

I had been friends with her long before *Dr. No* when she was in her *dolce vita* days in Rome. As a result of our friendship, Ursula asked if I would escort her to the Carnival. All things considered, I certainly had nothing better to do and eagerly accepted.

Rio is an incredibly beautiful city. Its warm sandy beaches carry romantic tropical names such as Copacabana, and Ipanema. These are filled with some of the most beautiful tanned bodies I have ever seen. The streets, and walkways are very wide, and the sidewalks are inlaid with colorful mosaics, while the city itself is surrounded by lush, green mountains, which seem round, full, even sensuous. They, too, carry colorful names such as 'Sugar Loaf.'

On the peak of the highest is an enormous statue of Christ with his arms extended. The name for this statue is 'Christ the Redeemer.' The statue is cast out of an opalescent white stone that seems to radiate a soothing white light in the evenings.

It gives one the feeling that He is somehow happy and benevolently embracing and blessing the city. And perhaps even forgiving all its extravagances.

The city is lush and tropical, and during Carnival, its inhabitants (they're called Cariocas) go absolutely wild. Each day, the streets are filled with a parade of beautiful women dancing the samba as they march down the streets. At night, the city is alive with Carnival balls, each with an exotic theme such as 'A Thousand and One

Arabian Nights.' The people begin these balls in masquerade clothes and generally end them wearing nothing, but each other's perspiration. Rio was my kind of town.

Another of the quaint local customs is to provide the Carnival queen with a slave. The slave is selected with care. Each year, the Brazilians search their entire, enormous country for the most beautiful young man. This year, they found him in one of the remotest villages along the Amazon River where it was rumored that a young man of extraordinary beauty lived. They were correct in their choice. Unfortunately, the young man could only speak an unintelligible Indian dialect. Even his fellow Brazilians could not understand him. Nevertheless, he was the best the country had to offer and was ceremoniously presented to Ursula — who, of course, was unable to communicate with him verbally.

Most people believe Ursula is from Scandinavia, but actually she's Swiss. The Swiss, like the Germans, tend to be serious-minded people and somewhat literal. Ursula took her gift very seriously and completely at face value. She treated her slave not unkindly, but as a slave. The actress, who created the majestic role of *She Who Must Be Obeyed* in the film adaptation of the Rider Haggard novel of an immortal empress, seemed to relish recreating her triumph with her cooperative slave. At nights, she ordered him to sleep on the floor at the foot her bed. This practice might have gone unnoticed, but for the fact that another guest of the Carnival was a remarkably beautiful woman who had fallen in love with Ursula.

The lady came from a very powerful family and was not accustomed to rejection. She was convinced that given the opportunity she could seduce the unsuspecting Ursula. Coming to me, she said, 'I would be so grateful if you would distract the slave. Get him out of her room. I just want a chance,' she pleaded.

So I gave it a try. I asked Ursula if I might borrow her slave as a guide. I kept him away for several hours. I introduced him to some of my Parisian acquaintances, and although communication was impossible, he impressed them in a Tarzan kind of a way. He impressed everybody so much, in fact, that I decided to bring him back to Paris with us — sort of like a tropical souvenir.

I introduced him to some of my PR friends, thinking they could use him as a model. I spent a good deal of time educating him and teaching him French and had such success that he established his own PR firm and became the live-in lover of an ex-minister of France. I guess you can take the boy out of the jungle. But to continue the platitude, you cannot take the jungle out of the boy. For after his enormous Parisian success, he became embarrassed by his humble origins and my role as his mentor and from then on was my enemy.

The combination of escorting Ursula, participating in the nightly Carnival frolics, and distracting the slave exhausted me. By the end of the long flight to Paris, I was completely worn out. As it happens, I had accepted an invitation to the opening of the Monaco Ballet for that very night. I got home in time to don my tuxedo and drag my worn body to the Opera House. (Its proper name is the Garnier Palace.)

Over the years as part of the Jet Set, I have learned many lessons. One of these is that a man should not be gauged solely by the stature of his friends, but also by the strength of his enemies. Being ostracized caused me shame and grief, but after a while, I realized that it also afforded me a certain mystique.

'There goes dangerous Massimo. Strike him off the guest list.' Ronald Perelman, the owner of Revlon, for example, a very powerful man, personally removed my name from his invitation list when he realized that I was the notorious Massimo.

This notoriety put me in a very unusual situation and ultimately ended my career as a bachelor.

The Monaco Ballet was a recent interest of Princess Grace. For its Paris premiere, Rudolf Nureyev was scheduled to perform. Several private boxes were reserved for society, but this posed a geographic challenge. Due to my tenuous status, it would be awkward to be seated in any box that contained a member of the royal family of Monaco. This left one available box occupied by Karl Lagerfeld and my ex-boss, Francine Crescent of *Vogue*. The two were friends and shared a low tolerance for boredom. They had a practice of spending their afternoons walking from theater to theater along the

Champs Elysées and watching a random ten to fifteen minutes of each movie until, losing interest, they moved on. Tonight I was to be seated in their box.

Francine was aware that I was no longer with Donina and seemed to be less distant than the last time I had seen her.

Exhausted after my trip, I was doing a poor job of trying to stay awake.

'Why torture yourself?' asked Francine. 'Stretch out on the bench, and I will wake you up when it is over.'

Next to her was a comfortably upholstered velvet bench that seemed awfully inviting. I took her advice and in seconds was sound asleep. She wakened me to announce that the show had ended and it was time to go to dinner. Generally after such an event, someone always organizes a dinner, and tonight it was to be at Maxim's.

Maxim's is one of those unusual restaurants that has survived time and fame without losing its charm. It was immortalized in the film *Gigi* where the suave Maurice Chevalier and the charming playboy, Louis Jourdan, took their newest conquests. In reality, it has not lost its belle époque charms. The walls are covered with beautiful murals of water nymphs and cherubs. There is a small stage on which a virtuoso plays a concert grand piano to the accompaniment of a roaming violinist who remarkably always stays in sync with the piano. The tables are arranged around a small dance floor rubbed smooth by a century of dancing socialites. It is a delightful place.

The dinner guests had seats assigned, and, naturally, I was exiled to the table furthest away from Princess Caroline, who already was at the brink of ending her marriage to Junot. Francine's place card put her very close to Caroline at the other end of the restaurant from me.

In what I considered a remarkable gesture, Francine went to the woman seated next to me and asked her if she minded switching places. This would be the equivalent of a first-class passenger asking someone in steerage if they minded exchanging seats. In addition to displaying an indifference to the privilege she was being offered, Francine risked the displeasure of Caroline and the other anti-Massimo factions. This, too, seemed of no interest to Francine. I was impressed. Was this a new experimental form of hyperminimalism — or did she really not care? I wondered.

As it turned out, it was quite sincere and done with an easy graciousness and without any expectation of thanks. I was truly moved by this act and what it represented. I drove Francine home, and now, free of Donina, I was able to begin dating her. After a very short time, I told the PR lady whom I had been casually seeing that it was over. I had no idea that my idea of casual was not at all the way she regarded the relationship.

Returning again to the film *Gigi*, there is a scene where Maurice Chevalier takes a confused Louis Jourdan to Maxim's to celebrate his first suicide.

'How did she do it? With insufficient poison?' asks a bemused Chevalier. In reality, being the catalyst for a person trying to take their life is not a reason that would bring me back to Maxim's. In another of the strange twists of the Jet Set, Ira von Furstenburg found my suicidal ex-girlfriend just in time

My luck seemed to have returned when I began to date Francine, and my enthusiasm as well. As I watched her run Paris *Vogue*, it occurred to me that I, too, might be able to manage a magazine. There was no real magazine devoted to the life of the Jet Set, and I thought it would be a good complement to my award. With Francine's advice and support, I began to publish my own magazine which, of course, I named *The Best*.

Now I had three vehicles with which I could play an active role in the evolution and life of the Jet Set. I had my PR work that assisted in launching people and even places into the world of society, an award that allowed my committee to reward what we felt was elegant, responsible behavior, and a magazine to chronicle our life-style.

Somehow, things had fallen into place.

I was a long way from the young man who lived off the allowance of Lydia Deterding. I had a lot further to travel, but my life was taking on a sense of independence and even began to feel as if it finally had some meaning.

13

DEATH OF THE ICONS

I developed a concept for my magazine and my public-relations work. My relationship with Francine and consequentially the fashion industry made it possible to merge the Jet Set worlds with fashion in my magazine and my social life.

Gianni Versace's career had skyrocketed since my profile. He was as disinterested in the Jet Set as it had once been in designers. But as his empire grew, he saw the need to reconcile himself with this influential group. Versace was becoming a fashion powerhouse, and now he wanted to launch a Versace perfume. The time had come to solicit the support of Parisian high society, and Gianni asked if I would help launch his perfume and in effect to launch Gianni himself into society.

I decided to do this in a big way and rented the entire Paris Opera House. This ornate, enormous edifice is the location of the legendary Phantom of the Opera.

It is built in titanic proportions out of finely cut light-gray stone. The building sits squarely upon a triangular island formed by the diagonal intersection of two major Parisian boulevards. Inside, one enters an enormous lobby with a monumental stairway leading upward to hundreds of elegant private boxes.

At the foot of the stairway, I organized my feast. This was done with large banquet tables. On the top of these enormous tables, costumed entertainers would perform acrobatics and juggle exactly as if it were a medieval feast. I filled the invitation list with the best names in Parisian and Jet Set society. After all, this was Gianni's party, not mine.

Everyone came.

The Rothschilds were there, Ira von Furstenberg, intellectuals like Sagan, fashion icons, and movie stars. The party was an enormous success. The press coverage was tremendous, and Versace and his perfume were accepted immediately by the Jet Set.

Gianni understood the marketing significance of this launch and next asked me to organize his first important Parisian fashion show. This, too, was an enormous success. Gianni accepted the need to maintain good terms with the Jet Set. He never really integrated into our world, but somehow coasted alongside it — occupied with his work and personal life, yet always accessible and receptive to us.

In August, he rented a house in Sardinia on the fashionable Costa Smeralda not far from Countess Marta Marzotto. He got a yacht and would take me out on day cruises, but rarely mingled with the Jet Set at night. He was content to mingle with us a bit during the day, but at night he preferred to stay at home with his companion, family members, and close friends and have quiet dinners.

I was fortunate to be counted among his friends and to be included in his very private world. As Gianni became more successful and consequentially very wealthy, he upgraded his standard of living to lavish.

He still maintained exactly the same pattern of being a homebody who enjoyed conversation. Whether we were sitting in the small, unpretentious bistros that he preferred or strolling along the avenue, his eyes were constantly moving, absorbing colors, patterns, and textures. He was attentive to his friends, but his mind was always occupied with his creations.

Lake Como is a beautiful lake in Italy's northern Lake District. It is bracketed by the Alps and surrounded by ancient villas. The Dukes of Milan had built a summer palace upon its shores. This, over time, had been turned into a luxurious hotel called Villa d'Este. It is one of those grand old hotels that managed to retain its charm, yet it is bathed in a certain melancholy and nostalgia as if the ghosts of so many happy couples haunt its marble halls. It was here that my old friend, the Duke of Windsor, took Wallis Simpson for a secret tryst when he was still the Prince of Wales.

Then as now, the Villa d'Este has a small yacht that takes out young lovers for an evening cruise on the still lake. Wallis Simpson loved that ritual and would repeat each night, 'Same boat, same night, same moon.' Meaning that she had found her version of heaven and wanted it to remain exactly as it was forever.

For Gianni, Lake Como was heaven, as well.

He bought one of the grand old villas next to Villa d'Este and had it restored to its ancient splendor. It was lavishly furnished in an architectural equivalent of his design concepts — somehow plush and comfortable at the same time. There was gold brocade everywhere and lots of overstuffed cushions. The villa was populated with an army of Filipino servants.

In that respect, it reminded me of Baron Langheim's strange island fortress in the Bay of Naples with its contingent of half-naked servants. Gianni, on the other hand, had his neatly dressed in a sort of white livery uniform. Despite all this splendor, there was still something very relaxed about Gianni's homes.

It was not unusual to see such stars as Madonna or Elton John visiting.

As the world turned Versace into a household name and as the Jet Set increasingly sought his company, Gianni became even more home oriented. When he built his lavish house in South Beach, Miami I was amazed to see how simply he lived. His home bordered a gay beach where you could often hear the carryings-on behind his fence. Occasionally in the morning, there were used condoms in his garden that had been tossed over the fence in a moment of passion or perhaps jealousy.

When I visited him, we would go out in a small group and walk along Ocean Drive among the crowds and tourists who frequented the strip of restaurants. Gianni would choose a typical restaurant and without fanfare or any security, we would sit outside and eat while Gianni watched the people, always concentrating on new design ideas.

After dinner, we would walk back to his house. He would unlock the door himself, and we would go in. Maybe that does not sound odd to you, but let me point out that Gianni's presence and wealth were well known throughout South Beach. Other community celebrities felt the need for security, and the real-estate developers created virtual fortresses for their exclusive clients.

Fisher Island, for example, was developed as a self-contained community for millionaires. In addition to its own security force, it had its own ferryboat. It could only be visited by a tightly controlled private boat, or, on special occasions, by a helicopter.

Another friend of mine, Thomas Kramer, increased his already enormous family fortune by building a complex at the southern tip of South Beach called Portofino. Here most apartments started at more than one million dollars. Part of the reason for its success was the Fort Knox-like security that it offered.

The security measures at the gatehouse were reminiscent of the immigration control at Heathrow Airport. In addition to a litany of questions, the license plate of your car would be logged into the computer system so the concierge could ensure that it was the same car that reached the tower and the same visitor who was exiting the vehicle. Kramer himself encircled his home with state-of-the-art alarm systems. Bodyguards surrounded his home, which featured a room straight out of a James Bond movie. Thomas would place his hand over a small scanner, and after the security system recognized the lines and contours of his hand, it would automatically open the vaultlike door. Inside the room was filled with every imaginable type of weapon. Handguns, machine guns, even a bazooka were readily available should the bodyguards require reinforcement.

As a strange aside to the somewhat colorful life of Thomas Kramer, I decided to feature Thomas and his beautiful fiancée on the cover of my magazine. It appears that the young lady was suffering from a physiological illness that was causing extreme depression. She tragically decided to take her own life and performed the dramatic act in a very bizarre way. Placing the cover of my magazine over her chest, she shot herself through her own cover photo into her heart. Thomas was distraught and in a manner similar to Juan Peron's insistence on leaving Evita's coffin in his bedroom, placed an effigy of his lost love in a coffin by his bed.

At any rate, people were getting a little paranoid about security. If anything, this tragedy somehow made Thomas even more obsessed about isolating and protecting himself. All this underscores just how startling Gianni's lack of security was by comparison.

Well, we all know what happened. One day, Gianni left his home without any form of protection, and a lunatic gunned him down for no apparent reason. And one of the greatest talents the fashion world ever knew was lost to us. It was interesting to see the people who attended the funeral. There were actors, famous singers, most of my old friends from the Jet Set.

Sadly, it was the last time we would see Diana, Princess of Wales. So shortly after this tragedy, we were to lose her just as pointlessly. And at that moment I would never have believed that I would soon be drawn into an international web of intrigue surrounding the question of whether her death was really a conspiracy.

In a way, the funeral illustrated how by this time the Jet Set was truly an integrated group of protagonists from diverse fields. It was a cross section of the uppermost strata of the world's elite, and they wept for Gianni as their equal. The attendance of royalty, aristocracy, and great wealth at a funeral for a clothing designer would have been unheard of twenty years earlier. That was the most cheerful thought I had on that sad day.

It is a strange addendum that even with the death of Versace, his choice of South Beach as a perceived Jet Set location caught on. Maybe it was the energy that the strip along Ocean Drive exudes, or maybe people simply needed to augment the old circuit. Whatever the reason, soon many of our circle were spending several weeks a year in that unlikely place.

My old friend, Riccardo Olivieri, who met with slightly more success during our screen test for Visconti almost thirty years before, realized that the Europeans felt out of place with American architecture and had the Bentley Hotel built in true European style. He contacted me after all those years to help launch his hotel the way I launched people into the Jet Set. I brought Gina Lollobrigida, Ivana Trump, and other members of our group, and I must say that it really caught on. So, even after the loss of Gianni, Versace's foresight in choosing South Beach resulted in a new venue in our travel circuit and even spawned the development of an infrastructure to accommodate it.

Shortly after my successful launch of Versace's perfume, I became intimately involved with another fashion star in a series of episodes that ended even more gruesomely than my friendship with Gianni.

Patrizia and Maurizio Gucci seemed to be one of the most happy couples I have known. They had everything. Maurizio was the last of the Guccis to personally run their vast fashion empire. The couple was clearly in love and had two beautiful little daughters. In a way, they reminded me of the way Onassis and Callas used to behave in their earlier days together. I met the Guccis in Acapulco in the very early eighties. I remember it well because Acapulco was still under the control of Lowell Guinness.

The place had been made fashionable in the forties by Errol Flynn, who would take friends there on his yacht, the *Sirocco*. Since then, a highly insulated community of enormously wealthy people created a compound in one part of the resort. It was as security-oriented as some of the South Beach complexes I described, except that in Mexico, guards are permitted to have machine guns.

Lowell Guinness was very English and very powerful. He was the only Jet Setter I've ever known who was headstrong enough to actually create his own time zone. You see, for the most part, our social group begins the evening with cocktails at nine, dinner at eleven, and then dancing and clubbing. Lowell rebelled at this, as Garbo had done in St. Tropez. He insisted that the group conform to his timetable.

In England, Lowell was used to having his dinner at eight, and so he imposed this regimen on his Acapulco domain. And he was successful. Many metabolisms suffered huge adjustments, and many Jet Setters walked around in a daze as they adjusted to what felt to them like constant jet lag. Lowell was impervious to their complaints and as punctual as an English barrister.

I've mentioned that in St. Moritz the event was Niarchos's New Year's party. In Acapulco, the same feeling was shared about New Year's at the Guinness mansion. Invitations were just as hungered for.

I met the Guccis just before the party and managed to get them invitations. It was a strange party, indeed. First, as one might expect, it started too early. Secondly, the guest of honor was Frank Sinatra. We were told in advance that Frank refused to be photographed, but that one could take pictures of the other guests. I brought a camera to capture some pictures for my magazine.

Doing my best to avoid even seeming to point the camera at Sinatra, I snapped a photo of the palatial ballroom. As the camera flashed, Sinatra went wild.

'What the hell is going on here?' he shouted. 'Stop him!' he screamed to his towering bodyguard.

The man jumped me and holding me several inches above the ground, unceremoniously took my camera.

'I was not photographing Mr. Sinatra,' I protested.

'Get him out of here,' shouted the still-irate Frank.

Guinness apologized to Frank, and I was allowed to stay.

It is safe to say that the festive mood of that New Year's Eve party was as effectively dampened as when Johannes compared Señor Patiño to a chimpanzee. Most of the guests avoided any form of eye contact with me or simply stared with hostility as if I had broken an unwritten law. A few more-lenient guests and some who hoped to get their pictures published by me were a little more understanding.

It was under these terms that I became friendly with the Guccis. Notwithstanding this misadventure, they were grateful to be introduced to society, and we began to socialize regularly. Maurizio had problems with the Italian tax authorities and sought refuge in Switzerland for a time. Patrizia remained supportive and loyal to her husband and as I discovered, had prepared a way to be with him.

I visited Patrizia in Milan for the fashion shows and to my dismay found that my hotel reservation had been canceled. It is a very busy time in Milan, and even Patrizia was unable to accommodate me in her home, but she trusted me enough to offer me a more secretive set of lodgings. She had me taken to a strange warehouse. The entrance led to a passageway that was concealed behind a sliding bookshelf. The basement had been converted into what appeared to be a bunker or bomb shelter, in the way some Americans had built concrete shelters during the Cold War. Patrizia had done a similar thing, but on a much larger and more luxurious scale. Inside were provisions of food and liquid to last two years.

The idea was that the exiled Maurizio could sneak across the Swiss border and pay conjugal visits to his adoring wife in the safety of their little hideaway. In those days, they seemed very much in love. I was so impressed with the couple, their contribution to the fashion industry, and their earnest attempts at courting society that I awarded Patrizia my *Best* Award in 1982.

Then something happened that I have often been falsely accused of precipitating. Maurizio became increasingly intrigued by the world to which I had exposed him. He began to ignore his fashion empire. Since he was the last of the Guccis to run the business, his new Jet Set addiction was of serious concern to the Gucci management.

The course of this addiction grew slowly at first, but by 1993 Maurizio had become a full convert into the Jet Set world. He sold his

284

50-percent interest in Gucci for $170 million, bought Niarchos's yacht, and even more astonishingly, he divorced his wife.

I simply could not believe it. At first I tried to maintain a friendship with each of them individually, but they were both too possessive and territorial.

During the summer of 1994, I accepted an invitation from Patrizia that led me into a surrealistic and gruesome story. She invited me on a three-week cruise of the Greek islands. She hoped that the diversion might free her mind from lamenting the loss of her husband. The rented yacht was staffed with a captain and a crew of seven. To this, she added her maid, butler, and chef, creating a staff of ten people for only four passengers.

Francine was unable to join me, so I brought my friend, Fabrizio. Patrizia had fallen under the spell of a strange, self-styled magician in Naples. She was an old, ugly, fortune-teller named Giuseppina Auriemma, and she looked exactly like those witches in *Macbeth* that were always up to no good. She was also a Rasputin for she held Patrizia under an almost-hypnotic spell.

Many Jet Setters, obsessed with their notoriety, self-absorbed, and bored, fall under the spell of astrologers and spiritualists. There is the strange case of Sarah Ferguson who trusted the self-styled Madame Vasso. Vasso taped their fortune-telling sessions and sold them to the tabloids, even offering a call-in number where one could hear the voices of poor Sarah and even Prince Andrew at the cost of fifty cents a minute.

But Vasso, bad as she was, turned out to be an innocent compared to Giuseppina.

Patrizia's old witch was well versed in black magic as well as manipulation, which perhaps is the same thing in the end. She realized that Patrizia was vulnerable and cleverly exploited her weaknesses. Patrizia still loved Maurizio and vacillated from being convinced that he would return to suddenly breaking into unsubstantiated accusations that he was really a homosexual. But her greatest fear lay in her belief that he was squandering the family fortune with his newly discovered Jet Set life and that he would have nothing left to leave to their daughters.

And so with this scenario, we began our cruise of the Mediterranean.

It was a stormy cruise with the magician creating a tempest. She would spend the day reading her tarot cards, muttering over her rune stones. For all I know, she inspected the entrails of the animals our chef prepared for dinner. She mixed conventional forms of fortune-telling with strange devices of her own creation, and before long, we had all fallen under her weird spell.

The highlight of each day would be the reading that she gave Patrizia. It would invariably portend the violent death of Maurizio. She saw blood and carnage and disaster in the offing. In a seemingly trancelike state, she would turn her head upwards and wail, 'Death! Horrible, violent death!'

She gave my friend Fabrizio a reading and predicted his impending demise with such vividness that poor Fabrizio was genuinely distressed.

We appealed to her for a means of averting this calamity, and she searched her secret incantations and spells and found a solution. A certain root existed, and we must find it and at the dark of the moon, burn it on an open beach. The root existed on an isolated portion of the island of Santorini. The captain was immediately consulted, charts were examined, various courses plotted, and we set sail for Santorini. Landing on the island, we followed the directions of the witch and, sure enough, located the root. That evening, we sat upon the volcanic sands of the deserted beach of Santorini and in a solemn midnight ceremony burned the root. Fabrizio survived.

No such remedy or expediency was recommended to ward off the violent death of Maurizio. The atmosphere remained very solemn and very frightening. We stayed at sea, once sending in the sailors to buy lobsters for us. I staunchly refused to allow the witch to read my future and was relieved when the cruise ended.

Unfortunately, the story does not end there. I tried to put the whole incident out of my mind. Maurizio was a little cold toward me after this for he felt that by accompanying his ex-wife, I had somehow sided with her against him. His anger toward me was brief for soon after the cruise, Maurizio was found dead. He had been executed gangland style — shot three times in the back of his head.

This might be enough to convince skeptics of

the power of the supernatural. Instead, it convinced a jury of twelve men of the reality of a plot of premeditated murder.

Patrizia and her magician and the hit man they had hired were convicted and sentenced to lengthy prison sentences. The supernatural alibi they had created did nothing to impress the judge.

14

THE JET SET GETS
SATURDAY NIGHT FEVER

And so the two great fashion stars I launched into society met premature, violent deaths. Nevertheless, the Jet Set had inextricably linked itself to the fashion world. It was not simply the society launches that were responsible for this cross-pollination. A new phenomenon had taken hold in New York City that radically destroyed the remaining barriers between the society Jet Setters, movie stars, and the fashion icons.

In the early sixties, society members isolated themselves to a great extent because their social activities were restricted and private. At that time, social interaction was dictated by the guest lists of hosts and mixing with other groups was not an option. Then, after-hours dance clubs began to emerge.

There had always been chic after-hours clubs, often for members only. Here socialites would dance and drink after their parties.

In London, Annabel's in Berkeley Square was such a place. It is discreetly situated in the basement of a large building on a typical London square — the type that seems completely uninhabited at night. This is part of its disguise. There is a stairway with a velvet rope leading downward, which you would miss if it were not guarded by a uniformed footman. Here one is politely informed that membership is required for admission. To obtain this privilege requires the sponsorship of two existing members. In other words, you are not allowed in unless you are already one of us.

Even with two sponsors, the waiting time for membership can take years. A set of rules exists that includes forbidding members to take pictures of the club or the goings-on within it. My friend and co-author Allan Starkie was expelled from the club simply because he described it in his book about Fergie. Such clubs require almost Masonic vows of silence. Clearly they are not conducive to the cross-pollination that society could have used.

But in the late sixties, another type of club developed that was slightly less restrictive. Clubs such as Regine's or Castel's did not require membership, although access was still somewhat limited.

Regine's was for all practical purposes a Jet Set club, and in protest, la bande Sagan taunted the guests by meeting each night at the entrance vestibule but never entering or mingling with the others. In a way, this too was an illusion, for members of la bande Sagan, although ostensibly anti-Jet Setters, were in actuality just slightly more eccentric members of our crowd.

For example, Porfirio Rubirosa was a playboy from the classic mold. He married and divorced American heiress Barbara Hutton and in the process clinched a million-dollar divorce settlement, placing him in the playboy hall of fame. This was hardly the act of a sultry intellectual rebel who detested the decadence of the Jet Set. Along with Porfirio, another member of Sagan's group was Roger Vadim. It was Roger who actually coined the term discotheque. That was to define this new type of club.

But these discotheques began with their own set of strange social restrictions and de-facto forms of insulation. Even my attempt at drawing members of my circle to Jackie O in Rome was short lived. In New York, the upper class still danced Fred Astaire-style at El Morocco and Le Club. *Women's Wear Daily* expressed disgust with this upper-crust conservatism, warning that 'society was suffering a premature hardening of the arteries.'

Then in 1977, something occurred that shattered the social barriers in an unprecedented way. Studio 54 was opened. A short man with tall vision and endless energy named Steve Rubell leased an enormous abandoned theater at 25 West Fifty-fourth Street. It had been built by the San Carlo Opera Company in 1927, and after a series of owners, ended its theatrical life as a sound stage for Columbia Broadcasting. It was home to such programs as Perry Como, Jack Benny, and even Captain Kangaroo.

Rubell managed a number of restaurants and was consumed with the concept of a mecca for the people of the night. He transformed the Studio into the leading after-hours venue the world had yet experienced.

To begin with, Rubell realized that the perception of exclusivity was essential to the success of his club. But it was not to be an exclusivity dictated by the names of your parents. He placed a barricade of velvet ropes strung along brass stanchions around the doorway.

Each night, Rubell along with his rope people would tightly and personally control entry. A small number of people would be culled from the enormous lines as if he were casting a play. He would call this 'making a tossed salad.'

People went to great extremes with their dress and behavior to be noticed and, they hoped, selected for admission. The feeling of anticipation at the door was part of the Studio 54 experience. Fortunately, Rubell quickly identified the value of admitting members of the Jet Set, and we were always allowed immediate entry through the roped-off VIP entrance.

Once you passed through this entry process, you felt as if you had been accepted into a secret fraternity. The rules that governed mortals were left on the other side of the velvet ropes. As you walked through the long entrance hallway, with each step the pounding beat of the disco music got louder and the excitement began to mount.

Often Steve would decorate this corridor in strange ways to create a special ambiance. One Valentine's Day, he had it filled with a dozen harpists all playing in unison. It was what one might expect the receiving line in Heaven to look like. On another night, he had a stage set of miniature furniture brought in and hired an army of dwarfs to partake in a miniature feast. All the utensils and goblets were made in half scale. They ate and drank impervious to our stares, as if it were a normal gathering.

Once past this corridor, you entered the massive Studio. The stage was still in place, but now used as a dance floor. It made the guests feel as if they themselves were the show. Above the stage was a huge moon with a man-in-the-moon face snorting imaginary cocaine from a huge spoon. This was symbolic of the fact that drugs were as much a part of Studio 54 as alcohol and sex.

The bar was located in the center and staffed by half-naked, well-built bartenders. I bet Baron Langheim would have loved it! In the early days, an area next to the bar had been cordoned off as the VIP area.

The most amazing features, however, were the mezzanine and basement. The mezzanine was the type you would find in most old movie theaters where teenagers went to fondle one another. As a matter of fact, it was reminiscent of the movie house where my friend Alex and I took Christina Onassis and her cousin to fondle them. In Studio 54, it did not stop at fondling — here it was used for sex, group sex, bi and homosexual sex, and all variations thereof. From the seats of the mezzanine, you could look down at the dance floor in a voyeuristic sort of way while all around you were the silhouettes of bodies in various degrees of undress and copulation. You could hear the sounds of oral sex behind and next to you to the pounding accompaniment of the disco beat constantly in the background.

The basement was a labyrinth of rooms reached by a door behind the bar. The stairs were made of roughly finished cement and led down to an unfinished series of rooms and cubicles divided by chain-link fencing. People would sit on broken furniture, crates, rolled-up carpeting, or on the floor. Overhead, the bare ceiling was crisscrossed with sprinkler pipes. Sometimes the half-naked bartenders would bring down the more adventurous guests and even handcuff them to these pipes to fulfill their sadomasochistic fantasies and the voyeuristic needs of those who were only there to watch.

The basement was really the venue for the hard-core drug users. Every form of recreational drugs was readily available, and if you ran out, 'Dr. Moon' was parked in his van outside the main entrance to sell you more out of his mobile apothecary.

From the very first day of its existence, Studio 54 attracted the Jet Set, smashing whatever social barriers still existed. A reporter for the *Daily News* said, 'When I came to live in Manhattan in 1976 the social order seemed to be ruled by the same network of families that had always ruled. That changed with astonishing speed and Studio 54 was the agent of that change.'

I could not agree more. Studio 54 was a final stage in the desegregation of the society. Everyone mingled. Recognizing the significance of Studio 54, I decided to hold my 1982 and

1983 *Best* Awards there. In a way, the worlds of high society, fashion, and entertainment that had been trying to unite themselves since the Rainier-Kelly marriage finally joined in this strange and unlikely place.

Studio 54 had its core group of regulars that included writer Truman Capote, the author of *Breakfast at Tiffany's*, and my old friend, Andy Warhol. It is odd now that he is dead to feel almost obligated to describe the significance of the man whose legacy will probably be his phrase 'in the future, everyone will be famous for fifteen minutes.'

Maybe Andy's immortality will be nothing more than the irony that much of the world has already forgotten his fifteen minutes. Andy was unique. He began his professional career as a commercial artist and became one of the pioneers in pop art along with Roy Liechtenstein. I'm sure people still remember Andy's famous paintings of the Campbell's soup can or his various images of Marilyn Monroe. He had a particular reason for this art style. Maybe in the final analysis, some people will never concede that it really was art. But it was original, and so was he.

Like the two Italians I so much admired, Alberto Moravia and Pasolini, Andy was multitalented. He created a weird studio called the Factory where he would produce the oddest films. They would be made for very little. He used nonprofessional actors. He would experiment with filming people sleeping, or masturbating, and very often just making love.

The actors volunteered their time, and the Factory was sort of a cult hangout with Andy as its strange, effeminate guru. He went on to make some real films such as *Andy Warhol's Dracula*, with very strong sexual content.

I met him in Italy while he was on a European tour setting up film deals with European producers. You might recall that I gave him a ride on my midnight speedboat excursion of the Venetian canals, and he repaid me with a photo of me that he signed. I must admit that I found him interesting and was glad to see him again virtually every time I went to Studio 54. Often he was in the company of some pretty diverse individuals. I spotted him once in a deep conversation with Liz Taylor, and shortly afterward, he was seen escorting Jimmy Carter's mother. Her Georgia upbringing had not really prepared her for the Studio, and the sweet old lady, looking rather baffled, shook her head and drawled, 'I don't know if this is Heaven or Hell.' We must be grateful that Mrs. Carter chose not to bring her son for he might have been torn with more self-admonishment for again lusting after a woman.

Andy was actively marketing his portrait business at the Studio. He would carry his Polaroid camera and snap people whom he found interesting or whom he felt were wealthy enough to want a portrait. The photos were blown up by his assistants and projected onto a large canvas. He would then highlight in paint the features that were most pronounced and create a form of portrait that was almost a caricature — or a synthesis of the most pronounced features of the subject. I believe he was paid about $50,000 for a portrait at the time.

He certainly invited me often enough, and I visited his Factory a couple of times. We had lunch, and I must have appealed to Andy too much because his boyfriend became hostile, and I never really felt comfortable visiting him again.

Another regular was the fashion star Halston. Indeed, it was at the Studio that I really got to know him. Prior to the opening of this strange meeting place, Halston did not go out at night. In his way, the Iowa-born designer was even more reclusive than Versace. But once he went to Studio 54, he returned almost every night thereafter. He particularly seemed to enjoy the mezzanine.

Other fashion stars also frequented the club. I became quite friendly with Calvin Klein and even brought Patrizia Gucci there in the days before she involved herself with witch doctors and hit men. The newest phenomenon, namely supermodels, also began to mix with the formerly diverse elements that now were happily groping each night in the dark. Movie stars were in abundance, and it was at the Studio that I forged my friendship with Brooke Shields.

Socialites were also there in large numbers. Debutante Cornelia Guest could be seen chatting with actor Sylvester Stallone. Younger-generation socialites would appear in their white evening dresses immediately after their debutante balls, often still accompanied by their West

Point cadet escorts decked out in full-dress gray. A regular among the society crowd was the untiring Diana Vreeland. As the editor-in-chief of America's *Vogue*, she actually was Francine's friend and was quite impressed with the way Francine was running Paris *Vogue*. But our real social relationship was a result of Studio 54 where the barriers were all so thoroughly removed.

Diana was a wild woman even though she was quite old and almost blind at this time. She, too, was an old friend of the Duke of Windsor, and we would often exchange stories about him. Diana had known him longer than I had. She met him at a polo match in the 1920s and ironically, while running a small lingerie boutique in Paris, had supplied Wallis Simpson with the batch of sexy lingerie she would wear on her first romantic weekend with the prince at Fort Belvedere. In fact, it was during one evening of sharing stories about the charming duke that I got the idea that some sort of event should be thrown in his memory. I organized such a gathering in Biarritz with the help of Ira von Furstenberg. I did not want him or the elegance that he represented to be forgotten.

Diana was no stranger to elegance, and her apartment in Manhattan had become a café society of its own. She was one of the last great hostesses who could entertain her guests with a broad range of fantastic stories. Her life was one long adventure. As a young girl, she learned to ride horses from Buffalo Bill. Moving to Paris as a young woman, she became close friends with the legendary Coco Chanel.

I had the good fortune to meet Coco once, but she was already very old, so I enjoyed listening to Diana's descriptions about how stunning Coco had been as a young woman. It seems that Coco had more suitors than even ex-Empress Soraya. Among them was the Duke of Westminster, who repeatedly asked for her hand in marriage. Coco's response was 'there have already been three Duchesses of Westminster, but there will always be just one Coco Chanel.'

Diana did have one extraordinary story about Coco and even had a souvenir to prove it. After the Russian Revolution of 1917, a number of high-ranking Russian aristocrats fled to France. Among them was Grand Duke Dimitri, the man reputed to have killed Rasputin. You know the story. Dimitri and Prince Felix Youssopov invited Rasputin to dinner and fed him enough poison to kill a horse. This didn't even upset the stomach of the bearded self-proclaimed monk. Several gunshots later, Rasputin began to feel ill, but still managed to take his leave. It took a midnight dunking in the icy Neva River to finally finish him off.

Dimitri had somehow escaped punishment for this assassination and with the Romanoff jewels in hand, made it safely to Paris and ultimately to the bed of Coco Chanel. He gave her the jewels, and it is, indeed, her copy of the Romanoff pearls that she had mass-produced and now can be found in various forms in most jewelry shops.

When Coco died she left Diana a set of these earrings, and it certainly gave Diana's story credibility when she would shake her head, causing them to twirl around for the final punctuation at the end of her tale.

Great artists would also come nightly to the studio. Among them was Salvador Dali. Having had a very long romance with the charming Amanda Lear, the first transsexual member of the Jet Set, Dali would often arrive with his retinue of attractive transvestites in various colors and shapes. With his bulging eyes peering eagerly, Dali would command them to dance with one another like performing seals.

Studio 54 was like going to the circus. Sometimes there were even animals. In the early days, Rubell's P.R. chief Carmen D'Alessio sent an assistant to the Claremont stables to rent a large white horse. He then body-painted a well-built black couple in gold paint — almost like the woman in the James Bond film, *Goldfinger*. They led the horse in as a surprise for Bianca Jagger's birthday party. Bianca was delighted and jumped on the horse for a photo opportunity that would delight the world press. See what I mean? In Annabel's, you are not even permitted to bring a camera. Studio 54 was designed to generate publicity for the guests, and that was an incredible attraction.

In this unprecedented melting pot, even royalty could be seen. The brother of an Arabian king came with his retinue of gofers. Steve Rubell hurried over to him and said he was welcome, but could he bring his brother the king next time so they could work out a solution to the Middle East crisis?

To sum it all up, it has been said about Studio 54 that 'it was where Sodom and Gomorrah met the High Street.'

Need I say that I found this to be an amusing place to wile away the evening after a society ball at the Waldorf? The VIP area became a meeting place where our social circle could assemble after attending various parties earlier in the evening.

Studio 54 succeeded in doing what I had set out to achieve in my early days with Donina in creating an integrated group of interesting people who were successful in their fields. In acknowledgment of this, I chose Studio 54 as the venue for my *Best* Awards for 1982 and 1983. I rented out the entire place, and it was closed to the public.

I remember those ceremonies well. Naturally I felt obliged to honor the man who exemplified the Studio, and so Andy Warhol was one of the award recipients. He seemed more impressed by the floral arrangements on the table than by the award and, at the conclusion of the party, gathered the flowering plants and took them back to the Factory with him.

Calvin Klein was another recipient. I got so choked up when it came to reading off his name that I pronounced it 'Calvin Clean.' As he made his acceptance speech, he thanked me for the extra honor of pointing out his fine personal hygiene and made a pleasant joke out of what otherwise would have been an embarrassment.

I was quite fond of the way the Reagans had added some elegance to the White House, and I awarded the prize to Ronald Reagan as well. He sent the governor of New York, Hugh Carey, to receive it for him. But the strangest event that occurred came about entirely by accident.

One of the more notorious Jet Setters of the eighties was Klaus von Bulow. As you might recall, Klaus was initially found guilty of injecting his diabetic wife, Sunny, with what was intended to be a lethal injection of insulin. She went into a coma from which she has never recovered. Klaus was sentenced to thirty years for this crime, but later the decision was overturned on appeal. A second trial resulted in a not-guilty verdict.

I knew Sunny when she was the happy-go-lucky Sunny Crawford. Unfortunately, I knew both Klaus and his mistress, too. A film, *Reversal of Fortune*, was made about this sad story in which Jeremy Irons portrayed Klaus and Glenn Close resembled Sunny in her happier days.

At the time of the party, thinking Klaus was in prison, I sent him an invitation as a kind gesture. I did not intend on giving him an award for trying to murder his wife, I was only trying to be polite. It turned out that Klaus had filed his appeal and was released pending a new trial roughly two hours before my party was to begin. Armed with my invitation, he had his chauffeur pick him up at the prison. He changed quickly from stripes to black tie and appeared promptly at the door. The newspapers had a frenzy, and the *New York Post* dedicated its front page to von Bulow's coming straight from prison to the *Best* Awards.

The story did not even end there. You see, this

odd situation appealed to the bizarre humor of the ever-insulting Prince Johannes von Thurn und Taxis. Traditionally, after my Best Awards evening, the recipients and friends threw a series of parties for the next several days.

Following the award ceremony, Klaus, reveling in his freedom, attended a number of these events. Johannes made sure to be present at one of these parties. Toward the end of a long evening, a lady approached the grand piano in the sitting room and began to play. Her playing was fair, but, alas, she decided to accompany herself by singing. It was gruesome. The other guests were embarrassed and tired, yet she continued.

Johannes had his opening. A man capable of alienating the Peruvian Tin King, insulting the ancient Orsini family, and annihilating a tank full of tropical fish with his deadly piranha couldn't miss the opportunity of baiting a man who had been convicted of trying to murder his wife.

'Herr von Bulow,' he said respectfully, 'may I ask you a personal favor?'

'Why of course,' replied von Bulow, obviously pleased to be of assistance to the greatly feared prince.

'Why don't you shoot that woman? You already have been given thirty years.' And for once, a Johannes joke met with the approval of the other guests.

Steve Rubell must have fallen under the same spell that seemed to entrance us all when we passed through the velvet ropes into the twilight of the Studio. Although he thought himself exempt from the mundane tax laws, the IRS did not agree. He was tried and convicted of tax evasion and went to prison.

For a while Studio 54 carried on, but the atmosphere that Steve had created was lost, and its era passed.

But Studio 54 served its purpose, and that strangely rarified social world I had entered in 1963 simply did not exist anymore.

The question was, what had replaced it?

15

LAUNCHES AND
LOVE STORIES

The world of the Jet Set was now considerably more accessible than it had ever been in the past. It is perhaps for that very reason that the label took on an ambiguous meaning. If anything, the easing of the social barriers encouraged more people to try to enter society. People actively sought my help as a patron.

There were certain developments in my personal life that made it easy for me to step into that role. After more than ten years of living and working together, Francine and I decided to wed, Princess Ruspoli, still grateful for my role in her happy life, hosted the ceremony in Palazzo Ruspoli. My best man was the Duke D'Orleans, pretender to the throne of France. The matron of honor was Gina Lollobrigida. The service was conducted by a bishop, who achieved fame as Grace Kelly's priest. Even as a bishop, he still was simply referred to as 'Princess Grace's priest.' He was liberal, and the speech he made at the wedding was considered shocking. He advised us to continue with whatever habits we had prior to uniting our lives and simply to be happy. He even allowed the in-vogue Jet Set band, the Paraguays, to perform inside the church. Later, the pope decided that this type of advice was not exactly what the Church had in mind, and the liberal bishop lost his assignment and was sent to an obscure monastery.

The wedding party was somewhat spoiled when servants of the host discovered that two of the guests had sneaked into the master bedroom and were happily fornicating on the princely bed. Somehow there was a strange ironic humor in the incident that I found amusing. At any rate, Massimo the playboy had retired and stepped into the role of helping younger people with their social careers.

My magazine, the annual awards, and my social network gave me the opportunity to introduce new faces, without old names, into the increasingly nebulous but still desirable world of the Jet Set. I noticed, too, that people regarded me as the society matchmaker. During my annual awards and the hundreds of parties that took place each year, I found that I was receiving lots of requests to make suitable matches between attractive people.

Various love stories resulted from my award ceremony being a magical event in which many Cinderellas were to find their Prince Charmings. And through it all, one particular point amazed me. Regardless of the perceived beauty and success of these people, they uniformly felt that they needed help with their love lives. The beautiful model Tiziana, for example, had fallen in love with Christopher Reeve. She begged me for the privilege of being the person to present him with his award. There on my stage, I watched the electricity between them, and it came as no surprise when they left together that night.

At least they had the good manners to wait until the end of the evening to leave.

In the case of Naomi Campbell, desire won over politeness. On stage, she presented the award in 1996 to Joachim Cortez, the famous dancer. When their hands touched, I think the audience could feel a jolt of electricity. Without another word, they left the stage and continued walking straight to the exit. Cortez was my guest at the Hotel Crillon. It would not take the skills of a Sherlock Holmes to re-create the course of their evening after their startling departure. The room-service bill from the Crillon vividly captured their agenda, which consisted of proceeding immediately to Joachim's suite where the evening activities included the consumption of three bottles of vintage Dom Perignon champagne. The relationship that began so dramatically was to continue with great intensity for a year.

Some of my introductions did not work out as well. Joan Collins has been a good friend since the early seventies. In the summer of 1989, I met a very handsome young Italian actor named Antonio Zequila. I felt sure he was Joan's type. I introduced the two at a party, and the chemistry seemed strong. They danced sensuously together and decided to stroll in the garden. It was an innocent moment, but as they walked side by side, a photographer jumped out from behind a tree and photographed them together. The story the next day was that Joan had a new lover. Antonio seemed distraught at the misunderstanding, and Joan soon recovered from her anger.

About a week later, I was invited to a party in Cannes on the theme of the Great Gatsby. We all found costumes from the Roaring Twenties and prepared for the evening with the extra enthusiasm that costume parties generally generate. Joan was to be a guest, so I invited Antonio again, hoping that they could resume their acquaintance.

The party was great fun, and we danced and got into the mood that the costumes and scenery were meant to induce. Once again, the suave Antonio escorted the gorgeous actress for a stroll in the night air. This time he leaned forward and kissed her. As their lips met, there was another explosion of light, this time induced by the flashbulb of a paparazzo who jumped up from behind a bush. This time Antonio's orchestration was a little too perfect to dismiss as coincidence. His plan for quick fame became even more obvious to Joan when the next morning he held a press conference at which he announced that they were lovers.

Joan has a great sense of humor and, although she was clearly very upset, said, 'Massimo, he really was quite good looking. If I had known he was going to take credit for it anyway, I might as well have gone with him.'

Yet even the great preparation that Antonio expended in trying to win his prize fades in comparison to the strange case of Brigitte

Nielsen. I had met the stunning ex-wife of Sylvester Stallone at a party in Rome. A short time later Brigitte came to Paris, and I took her to a small dinner party. I sat her next to a handsome playboy, Philippe Richard. Although not rich, Philippe was one of those people one often encounters on the fringes of the Jet Set. He owned a Ferrari (or at least he could be seen driving one) and went to ridiculous lengths to give the impression of being extremely wealthy.

During dinner he did his best to impress Brigitte, but was having absolutely no luck until he accidentally mentioned horses. Brigitte really loves horses, and not missing a beat, Philippe described his horse farm, polo ponies, and any other interesting quadrupeds he could invent.

'You must come to my stables to see my new string of polo ponies,' he said enthusiastically. Her attention finally seemed slightly awakened, and he entered into a tirade about the various breeding and training methods. It sounded pretty impressive. Despite this, Philippe was unable to talk Brigitte into going home with him that night. Or even to make a firm commitment to look at his ponies.

She was staying at the elegant George V Hotel and the next morning was awakened by a confused concierge.

'Madame,' ventured the timid fellow, 'there is a large white stallion here in reception with a ribbon around it and a note saying it is a gift for you from Philippe.'

I am not completely aware of the livestock codes in the particular quarter of Paris, but I doubt that the George V was equipped for their new guest. In a sense, it probably was an idea that Philippe had stolen from Steve Rubell and that wild birthday party for Bianca Jagger.

Brigitte was startled and perhaps flattered too. She immediately telephoned Philippe to thank him for the gift. She asked if he could care for it while she was in Paris and then arrange for its shipment to the United States.

The smooth playboy was prepared for this contingency, and soon the stallion was led away to Philippe's imaginary stable. In return, Brigitte had agreed to a dinner date, which, at least in Philippe's account, resulted in a very satisfactory evening. The next day Philippe was nowhere to be seen — nor was any trace of the stallion ever found. A sad stain on the reputation of French playboys had been perpetrated that night.

But one of the most amusing examples of the power of love and Italian-watch technology occurred at a party at which I was honoring ex-Empress Soraya. I held the party in the ballroom of the Hotel Royal Monceau in Paris. The Royal Monceau is elegant, spacious, and has always been accommodating in hosting large numbers of my guests for events that I hosted in Paris.

One of the responsibilities of a host is to ensure that there is an equal number of guests of both sexes present. I realized to my horror that I was one man short and also that I had not really invited anyone who might appeal to Soraya. The Royal Monceau has always been particularly attentive to me, and questioning the concierge, I learned that the American actor, Matt Dillon, was staying in the hotel. This was a stroke of good fortune.

Without even calling for an appointment, I went to his suite and knocked. Matt answered the door looking a little confused that I was not wearing a room-service uniform. 'Hello, Matt,' I said, as if we were old friends.

'I'm afraid I don't know you,' he answered, with a tone of suspicion.

'I am Massimo Gargia, and I'm throwing a party downstairs. Would you like to come as my guest?'

Now Matt really looked perplexed. 'Why would I want to do that?' he asked. Not in an unkind, but simply in a genuinely curious, way.

As he spoke, I glanced down at my watch trying to calculate how long it would take to persuade him. He noticed the glance and followed my eyes to the Bulgari watch I was wearing. Noting that he seemed impressed with the attractive gold watch, I quickly answered, 'Because if you come, I'll give you this watch.' I took it off and placed it in his hand. He looked at it with interest but continued suspicion.

'And all I have to do is to come to your party?' he asked, perhaps suspecting that I was some nutty fan with a dangerous agenda.

'I promise you, that is all,' I assured him. 'Furthermore, you will be seated next to the former Empress of Iran.'

'Give me ten minutes to get dressed,' he said quickly.

Soraya seemed very pleased with her table-mate, and not surprisingly Matt seemed totally impressed by Soraya. At the end of the evening, I was pleased to see that they left together. I never asked, but I always had the feeling that Matt ended that night with more than a Bulgari watch.

Sometimes my role was not limited to making introductions, but even including acting as marriage counselor for relationships. LaToya Jackson is a prime example of my ill-fated attempts at such counseling. She came to Europe to spend some time with Francine and me and brought along her husband of the time, a man named Jack Gordon. The four of us traveled through Europe for several days, and the tension between the couple was so horrendous that we began to fear for LaToya's safety.

Francine, ever discreet, broke her normal behavior and demanded that Jack speak less abusively to his poor wife. LaToya burst into tears and told us that she was used to such abuse — that indeed her father had abused her in many horrible ways, as he had all her siblings. We felt very sorry for her and were relieved to learn that the couple divorced soon afterwards.

In addition to the various introductions and attempts at counseling that I now found myself facilitating, I was also often asked simply to launch people into society. It is funny, but even today if you are completely penniless, but possess a great family name, it isn't difficult to get on the very best guest lists. If on the other hand, you come from an unknown family, but are very rich or very famous, with a little coaxing I can guarantee at least a fair number of invitations. However, if you are neither of these things, it makes my task a true challenge.

I was confronted with such a challenge in 1993. A sweet and very beautiful woman named Marina Castelnuovo came to me. She and her husband were well off, but not fabulously wealthy. Their family was middle class and carried no social clout. But Marina wanted to live a social life and even to become famous.

I found her charming, sincere, and kind. In a way, it would be a shame to disturb her natural trust in people by introducing her to the superficial world of my circle. Nevertheless, she wanted it so badly that I decided to be creative. The one unusual thing about Marina was the way she looked. I guess that everyone has a double, and Marina happened to be the exact double of Elizabeth Taylor. Although younger, she bore such a close resemblance that it reminded me of the *Prisoner of Zenda* where a king is replaced with his double and almost nobody figures it out. With a little modification, I felt sure that Marina could almost pull off such a switch.

We coifed her hair and made her over to accentuate the resemblance, coached her on her carriage and speech, and even had the famous garments of Taylor's wardrobe copied. When we finished, I wonder if their best friends could have told them apart.

And so we began to escort her to parties, and people uniformly assumed it was Elizabeth. The press naturally got wind of this and began to really follow Marina as she traveled throughout the world in her new persona. In a way, she did become something of a celebrity. At first, Elizabeth was amused. They even met and had a laugh about the situation.

Although I can't count Elizabeth Taylor as one of my close friends, we've known each other for a long time, and she was tolerant of me. We both remembered the time when she, Richard Burton, and I drank together late into the night. I think Liz would have put up with the double if an unfortunate incident hadn't occurred during the Cannes Film Festival. There was the premiere of a new film and naturally a reception afterward. Liz was not feeling well and decided not to attend. Marina, dressed to the nines, went in her place. The press assumed she was the real thing and happily snapped away.

Liz was furious. It is one thing to have a double and quite another to have a real-life replacement. She came to the reception and told off Marina in harsh language and later complained to me. My friendship with Liz never really recovered from this episode, but the story of Marina goes on.

In 1996, I decided to make a political statement with the annual awards. The Cold War was over, and it seemed pointless that Cuba and the U.S. still were on such terrible terms. I decided that I would select both Clinton and Castro for the award. I hope this settles the confusion that may have existed that mine is a 'best-dressed award.'

Both leaders were perplexed about how to handle this invitation. Neither wished to offend, and, of course, both probably concluded that the formal end to Cuban-American hostility was not to be consummated on my stage. So Castro sent his ambassador, and President Clinton sent his brother, Roger.

Roger Clinton is a down-to-earth, good-old boy from Arkansas. He lacks the sophistication of his brother, but has a natural charm and is unpretentious. He brought his banjo along and when presented with the award, insisted on playing 'La Marseillaise,' singing enthusiastically in his Arkansas-style French. The French, who as we all know are rather fond of being French, were honored and touched.

Roger had a great time and decided to visit some of his new friends in Europe. Traveling to Rome, Marina offered to be his hostess and guide. This innocent event was to play an unexpected role in the Monica Lewinsky case. As it turns out, Marina insisted on buying a silk necktie for Roger's august brother, the president. They selected an attractive blue-and-gold tie, and Roger later presented it to his brother. The president was grateful for the gift and for the hospitality that Marina had shown Roger and invited Marina and her husband to Washington to a number of parties honoring his reelection. The president charmed them both, and they left Washington feeling quite bonded with the Clinton brothers.

Later Monica Lewinsky took credit for the purchase of this particular tie, and it found its way into the depositions. The press even regarded this as significant, and it was reported that 'the former White House intern later told prosecutors she gave Clinton the necktie on his 50th birthday in August 1996. She said she did it because it would act as a symbol of their relationship when they were apart.' Monica claimed to have told Clinton, 'When I see you wearing this tie, I'll know that I'm close to your heart.'

Marina was insulted and wrote to Washington sending a copy of the receipt and various other material to Clinton's lawyers. To show you just how ridiculous (and expensive) the investigation had become, the prosecution and defense both found this a significant point. Letters of clarification were exchanged, and Marina was told she should be prepared to testify under oath that the necktie was indeed purchased by her. A crucial legal point would you not agree?

Marina's career as the Liz double peppered now with international neckwear intrigue became so interesting in Europe that a book was published about her. I was quite proud of the success I had with Marina's launch into the somewhat more accessible world of the Jet Set. But a much more interesting case was to follow. In fact, I was to lose control of the next launch, and it would pull me into the weird world of the British royal family.

16

THE PLAYBOY AND
THE PRINCESSES

The Jet Set has always been intrigued and plagued by playboys. These men are a different breed than the garden variety that one might find at any nightclub. For the most part, Jet Set playboys are members of the Jet Set who happen to be playboys. They are typically from very wealthy families and have managed to distance themselves far enough from the source of wealth not to be tainted by either its roots or the need to participate in its future availability.

Generally, playboys have been trained from an early age to master all the activities and sports that are necessary to allow them to participate with seeming effortlessness in such diverse activities as dancing, hunting, skiing, and making pointless small talk sound important.

Mostly, though, playboys must be masters in the art of flirting. In my time, the press has kindly attributed the rank of playboy to such people as Ali Khan, Gunter Sachs, and even me. Yet few people have ever embodied the characteristics of this rare breed as has John Bryan, the man forever linked to the toe of the Duchess of York.

Our paths crossed over the years, particularly

in the dark corridors of Studio 54, but I only began to pay attention to him after he made his fabulous splash with the St. Tropez pictures. Not only did it dwarf my small splash with the Garbo photos, but John managed to persuade the gullible Fergie that he not only was blameless in the scandal, but that he had done his manly best to prevent publication of the sensational photos. And so the couple continued their relationship for four more years of free press coverage. By the end of that period, John was regarded as a de-facto member of the British royal family. I was intrigued by his success and decided to research his background and perhaps even aid him with his career.

John was fortunate enough to receive the finest education in preparation for becoming a playboy. He was thrown out of the most exclusive private schools in America. This gave him a reputation for wild unconcern. The Jet Set, obsessed with Garbo-esque minimalism, is quite intrigued by wild unconcern. His father married Josephine Abercrombie, who in the 1950s was one of the richest women in America. During most of John's youth, the Abercrombie name and wealth gave him access to the best families. He was deliberately tutored in how to master all things that were considered important to such people.

By his late teens, John was adopted socially by Whitney Tower of the New York Whitneys. Now he had a second sponsor, a younger yet socially even-more elite guru. Through Whitney, John met everyone from princesses to rock stars and charmed them all. He boasted that Mick Jagger was his best friend, and indeed, could be found dining alone with Mick at New York's elegant restaurants. In fact, in anticipation, the restaurant owners would cordon off a table so the pressing fans would not disturb the two friends.

It was in this venue that John learned some of the secrets that later became the hallmark of his adult philosophy. It appears that despite the wild enthusiasm with which girls greeted an invitation to join the Jagger-Bryan table, these young ladies sometimes refused to have sex with John at the end of the evening. Mick explained that it was imperative 'to make the deal before leaving the table.' It turned out that most girls would keep their word if they had given it in front of Mick. The second lesson John learned was to go through the seduction process as quickly as possible. He coined this 'going for the 'no' early,' concluding that if a girl is not willing to sleep with you, it is better to learn this sooner than later so you can move on to the next candidate.

The neophyte playboy was learning the ropes with the best possible instructors when disaster hit. Tony Bryan was unable to stay faithful to his jealous Josephine. The resulting divorce deprived John of the fortune and life style to which he'd become accustomed. No more private jets to fly back to school. No more automatic invitations to the best parties at the best places. John had to fend for himself.

His contrite father tried to appease his disappointed son by providing him with jobs he could not handle and by buying him companies he was somehow unable to manage successfully.

In the early nineties, John was to come into his own. Tony and John bought a publicly traded English oil-support company called Oceonics and moved together to London. Within a matter of months, John was the boyfriend of Lady Ogilvy, the daughter of the powerful press baron, Lord Rothermere, the husband of Bubbles Rothermere. John became of interest to the British public and received privilege and protection from the British press. But John had his sights on bigger fish. Through his distant cousin, Steve Wyatt (son of my old socialite friend, Lynn Wyatt), John met the Duchess of York.

She was then not-so-happily married to His Royal Highness Prince Andrew. Acting as self-appointed relationship and financial consultant, John managed to replace Wyatt in the Duchess's heart and bed. At the same time, he successfully ingratiated himself with virtually every member of the royal family.

Prince Charles showed John his book of watercolors, hoping for an approving nod. Prince Andrew allowed John to virtually live at Sunninghill Park. There, John satisfied the erotic needs of the Duchess while Andrew retired to watch videotapes. Even Prince Edward bounced a couple of business ideas off the self-appointed expert. It was in John's presence that the Queen Mother was to try her first spoonful of canned tuna, and it was with John that the Queen was to discuss her impending journey to Russia.

These quaint family scenes were abruptly discontinued following the publication of the south of France photos.

It was here that I entered the picture.

After conducting my own research, I sent a representative to London to invite John to accept my *Best* Award. I received a polite answer from his office asking me to provide a list of the former recipients. This list, which included virtually every royal family member as well as a number of American presidents, seemed to satisfy John, but it was really a coincidence that prompted him to come. Since the south of France photos, John and Sarah had lived together in disgrace and virtual exile in her small rented home called Romenda Lodge. Evidently they were driving each other crazy, and the Duchess encouraged John to accept my invitation, grateful for a few days' break from him.

I worded the invitation to appeal to the ego I had heard so much about. And so John came to Paris with his business partner, Allan Starkie, fully convinced that he was about to be hailed as a great international businessman and overall elegant fellow. He even prepared an odd acceptance speech, which would have amused the other guests had they been able to understand it.

A number of other people were being honored that night including Roman Polanski, Vanessa Redgrave, and Naomi Campbell. The latter two were staying in the Plaza Athénée, and John lost no time in introducing himself and exerting his charm on both Naomi and her gorgeous mother, Valerie. I sent cars to pick them up, and they were deposited at the entrance to the Carousel of the Louvre.

I must admit that I had underestimated how famous John was at that time. The combination of Naomi Campbell and John Bryan had obviously resulted in the recruitment of every able hand in Paris that could wield a camera. The entrance and the long corridor to the Carousel were mobbed with hundreds of photographers. *Paris Match* and *Hello* planned to devote several pages each to photos of Bryan as he made his triumphal entry into the playboy pantheon. Naomi took a more flirtatious approach with the press and, whipping out a small instamatic, began photographing the photographers.

The evening went well. John was a hit among even my most snobby guests. It might be hard to explain why he was such a hit after so much negative press appeared about him. Let me simply say that he exuded a childlike spontaneity and charm that seemed to mesmerize people. Almost completely bald and developing a midriff bulge, he still carried himself with such sexual confidence and awareness that people invariably found him to be as attractive as he was charming. Additionally, he exuded that 'All-American' quality that one sees in an old Frank Capra film. He was a mixture of Jimmy Stewart's credible good sense, Kevin Costner's smile, and Bruce Willis's wild abandon. When one sums this up, the bottom line is that he was dangerously devastating to women and yet somehow nonthreatening to men.

Roman Polanski was so impressed that he

invited John to join him at the popular nightspot, Les Bains, after the awards. (This was the premier after-hours club where Dodi Fayed spent many fun evenings.) John demonstrated that childlike spontaneity when in his joy at receiving such an invitation from the genius film director, he shouted the invitation in overly superlative terms to Allan seated at a distant table. There was little doubt that John meant his praise as a great compliment, but he offended Roman enough that the director withdrew his invitation.

The unperturbed Bryan grabbed Naomi, her mother, and an assortment of other beautiful ladies, and we went as a group to Les Bains. John danced in a frenzy of sexual energy with the two Campbells, screaming in a stage whisper that none could miss hearing that he was sure he would get a threesome out of them. Here, let me say that not unlike Gunter Sachs, John Bryan prided himself on threesomes with two women. He would often philosophize on the rules that govern this type of interaction and the various forms of preparation required for its success.

As the night wore on and even the robust Campbells wore themselves out, John frantically sought another available partner with whom to vent his sexual tension. I have always sprinkled a number of available ladies at my social events for just such contingencies. I encouraged my friend Jessica to dance with the frustrated Bryan, and in no more than ten minutes, they were headed back to the hotel.

Bryan was sharing the room with his niece

who aspired to become a famous model. The sleepy young lady was unceremoniously evicted and told to wait in the hall while John expended the lust he had accumulated and reserved for the Campbells. Finally satisfied, he sent Jessica on her way and allowed his niece to return.

Pleased with the evening, John decided to fly back to London on the earliest available plane to relate his social triumph and overall popularity to his royal concubine.

The following morning, I hosted a brunch for the award recipients. John was conspicuously absent. I seated his partner next to a group of television journalists who had asked me to arrange for John to appear on their talk shows. In his absence, they spoke to his partner. It was then that Jessica sat down in the midst of this group.

I was not quite sure where she spent the night, and she wasn't either. She had apparently not understood with whom I'd sent her the night before because she began to enthusiastically relate what a wonderful lover John Malkovich turned out to be. I tried to catch her attention when it dawned on a number of the other people that she was describing her night with John Bryan. We spirited her away from the table before the journalists could realize the scoop they had almost gotten.

Allan Starkie made a series of frantic calls that resulted in a deal being made. Jessica would spend that night in the intimate company of Allan and his girlfriend, Edda. It would be made obvious that Jessica was involved in a threesome that had begun the night of my award dinner. John would pretend to be impressed with such an exploit and tell Sarah about it, even inviting her to meet Allan and Edda's new girlfriend. Jessica would seal her lips in return for an invitation to the Christmas party thrown the next day jointly by the Duke and Duchess of York.

Jessica could not believe her good fortune. Calling me in amazement, she related the situation in which she found herself.

'Go to London, Jessica,' I suggested. 'Maybe you will be able to attract Prince Andrew. He's available right now.'

With happy expectations, Jessica went to England.

Although unaware of the romantic link between Jessica and John, the Duchess took an instant dislike to Jessica and pulled Allan aside to suggest that Jessica be escorted to the airport as soon as possible. But in the intervening moments remaining to poor Jessica, she managed to edge up to the Duke of York and began flirting frantically.

Dropping all protocol, she addressed the astonished prince as Andrew while rubbing herself against him and smiling seductively. The unfortunate Jessica (who boasted a sexual collection of twelve princes) was to leave England without attaining her goal. But for John, at least, the evening was a success. Jessica kept her promise and remained quiet, for the rest of her life.

I remained good friends with Jessica and enjoyed hearing her speak of these strange adventures with John and Allan. Regretfully, she would develop a serious illness, and I was shocked to see how most of my Jet Set friends who had enjoyed Jessica's witty, fun-loving personality ignored her in her time of need.

There was one notable exception. Prince Egon von Furstenberg (Ira's brother) insisted on paying all her medical bills until her death. I look upon his gesture with a great deal of admiration.

I was so amused by the Jessica-John episode and by John in general that I decided to let him participate in the full circuit if he wished. And indeed he wished. The following weekend, I invited him to Paris to a dinner party I was throwing for a few people who had voiced a particular interest in seeing more of the dangerous American.

Now, as I pointed out earlier, Dewi Sukarno is a woman of considerable passion. She had been at the party at the Louvre and found John devastating. In addition to Dewi, I invited HRH Princess Esmeralda of Belgium and her scruffy, bearded Tunisian boyfriend, Albert. John was accompanied, as always, by Allan Starkie.

Dinner was an interesting spectacle insofar as everyone had a different agenda. Dewi's was the clearest. John wanted to be accepted by this group and was ostensibly seeking business opportunities for his never clearly defined business. Esmeralda, in an odd choice of careers for the daughter of the king, was the journalistic partner of the considerably older Albert. The two were hoping for a society interview first with John and then with Fergie. They were to achieve all this and more. In fact, everyone was to accomplish his agenda with the exception of Allan, who was there to keep John out of trouble.

After dinner, we went to a number of nightspots and ended up in the old favorite Calvados. Here in the wee hours of the early morning, the tradition is to drink Bloody Marys and eat spaghetti Bolognese. It is sort of a ritual of renewal. When we entered, the owner and the ever-present mariachi band immediately recognized Dewi and started playing 'Don't Cry for Me Argentina,' to which she would sing 'don't cry for me Indonesia.'

Upon spotting John, they launched into composing a ballad to immortalize his sexual and romantic exploits. Comically, they had thought him to be Princess Diana's and not Fergie's boyfriend, so the words they improvised did not quite fit. Dewi then ended the evening by inviting John and Allan back to her magnificent apartment on Avenue Montaigne. It is, in fact, Marlene Dietrich's old building, and one could often catch a glimpse of that grand lady in Garbo-esque exile.

The second success from my small dinner party was the odd relationship that developed with Princess Esmeralda. She followed up on my introduction to John and persuaded him to give her an exclusive interview to talk about his life and about the Duchess of York.

John had made a number of glaring blunders with the press such as his famous line to the tabloids that 'I have the palace by the balls.' But these remarks did not constitute an exclusive interview. Esmeralda truly pulled off a coup and sold the story to a number of magazines.

Eager to pursue the match I had made, Esmeralda talked Allan into introducing her to the Duchess of York. He set up a meeting at his apartment in Frankfurt for the two princesses, and the sexual chemistry was good. Sarah trusted Esmeralda and what was to follow was amazing. Esmeralda was to become sort of a secret press agent. She lurked near the Duchess on charity and business trips and at a predesignated time would have her cameraman snap an exclusive picture and somehow manage to print it with an appropriate quote.

Sarah and Esmeralda were partners, and both profited well from the alliance. It is funny, but when someone feels indebted to you, how fervently they try to avoid your company. I have rarely seen Esmeralda since I created this royal alliance. In fact, when the Duchess, Esmeralda, and Allan decided to establish a German charity, Esmeralda seemed to sabotage me.

Allan had convinced the Duchess that I should organize the first charity gala. They dared me to succeed in raising 250,000 pounds the first night, and I was sure I could manage it. Then Allan called to say that Esmeralda was advising against associating the charity with me. The Duchess withdrew her request, and that is how I was repaid for the introduction. It reminded me of the way that the Romanian refugee I had launched took Donina's side after our breakup and treated me not with gratitude, but with anger and contempt. Helping other people is often a risky business.

As time progressed, I became increasingly fond of John Bryan. He was loud and arrogant, but always charming. My guests enjoyed his company, and he livened up my parties. I decided to invite him to one in Rome given in my honor by the Crown Prince of Libya, Prince Idris. Idris had married a beautiful Spanish aristocrat, and the two enjoyed a relationship with King Juan Carlos of Spain. Nevertheless, Idris wished to expand his social network, and I was to be instrumental in expediting this.

John came to this elegant affair accompanied by Allan, who was there to repair any of John's transgressions. I introduced them both to Prince Idris since I thought they might be able to conduct some business together. Prince Idris had made a great amount of money with some very clever deals.

John found this interesting and hoped to form an alliance. The two hit it off and struck up a guarded friendship. Idris made the common mistake of trusting John's discretion and believing his self-proclaimed importance. Believing John to have powerful political connections, Idris, under a strict promise of secrecy, told John that Qaddafi had invited him to be prime minister. Idris felt that if John were in contact with the CIA, they could use this opportunity to overthrow the Libyan government.

John nodded solemnly, as if he assisted in such transactions on a daily basis. He assured the young prince that 'Pop and I have just the right people for you to talk with.' In actuality, the only person John did talk to was a journalist named Elizabeth Kaye, who wrote about the invitation in an article for *Esquire*.

On this particular evening, I sat John between Valerie Campbell, whom he had so eagerly tried to seduce when Naomi was last with us, and Francesca Dellera. Francesca is the gorgeous movie star who had the unusual experience of being the girlfriend of the rock star Prince as well as of the muscular *Highlander* star, Christopher Lambert. It is hard to imagine the contrasts she must have experienced.

I figured that John (at least his body type) might constitute a reconciliation between such extremes. John was polite and charming, and in a very short time, it was clear that Francesca was about to be seduced. She was wearing a low-cut dress and would often lean over to allow John a more complete look at what might lie ahead. She has strikingly beautiful eyes, and that night she wore dark-rimmed glasses deliberately to create the look of an average office secretary. John has always been partial to secretaries.

Just as the dancing was to begin, John and Francesca disappeared. Reemerging before the festivities ended came a very self-satisfied John to tell us all about it.

'Massimo, she was great, just terrific!' he began.

I am not crazy about discussing these things in too much detail, but John provided a rather graphic account of his exploits. Francesca must not have minded John's enthusiasm too much as she said to the press the following week,

'Johnny's a lovely person. I like men who are young, good looking, and dangerous.'

To compensate Francesca for any inconvenience that my introduction to John might have caused her (despite her brave words to the press), I introduced her to Victor Emmanuel's son, the Prince of Venice. He is considered to be one of the most handsome young men in the Jet Set. They became extremely close friends.

I decided to test my new sensation on the more staid Monte Carlo crowd and brought John with me to the Grand Prix weekend that May. The Grand Prix weekend is one of the staples of the Jet Set's social world. The event actually predates the Jet Set and is conducted not on a racetrack, but through the streets of Monte Carlo. As always that meant a suite in the Hotel de Paris so we could watch the races from our terrace and then partake in the celebrations that usually began in the hotel.

By now, John was feeling like a regular and was being greeted with acceptance by my friends. That night I was amazed at what followed. We ended up in a party where Prince Albert was present. I had been very careful around the Grimaldis since my breakup with Donina, but John grabbed Prince Albert, who recognized him immediately, and the two were inseparable for the next several hours.

It seems John already had some experience with this amazing family. He had been friends with the actor Rob Lowe during the time Lowe dated Princess Stephanie. At some point, Rob had made the mistake of leaving John alone with the beautiful princess, and John naturally tried to do his usual thing when left alone for more than five minutes with a woman.

Stephanie was reticent, so John withdrew. He later explained that he could never seduce the girlfriend of a friend. At any rate, he was not shy around her brother, and the two hit it off. At that time, John's association with the British royals was so widely known that he truly was regarded as something very special, almost as if he were part of that crowd. It seemed to even impress Prince Albert.

With John's growing social success and notoriety, I decided he was ready to participate in one of the Jet Set rituals, the Costa Smeralda of Sardinia. It was where we would spend the last two weeks of August. This suited me perfectly as my birthday falls in this period. As a result, I have the good fortune to celebrate my birthday at a location in which all my friends are always available.

This has turned into such a ritual that many television stations have televised portions of my parties because of the guest list. On this occasion, I had a great one planned. A new hotel had opened and felt that hosting my guests and my party would give them free publicity. Most of my guests were staying on their own yachts or in their villas, thus making it a not-too-expensive gesture for the hotel.

The hotel staff was in a frenzy to prepare for the festivities. As a diversion for the other guests, I invited the astronaut Buzz Aldrin. Although his feet actually followed Armstrong's, we politely referred to him as the first man on the moon. Before either John or Buzz arrived, I overheard a conversation that I have often thought of as the perfect example of mindless star admiration. Two maids were in the hallway outside my room and one said to the other, almost apologetically, 'Who is this man John Bryan?' The other, laughing and in a superior tone said, 'Don't you know anything? He was the first man to walk on the moon!'

The hotel was perched on top of one of Sardinia's typically barren, rocky hills. From our vantage point, we could look down at the coast and at the port as it began to fill with the yachts of my friends. Naturally there is an unspoken contest regarding the size and splendor of these craft. I imagine Freud might have had a lot to say about that.

The winner that year was Sergio Mantegazza, who for a long time has been one of the richest men in Europe. He came in the *Lady Marina*, which had a crew of twelve and had original Rembrandt etchings in the staterooms.

Sergio was a rare species of Jet Setter of the likes of Onassis. He managed an enormous financial empire that he himself had built, participated with enthusiasm in our travel and social circuit, and even sponsored us. By this I mean that he, quite like Onassis, was generous with his huge resources. He would fly us to the Feria in his Falcon jet, sail us around the Mediterranean in his yacht, and host us for lavish parties. In a way, he was sort of a replacement for the loss of Onassis. According to

Forbes magazine, Sergio's fortune of two billion dollars makes him one of the richest men in the world and in today's terms is essentially the size of what Ari's fortune was in the early seventies.

The Jet Set often reminds me of migratory birds that take off together and fly in a formation with no apparent reason for their choice of direction or the selection of where they will next land. It is impossible to really understand why we have selected the migratory habits that have become almost institutionalized or why other new locations suddenly attract the flock of birds.

One thing is certain, however, and that is that we are grateful when the large industrialists provide us with the means of traveling elegantly. I have been indebted to the Agnellis, the Rothschilds, Onassis, and Sergio for their kindness in making our strange migrations comfortable and discreet. A new addition to this group of Jet hostesses is Hussa Adham, who went as far as outfitting her private jet with three luxurious guest bedrooms.

Ivana Trump was with her fiancé, Riccardo, aboard his little boat, and we all were amazed by her decision to even sleep on the tiny boat. My friendship and respect for Ivana continued to grow, and I found myself always amazed at her loyalty to a man who offered so little, yet demanded so much from her.

A group of my other friends pulled into the harbor aboard Elizabeth Taylor's former yacht, the *Kalizma*. Although not the largest, it was the most elegant yacht by far. It had a smokestack and old brass portholes, the decks were covered by a striped awning, and the prow and stern had built-in upholstered seats. I could only imagine the parties that must have taken place when Burton and Taylor sailed the *Kalizma*.

The majority of my guests had arrived, and I eagerly awaited the arrival of my favorite playboy and his friend. John must have filled the cargo hold of the plane with enough luggage to outfit several gigolos, a camera crew, and even Jacques Cousteau. As the porters labored with cases of clothes, Aqua-lungs, and video cameras, John walked cheerfully over to me, already extending his arm in an exaggeration of a handshake while still three yards away.

'Massimo,' he purred, as if it were not a name but his favorite type of pleasure. 'I am so glad to be here.'

He was wearing a cream-colored shirt, and where initials might be, I realized he had his phone number embroidered — 071–371–3719. Noticing that I was staring, he said, 'Yea, it's a gift from Sarah. She says it will save time, ha, ha!'

'How is the Duchess?' I asked.

'Who knows? We have a moratorium on speaking for the next two weeks, beginning today, and I haven't spoken to her in over two hours!'

At that moment the phone rang, and it was, of course, Sarah. I had explained the various relationships to the concierge, and he nervously approached John. Feigning disinterest, John gave us a slow smile and, looking over at Allan, said, 'See what she wants.'

Five minutes later, Allan returned to say that she simply wished to see if we understood that the communications moratorium was in effect.

'Good,' said John. 'See Massimo, it's just like I told you. It's a test to see if she can get along without me for a while. She will see . . . '

It was getting late, and we had our first party to attend that evening. We went our various ways to get ready. In Sardinia, much like St. Tropez, men do not dress for the dinner parties, but the woman often wear elegant evening gowns. The parties are hosted at various villas on either side of the island.

On this night, we were the guest of a beautiful French countess who had married the Prince Sabet D'Acre. It was the first party of the season, and Countess Florence had gone to a lot of effort to see that it was stunning.

We met in the hotel lobby at nine and drove through the clear night to Florence's home. The house was built of local stone. It contained a huge vaulted ballroom plastered in white with double height glass arches facing the sea. From these enormous windows, one could look down to the sea where a large catamaran was moored under a full moon. Some of Florence's guests had just sailed in on it and were debarking to join us.

The party was to be held in the large garden which overlooked the sea. It was a somehow eerily ancient setting. The garden was bracketed by rows of gnarled trees that met at the top to create a long corridor of an arbor in which two long banquet tables lavishly garnished with silver and crystal awaited the guests. The remainder of the garden was furnished with massive, rough-hewn stone benches. On the rough stone lay comfortable cushions, while between each pair of benches lay a massive slab of stone like some Druid sacrificial altar. Upon these slabs were hundreds of flaming oil amphorae, casting a magic spell of ancient times on this otherwise timeless scene.

The setting was wrapped by a sky of brilliant stars, one of which sped downwards through the heavens — a sacrifice to complete the aesthetic of the night. That night and so many like it sums up why I wished to spend my life in the Jet Set. This was a world in which deliberate, almost singular attention is paid to creating a fleeting aesthetic of sublime social beauty. Watching the faces of my friends illuminated in the flickering firelight, looking at the moon rise over the dark sea, we felt that we were safe in a world inhabited by just the group of us.

Florence came to greet us, her beautiful green eyes twinkling with pride at the pleasure she knew her party was giving us. John was circulating, 'working the room with Allan,' as he later put it. He stopped suddenly when he spotted someone who caught his particular interest. The woman was the Princesse Zibeline de Montfort d'Ancy.[1] If France were not a republic, she would have been a royal princess since her family dates back to the days of the Battle of Hastings. Their title was given to them

---

[1] Not her real name

in perpetuity by the Pope himself, and as a result the papal crown remains one of the insignias of their coat of arms.

There have been few women more suited by nature to fill the role of a true socialite princess. She seemed exactly like the first wife of Maximillian de Winter in *Rebecca*, the wife who is already dead when the book begins, but whose strength haunts the household and dominates her successor.

Zibeline was of medium height with a mane of dark brown hair and large almond eyes of a hazel-green. Her skin was always darkly tanned, and her features were almost too perfect. When she smiled, her perfect white teeth contrasted with her tanned skin and would capture immediate attention.

Zibeline is a Jet Setter. She is a perennial member of our circle and participates with great enthusiasm in the circuit. She has created a strange persona for herself in our society with her extravagant behavior. She seems to require no sleep. She dances all night every night — and has the unusual habit of smoking big cigars.

It is not so much the smoking of these Churchill-size Havanas that excites such interest and curiosity as it is the ritual she has developed for igniting them. Zibeline takes the cigar and slowly slips in into her mouth in a gesture that is clear to all who watch. She then puckers her mouth and slowly rolls the cigar along her slightly extended tongue. When she is satisfied that it is moist enough, she bites off a piece of the end and spits it out loudly and contemptuously on the ground. At this point, satisfied that she has symbolically aroused then emasculated any male who is watching, she lights the end and puffs away with a self-satisfied smile. It was upon this display that John's attention was now riveted.

Zibeline was midway through the ritual castration when their eyes met. She actually stopped what she was doing, then finished the show in deliberate slow motion.

John stood smiling all the way through and when she was about to light the cigar, he grabbed the lighter out of her hand and did it for her. This show of postcastration male dominance was perhaps what she had waited for all along. She was stunned. Letting the smoke slowly escape from her lips, she eyed John warily. Then she flashed him one of her smiles.

'John Bryan,' he said, as if this were not just his name but an explanation. Taking her arm, he walked her down to the furthest stone bench dimly illuminated by the amphora light.

As the night wore on, one of my friends suggested that we take a midnight cruise on the *Kalizma*. It sounded like a fine idea, and soon the tenders were carrying us out to the harbor. Once on board, we sat together in a circle on the aft deck drinking wine. The indomitable Zibeline could not take her eyes off John. I had never seen her like this before. John seemed intent on impressing Zibeline with a dissertation on the status of the royal family.

'The Queen is taking advantage of Sarah. It's a

joke, and I won't let it happen. Sarah is getting shit out of the divorce, and there is nothing she can do about it! But Diana, well that is another story. She comes over to Romenda Lodge every Sunday, and I have got to say she is very impressive. She does everything right, and she is going to cream Charles in the divorce. She really is jealous that Sarah has someone like me to help her, and so I give her lots of advice. I take Prince Charles' part, and we go through playing devil's advocate with what he would say and do in the divorce. We have him nailed, now that he has admitted adultery.

'What a dummy! But the Queen, she has abdicated her role as head of that dysfunctional household! Either a bunch of palace assholes are running the show or Phillip is calling the shots. She is absolutely terrified of him. They all are. Boy, Diana really can handle that family, though. I wish Sarah could. Do you know what happened last Christmas? They made her stay at some fucking farmhouse outside of Sandringham, and she wasn't allowed to attend any of the family stuff.

'She had to dress up her daughters and send them off alone. Unbelievable! You bet that they wouldn't get away with that shit with Diana!'

John held us all in a state of amazement as he poured out his royal report. I must say he did capture everyone's attention. It was getting to be about four A.M., which is pretty much close of business for our trade. So we were spirited away to our various accommodations.

Although Zibeline was a guest on the *Kalizma*, I noticed that she was taking one of the tenders to shore.

The next morning, my suspicions were confirmed.

17

TECHNOLOGY MADE ME POSSIBLE

The Jet Set night life of the Costa Smeralda is concealed from the curious eye of the average tourist by the fact that it is enacted primarily on large yachts and private villas. Nevertheless, even Sardinia has its equivalent of Studio 54 in which those members of our group most impervious to fatigue are wont to spend the final hours before dawn. It is called the Country Club and, contrary to the confusing names of most discos, even looks its name.

The expansive structure is secluded within a forest featuring a large private park with an outdoor pool. The building itself is a concrete structure with huge glassless windows. This allows the subtle Sardinian breeze to cleanse the room of excessive smoke and to temper the ambiance with a feeling of cool serenity. It was here that the tireless Zibeline planned to dance away the feelings that John had apparently awakened in her. It was here that after two hours of wild dancing, the still-uneasy princess asked Prince Carlo Giovanelli (you may remember him as the prince addicted to Swiss honey) to drive her back to John's hotel. And so the unlikely situation arose in which a prince of the Holy

Roman Empire delivered a princess of France to seduce the lover of a princess of the British Empire. When I pointed out this complex constellation to John the next day, he shook his head at the thought and said with enormous pride, 'I bet that never happened before, I mean some dude sleeping with two different royal ladies within the same twenty-four hours.' In fairness, his ever-practical friend, Allan, pointed out that only air travel made such a thing possible. John thought about this for a moment then retorted with satisfaction, 'Yeah. Technology made me possible.'

I was to learn the next morning that the aroused princess was duly delivered to the spacious suite of the sleeping playboy. John, ever hopeful, had left the door to his rooms unlocked and lay naked and presumably ready for the nocturnal visit. The confident playboy was, nevertheless, astonished by the unbridled passion of our tanned princess. She entered the suite without sound or light and was equally naked by the time she reached his bed.

In the mild light of the very early dawn, all that John could see as he struggled to awake himself were four streaking white smudges in the darkness. These of course were the luminous eyes, the flashing teeth, and the two-inch square spot where Zibeline's skin was not tanned. By this time, John had discerned the identity of his visitor and with satisfaction lay prostrate and attempted to enjoy his surprise with as little thought as possible to its potential similarity to the famed cigar-lighting ceremony.

It was late the next afternoon before the tired couple emerged from John's suite. Zibeline contradicted all her habits of the past and remained at the side of her new lover. Together they joined us for a lunch at which the couple seemed unaware of the existence of any other human beings. They ordered spaghetti and teased one another, sharing each string of pasta and slowly sucking it in from both ends until their lips would meet in a saucy kiss Bolognese.

I was aghast. Although sexuality plays a dominant role in the life of the Jet Set, oddly, discretion is generally exercised and public displays strongly discouraged. No one was prepared for the spectacle that now confronted us.

Declining the dessert offered by the house, John and Zibeline hurried back to their suite while the rest of us tried to act natural. Allan Starkie looked particularly concerned and pointed out that the Duchess had spoken to him three times already that day to check on John and to confirm that the moratorium on communications was still in effect.

That evening, we were all invited to a party by the fashion star, Krizia. Her home was built in a cul-de-sac and was protected not only by a high wall, but by two policemen whose cars were indiscreetly parked in front of her gate. The gate itself was reminiscent in massiveness of a castle drawbridge.

When one was announced, the huge metal door would grudgingly slide open. Once entry was thus obtained, the sheer magnificence that confronted you was explanation enough for the severe security. Not only was Krizia's home carved out of the mountain, she had decided to carve it a little extra deeply and create her own stone valley. The sides of this valley were cut steeply into the stone creating a large crevice in which the home rested safely.

Terraces had been carved into the sides of the mountain forming a natural amphitheater. In the center she had a large, raised, wooden dance floor installed so the dancers were actually onstage in this Greco-Roman theater. The side of the house facing the valley was a series of glass doors which, when open, allowed the interior to flow into this extraordinary setting. On the other side of the house, she used the immense garden to place separate dining tables for perhaps 100 guests.

Krizia dressed in an outfit of her own creation. It resembled a suit of chain-mail armor. One would have expected Zibeline to be the best-dressed person in a party of only 100, but on this occasion she was wearing a dress clearly not made for her. As it turns out, she was so hesitant to leave the bed of our illustrious playboy for even a couple of hours that she borrowed a dress from Allan Starkie's beautiful Norwegian girlfriend. Although in possession of a wonderful body, Zibeline lacked the full range of feminine charms required to fill out this particular outfit. Unperturbed by this, she remained a few inches from John the entire evening. When the dancing began in the amphitheater, Zibeline either danced with John or sat puffing on a large cigar as she watched him spin the other female guests in his personal step that we dubbed the John Bryan Universal Step as he could do it to any form of music. After the party broke up, John accompanied Zibeline right back to his room.

By the next morning, the joke was that the Jet Set had a hostage crisis and that Zibeline was in her third day of captivity. Room service and the wardrobe of Allan's girlfriend seemed to be the only form of interruption that the couple was willing to tolerate.

That afternoon was to prove an exception. The affair, which until now had remained contained among my closest hundred friends, was about to attract global interest.

I had been invited to go on a cruise on the *Kalizma* and asked John and Allan to join me. Sardinia boasts few sandy beaches, and it was proposed that we sail to a neighboring island where we could enjoy an isolated beach. Allan convinced John that a short separation from Zibeline (particularly in public) would be advisable, and so the two friends accompanied us on our short cruise.

We sailed for four hours until we reached our destination. Just as we were about to drop anchor in what appeared to be the most isolated spot in the Mediterranean, a speck that I had seen on the horizon began to grow into the shape of a boat of astonishing speed and sleekness. It could only be the custom speed cruiser built at enormous costs by my friend Carlo Cilia (who, with the Duke D'Orleans, had

346

been best men at my wedding). It is essentially an oversized racing boat that can sleep ten people. It must have made the trip in a quarter of the time it had taken us. The speedboat dropped anchor fifty yards away from us, and there on the prow stood the topless, bronzed body of Zibeline, like a figurehead carved out of mahogany. John must have spotted her at exactly the same time for he ran straight to the prow of our own ship. Then, as if in an Esther Williams movie, the two sprang onto their respective rails and in one synchronous fluid motion each dove into the sea.

With deliberately exaggerated strokes, they swam toward each other with all the other passengers staring in disbelief from the sides of the two vessels. They met at exactly the point equidistant from both ships and embraced. This was Hollywood. What none of us realized at the time was although Zibeline had written and directed the scene, she had also brought a camera crew to capture it. It seems that Zibeline required an income to support her Jet Set life-style and was working for *Point de Vue* magazine, sort of undercover.

John had been set up, but Zibeline was not satisfied with just these aquatic snapshots — she had a more devious plan ahead. Meanwhile John, unaware that his every movement was being immortalized, got others to join him in the ocean and began to play water volleyball.

As Zibeline smashed at the ball, her five-century-old signet ring flew off her finger, and in slow motion we watched it arc into the air, then soundlessly disappear into the sea. Zibeline was distraught with what might have even been real grief. John was photogenically consoling.

After several abortive attempts to find the ring, John offered to replace it if he could get a picture of how it looked. Zibeline was ready for such a contingency. Pulling back the side of her microscopic string bikini pants, she exposed a tattoo of the lost crest on her shapely right buttock. With this to refresh his memory, John promised to have the ring replaced. As we sailed back to our next party, we passed another speedboat with a team of salvage divers in full scuba regalia whose very presence silently testified to Zibeline's confidence in John's word.

The next morning, Zibeline (still accompanied by her photographic team) told John that she was helping me to do PR work for the hotel and wanted a photo of him by the pool. John always believed that he had special protection from any new scandal not of his own creation and readily agreed. Zibeline slipped off her bikini top and raising one bronzed leg, assumed a very convincing reenactment of the Fergie south-of-France scene. It almost looked like one of those dramatizations that are made after great crimes.

The photos were taken and within hours appeared in dozens of newspapers with the caption 'His new love is a princess on both sides instead of a duchess by marriage.' Fergie was livid — not with John, but with Allan and me for not watching him.

John accused me of collaborating with

Zibeline, which I am sorry to say I did not do. With all this uproar, we politely managed to celebrate my birthday, then retired to lick our various wounds.

John avoided me for a few weeks to prove to the Duchess that he agreed I was a bad influence on his morality. But when I invited him to a party given in Paris by the Duke D'Orleans, he decided that it was time to be friends again. Naturally, Zibeline was at the party, and naturally we ended the evening at our old haunt, Calvados.

John's fame in continental Europe had only been increased by the Sardinia photos, and the mariachi band, delighted to see him again, burst out into the song they had written for him the previous year. New verses were added in honor of his current conquests. One could imagine that this is how the glories of Achilles were first passed from one generation to another until Homer set them down on paper.

John pretended to ignore Zibeline, who responded to this snub by flirting with Allan. This was, of course, too much for John to bear. He immediately began to fondle her legs under the table and reassert himself as the most worthy of possible playboys. At an alarming speed, Zibeline and John relocated themselves to the first stall of the unisex toilet. At first their absence was hardly missed. Then a strange thing happened. Sounds emanated from the toilet with increasing volume and intensity. First there was a pounding against the stall walls like the distant beating of jungle drums, then the sound of gasps and finally screams.

The mariachi band, noticing this disturbance, played louder in an effort to drown out the noise. Finally, when the din of pleasure was at its loudest, they realized the futility of their situation and putting down their instruments with manly resignation, took a coffee break until John was finished. In the meanwhile, I looked over at Allan. It was clear he was searching the room for his friend, desperately hoping that John was not the source of the phantom groans.

Finally he looked at me and asked plaintively, 'Have you seen John?'

The answer came from Michèle Mercier, the French film star, seated by my side. 'Yes, he is fucking Zibeline in the toilet.'

I suppose it would have offered Allan little solace if I had pointed out that technology made John possible.

18

PRISONER OF LOVE

I remained involved with the strange world of John and his friends. But just as I had experienced with Donina, John Bryan and his world were built out of a house of cards. It required only a small breeze to set it tumbling, and I watched with horror the carnage and destruction as it went down.

In actuality, the relationships among John, Sarah, and Allan were so complex, overlapping, and interconnected that it seemed certain to me that if one of them failed, it would bring down the entire complex. On top of this, they had combined their business interests in just as complicated a manner. And, indeed, it all fell apart one sad spring day in 1995.

The financial empire that John and Allan controlled toppled in such an abrupt way that the banks that financed them were furious. An investigation was requested. John never was noted for his courage and fled Europe leaving all his possessions for his shocked secretary to pack and ship. Without his magnetic personality and seeming control of Sarah, their romance of four troubled years soon disintegrated.

Allan Starkie, determined to hold their world together, remained in Europe. The German

351

authorities were convinced by John's hasty departure that some wrongdoing had occurred. Their reaction was to imprison Allan.

For five months, he remained in solitary confinement as the investigation dragged on. In the end, it was concluded that no offense had been committed. Nor were any charges ever filed against Allan.

German justice is peculiar. John, like many other businessmen, had taken full-page ads in my magazine, *The Best*. Days before Allan's arrest, I received a personal check from Allan to pay for all of John's outstanding bills. I found this act of personal integrity so touching that Francine and I decided that we would try to help him. Despite our best attempts and even utilizing our international network, we were unable to even send Allan a letter.

I was upset to learn that he was facing this alone. Once again I was made aware of the superficiality and lack of real commitment toward friendship that typifies the Jet Set. Within a very short period of time, this lesson was to be brought home to me in an even-more personal way.

Not a man to quietly accept martyrdom, Allan used his time in prison to write an international best-selling account of his years with Sarah and John. This so impressed me that I decided that I would solicit Allan's assistance in writing my own memoir, and, indeed, he is the co-author of this book.

We began our project in an unlikely setting and one that would result in the opportunity to share the fate that Allan had just experienced.

My life had fallen into routine. Each month, Francine and I produced our magazine. Each year, too, we coordinated the complex selection and award process of the *Best* Awards. The time in between was filled with parties and launches.

The PR business had grown to the point where I was flying my network of celebrity friends all over the globe to participate in gala openings. I accepted an offer from a gentleman named Alberto Cilona to help him launch his new casino-hotel in Marrakech, Morocco.

Marrakech is full of contradictions. It is lavish and filled with Arabian splendor, and yet large sections of the city are filthy, dangerous, and poor. The city is dominated by a twelfth-century stone tower that stands almost in the very center. It is an historic mosque, and its rough walls made of hewn stone block are illuminated at night. This monument is ringed by streets filled with luxury hotels and elegant Arabian villas built around large, tiled courtyards with magnificent fountains that create a cool and idyllic atmosphere

In the center of town is the enormous market, or souk. It is a labyrinth of stalls and small shops entirely covered either by a roof or by cloth. It gives one the sensation of walking through an endless series of dimly lit tunnels filled with exotic treasures.

Ornately worked brass oil lamps flicker, creating a shadowy landscape in which the animated faces of the bearded vendors in their traditional garb and headgear seem like the images of a silent movie. The shoppers are often pulled into the small cubbyholes where they are shown a myriad of objects, such as an arsenal of antique flintlock rifles and pistols with hand-worked silver barrels and curved stocks made of carved animal bone inlaid with silver and golden studs.

Then, of course, there are the inevitable rug merchants. With charm and painted smiles, they lure you into their domain. Once inside, you are politely held prisoner while being served gallons of sickeningly sweet green mint tea that you drink from glass bowls trapped in a silver-handled frame that scorches your hand while upsetting your stomach. To escape this torture, many tourists drop all resistance and agree to purchase a carpet.

The market goes on forever, and for those foolish enough to brave its exploration without a local guide, the exit is quite often elusive. Once outside, at the end of the day, the square is filled with magicians (Patrizia Gucci would have loved it) and snake charmers. After the excitement of a day of shopping adventures, one can hire a horse-drawn carriage or even a camel back to the hotel.

During the period when I dated ex-Empress Soraya, I had often been a guest at her neighbor's villa in Rome. Soraya lived on the eerie old road that leads out from the gates of Rome called Via Appia. It was used as the cemetery in ancient times because the Romans had a revulsion to burying their dead within the city walls. The road is scattered with ancient decaying monuments and tombs. Underneath are the famous catacombs that early Christians had used as secret meeting places.

During the sixties, the Via Appia Antica had become a favorite living spot for movie stars and Jet Setters. Gina Lollobrigida still lives in one of those enormous villas. Next to Soraya lived the sister of the King of Morocco. We would often be invited for Moroccan food and belly dancing. As a result, I felt quite familiar with the customs of the country. I also felt protected by their royal family. My old friend, Omar Sharif, had a house outside the city, and that, too, was an attraction. So I didn't hesitate to take on the assignment of launching the hotel.

All I had to do was to bring some of my celebrity friends once or twice a month and have fun with them. We were requested to spend a couple of hours in the casino, but never required to actually gamble. The idea was just to be seen.

I made a number of trips, each time bringing one or two old friends like Gina Lollobrigida, Dewi Sukarno, Ursula Andress (this time provided with no slave), actor Ben Gazzara, Amanda Lear, and a number of attractive European starlets. Allan had achieved some notoriety with his book, and the management was happy to invite him, too.

And so we began to write my memoirs in Marrakech.

At this time, my good friend, Ivana Trump, was going through some rough times with Riccardo, now her husband. I had thrown them an engagement party and was amazed at the tension between them. Unfortunately the marriage did little to change the dynamics, and in June, Ivana called to tell me it was finished.

'Is there anything I can do?' I asked.

'Start looking,' she responded with a laugh. But I decided to take this pleasantry seriously and began to search for a man worthy of this talented and beautiful woman.

A few weeks after the above conversation, I ran into a startlingly handsome Italian whom I had known since his early childhood. His name was an impressive list of titles that connoted the fact that he came from one of Italy's oldest and most respected families. Count Roffredo Gaetani Lovatelli dell'Aquila d'Aragona was the elder son of the Count and Countess Gaetani.

As a young man, I had the opportunity to visit them at their palace by the Colosseum in Rome. They were a very popular couple in a traditional, yet open-minded way. What I mean is that their palace seemed to come straight out of the past. It was filled with antiques and white orchids.

The butlers and footmen still wore livery with the family crest upon their breasts. Yet within this traditional — almost museum-like world — the couple frequently hosted a most interesting assortment of Jet Setters and movie stars. Cary Grant was a frequent guest, as was heiress Barbara Hutton. One of the things that seemed to draw these guests was the pleasure of watching the way their hosts interacted. They were absolutely crazy about each other. They had produced six very beautiful children who were raised with the politeness and good manners that

356

also seemed from a bygone era.

I remember during one early visit that Roffredo and his brother, Gelasio, were brought downstairs by their governess to bid the guests good night. Although not twins, they were dressed in identical white shirts and little black shorts. They politely approached each guest and either shook hands or bowed as they said their good nights. Sadly, wonderful worlds do not last, and Roffredo's father died. His mother never recovered from the loss of the man she so adored. She retired to their country estate.

It was these memories that filled my head as I saw the tall, handsome man Roffredo had grown into. I decided that this man could be a candidate for Ivana.

'Roffredo, have you ever met Ivana Trump?' I asked.

'I have seen her, but we never have been introduced,' he responded.

'What do you think of her?' I continued.

'I find her physically to be fantastic,' he said enthusiastically.

Perfect, I thought. 'Then come to dinner next week at the Hotel de Paris in Monte Carlo.' I knew that Ivana would be there at a party given by a good friend of mine, Fawaz Gruosi.

I had to do a small makeover to assist Marina to become the double of Elizabeth Taylor, but Fawaz needs no help in being the twin of Tyrone Power. I wonder if Linda Christian could have told them apart. In addition to his extraordinary good looks and charm, he is a successful businessman and married to Caroline Scheufele, the beautiful heiress of the Chopard family, the manufacturers of exclusive Swiss watches.

Fawaz is another of those rare members of the Jet Set who runs his own business. He had, in fact, pioneered the commercial use of the black diamond with such success that the openings of his exclusive boutiques are of great interest to the highest members of society. When he opened his London boutique, there was a slight conflict about who might attend the opening and later the reception that was hosted by Salima Aga Khan. Camilla Parker Bowles (the mistress of Prince Charles) was quite interested in a black diamond, but so apparently was my old acquaintance, Princess Margaret. The Royal Family is not very approving of Camilla, and one of those civilized British understandings exists in which they take care not to ever participate in the same events.

I do not know exactly how such things are coordinated, but somehow it seems to work. In this case, Camilla came to the opening and had a chance to gaze at the black jewels while Princess Margaret appeared later at the reception. I had not seen her in two years, and she had aged and appeared to have shrunk. It has been a difficult time for the Windsors, and I felt sorry for her. She was certainly not the lively, flirtatious woman I had known in Sardinia almost thirty years before.

Fawaz was hosting a party that August 5 on 'the Terrace' of the Hotel de Paris, and I made sure I had the opportunity of introducing Roffredo to Ivana. Remember how I described the electricity between Christopher Reeve and Tiziana and between Naomi and Cortez? Well, those were childlike infatuations compared to what I now witnessed.

Ivana had rented a yacht and was traveling with a wealthy Texan. In two days, the poor Texan was gone. From then on Roffredo and Ivana were inseparable. I was pleased with my matchmaking success.

I was writing a society column for an Italian magazine. Between coordinating the PR work, writing my column, and publishing my magazine, the days flew by until suddenly time stopped. As I went through my ritual of bringing friends to Morocco and spending the late hours in the casino writing my book with Allan, I was unaware that something unusual was going on in the background.

The Italian government has a special team called DIA. For months, they had been watching the operation of Mr. Cilona and were ready to act. They alleged that he had fixed the gaming tables.

The DIA staged a massive raid. The casino was closed, and virtually everyone associated with it was arrested. I was in Paris at the time when I learned that a warrant had been written for my arrest. The charge was unclear, but suddenly I found myself in the position not unlike the one that Allan had been in a short year before.

In times of crisis, I have always found comfort in the company of Sagan and I went to her now. In addition to her home in Paris, she spent much of her time at a country estate near mine in Normandy. Here, she would consort with nature. She loved horses and would leave the door open so that the animals could wander in and greet her in the morning as if they were dogs. She offered me this refuge for a short time so I could decide what to do. There was only one possible course of action. I had committed no crime. I had to report to the authorities.

Respecting my cooperation, the Italian judge promised me that I would be allowed to spend my incarceration, during the early stage of the investigation, under house arrest. Under these terms, I boarded a plane and accompanied by Francine, flew to Italy.

As we exited the aircraft, a reporter snapped a picture of me. It is even hard to recognize that the agonized face that appeared in the newspaper had any resemblance to my own. I was taken to the police station and went through the usual demeaning procedures. Frightened and exhausted, I was sent to my apartment where I was instructed not to exit or even make telephone calls. Sometime during those night-marish first hours of confinement, I was notified that Donina was dead.

Despite the bitterness at our parting, she remained one of the greatest loves of my life. Six months before her death, when the severity of her illness became known, she requested a final meeting with me. It took place at a party in Cap Ferrat.

She ran to embrace me in front of many of the people who had been polarized and scandalized by our vicious separation. As she embraced me, through her sobs, she kept repeating, 'Forgive me, Massimo. Forgive me.'

Suddenly, I had to face my solitude with the additional shock of her loss. My lonely apartment was filled with ghosts of the past.

Any form of involuntary confinement is prison. Regardless of the opulence of my surroundings and the familiarity of my possessions, I felt trapped. Not surprisingly, few of my friends would defend me or even associate themselves with me. I learned whom I really could trust.

Sagan had shielded me and continued to write letters of protest to any newspapers that unfairly accused me. Gina Lollobrigida and Ursula Andress actually flew to the tribunal in Sicily to testify on my behalf. Gina with her usual strength of character lambasted the judges for their unfairness and assaulted the press for their complicity.

Two of my American friends were also to prove their loyalty. Ivana Trump spoke daily with Francine, offering support. Allan Starkie went one step further. Understanding the pain of unjust imprisonment, he petitioned to be allowed to visit me during my confinement.

With the exception of Francine, the courts had refused all other visitors, but they did grant Allan permission to visit me each day. Francine and Allan divided their time so that I would not have to be alone. With their help and from the strange perspective of this confinement, I was able to confront my past and try to understand it.

Allan and I would sit on my window box and stare at the Roman Colosseum as we spoke of my past. It was easy to feel that I might be Claudius, writing my memoirs from my final prison. I learned one thing from this confinement. There was no way I'd allow myself to be placed in jail.

I decided that if the courts would not agree to release me, I would take my life. Francine did not discourage this. She simply said that she would join me.

Shortly before Christmas, the tribunal was to meet again and decide my fate. I hoped that by that time they might be able to determine that I had no involvement in the crime situation in Morocco. I was hired simply, and only, to promote a hotel.

The decision finally came — I was free.

I can't fully describe the elation I experienced when I was permitted to open the door and just step outside. My familiar neighborhood seemed strange, endlessly large, and beautiful. Life seemed possible again — but on new terms. All the things I had valued now appeared to be very insignificant.

I needed to get out of Europe.

For the first time since 1976, I had canceled my *Best* Awards. Instead of rescheduling it, I simply flew to America. There, among friends and in a country where one is not imprisoned without a charge being filed, I felt free.

When I returned to Europe, I went to my country home and spent hours walking along the deserted beaches with my two dogs, accompanied by the ghosts of my past. The silence and the size of that desolate beach soothed me and calmed the claustrophobia I occasionally carried after my confinement. But things weren't the same. I kept questioning everything I'd done and that I'd believed.

The only therapy for agonizing over how and why I'd spent my life was to continue writing my memoirs. I became more introverted and convinced myself that I had to find a different direction to my life.

The addiction of needing to profit from relationships that developed, starting with Lydia, had dissipated — but in its absence, I found that my life lacked direction. Although I had supported myself for many years, I hadn't accomplished very much in which I could take pride.

I was in a uniquely privileged position and had to find a way to use this productively.

My reveries were disturbed by a turn of events that drew me into a world of international intrigue.

An acquaintance of mine had been contacted by a member of a European intelligence agency. The agent had a document that he alleged revealed the nature of the plot that resulted in the death of Princess Diana and Dodi. It provided the names of the people involved and even the means they purportedly used to throw Diana's car out of control. The man had tried to contact Dodi's father, Mr. Fayed, but failed. He heard that I was collaborating on a book with a man who had known Diana and felt that perhaps

I might be able to expose this horrible secret.

After my trouble with the Italian authorities, I was too fragile to get involved in an international scandal, so I asked Allan if he would be willing to reach Fayed.

I trusted Allan and knew of the years he had spent in the espionage world as an officer for both army intelligence and the Defense Intelligence Agency (DIA). Allan agreed and was shown the document. He believed that it might contain valid information, but simply couldn't be sure. I tried to schedule a meeting for him with Fayed through Adnan Kashoggi, who is related through marriage to the Fayed family.

Not receiving a response, I called a man named Klein, who managed the Ritz Hotel in Paris. It was owned by Mr. Fayed and was the origin of the ill-fated drive that led to the tragic crash. Allan met the manager and explained the unusual situation in general terms.

Klein was pleasant, but declined to become involved. He suggested that Allan go to the judge handling the case or simply write a letter to Harrods, the London department store that is also owned by Fayed.

The agent who supplied the information required a promise of secrecy, as he believed that his life would be in danger if it were known that he revealed what he knew. He agreed to attest to the verity of the document if his safety could be guaranteed.

Allan was reluctant to trust such a responsibility to either Harrods or some unknown judge. We decided that we needed to at least verify the authenticity of the document. I did not anticipate then that this would lead into the dark corridors of the KGB.

It was now December, and after a year of dwelling on the past and trying to make peace with its ghosts, it was time to reenter the world of the living. I reinitiated my *Best* Awards after the year's hiatus. It was held in Paris at the large studio of Pierre Cardin — the man who whom I had met in Capri almost forty years before.

I wanted the ceremony to be meaningful this year. The selection criterion was expanded to reflect my new perspectives about social responsibility. Even the award itself was more lavish than usual. I gave each recipient a solid gold Chopard watch with a diamond face.

Not wanting the event to appear too serious, I decided that after the presentations and formal dinner, I would arrange for my guests to let their hair down at a wild new nightspot called Cabaret. There, within minutes, the bejeweled, formally dressed socialites would be drinking and dancing with their usual enthusiasm.

I wanted to express something about what I had learned by the selection of people. And so, among those chosen, were Count Roffredo and Ivana Trump. He is a man who reconciled manners and elegance from a past era with the energy and drive of this century. And I felt that their relationship also combined the precious elements of elegance and energy.

Also among the recipients this year was Lili Mahtani, who embodied a combination of talent and social concern. She is currently writing a book based on the life of the composer Puccini. In addition to this, she is on the board of the Almeida Theatre in London and is an executive member of the Royal Academy of Arts. But I selected her more because of her devotion to charity. Lili, as a member of the Foundation against AIDS, created a substantial grant to fund research at Boston General Hospital. She hopes to support young doctors, researchers, and biochemists in finding a cure for or means of prevention of this terrible disease.

Her next project is to build her own research clinic. Typically, Jet Set charity sponsorship is not very hands on and often is an excuse to hold gala charity events. I wanted to acknowledge that a direct contribution to a worthy cause is more significant than giving thousand-dollar-a-plate charity balls.

In keeping with a mood of reconciliation, I gave the award to Emma Parker Bowles, the niece of the much-maligned Camilla. After the loss of Princess Diana, the ghastly press coverage of John Bryan and the Duchess of York, and even the burning of Windsor Castle, I felt that the world could be a little more tolerant to the Windsors and particularly to the love that Prince Charles and Camilla shared.

Emma is a beautiful and sweet young lady, and the British press, amazed at my selection, gave her a lot of coverage. It is hard to say if this publicity was solely responsible for what later happened, but several weeks after my award ceremony, Emma began to date Prince William, the future king of England.

I would like to think that somehow the fabulous photos of Emma in her golden evening dress caught Prince William's eye and that I might have contributed to the odd romance in which the son of Princess Diana fell in love with the niece of her rival. But, as I said, reconciliation was the theme this year.

I had chosen to give the award to two Russian aristocrats as well. The Grand Duchess Maria de Russie is the highest-ranking surviving Romanoff. She was invited by Yeltsin to return to a Russia that executed her ancestors and to reconcile the past with a brighter future. Accepting this offer, the Grand Duchess also pledged her fortune to build hospitals for the poor.

I also selected a dashing Russian prince named Prince Umar Dzhabrailov. Although a man who could have enjoyed the social world offered him by his title, he had become one of the great new Russian entrepreneurs. He created and personally directed the Plaza Group that was perhaps the largest developer organization in the former Soviet Union. His hotels have hosted President Clinton and Vice President Al Gore. Fearless, yet polite, Prince Umar is one of those success stories of the brave new Russians who struggle to push their economy forward.

Out of gratitude for the award, and also to acquaint me firsthand with his work, Umar invited Allan and me to visit him in Moscow. There we were offered some of the most incongruous, yet fantastic spectacles I have yet seen and also a little more international intrigue.

We were invited to attend the world premiere of an epic Russian film. We also had another agenda. Allan was convinced that there existed at least a possibility that the information we had been given regarding the death of Princess Diana might have some basis in truth.

After the lukewarm reception he had received at the Ritz, he decided that another approach at testing its verity should be found. At this point, Dodi's father was in the middle of a tedious process of trying to obtain information from the Defense Intelligence Agency and the CIA. Allan was sure that whatever information we might provide either agency would immediately disappear into a black hole of bureaucracy and secrecy.

He knew a former KGB general who had headed state security for ex-Soviet Premier Andropov. He decided to use this contact to try to verify the source of the information. Ensuring that the contents of the top-secret document were themselves not revealed, Allan produced the form and headings of the missive. Within hours, his source was certain that the document itself fitted the format used by the agency from which it was purported to have been produced.

We had come one step further in unraveling the riddle. Upon our return, we would see that the document found its way to the appropriate authorities. We could now devote our time to our host and the premiere.

The Russian film industry had produced its first epic film in decades, titled *The Barber of Siberia*. The first showing was at the Kremlin.

Allan and I were driven in Prince Umar's bulletproof Mercedes to the steps of the auditorium. It felt odd entering the forebidding gates of the Kremlin, driving through the expanse of Red Square, past the colorful onion domes of its famous cathedral, to the very building that had housed the highest echelon of our Cold War enemies. Once inside, surrounded by bodyguards, we watched the strange spectacle of Russians trying to reinvent a social world.

For more than eighty years, elegance and society were criminal offenses. Now a population beginning to enjoy affluence was trying desperately to define a social standard and sense of aesthetic. Within the massive, ice-cold social-realism architecture of the auditorium, whose only adornments were stark mosaics of the hammer and sickle along with the symbols of the Politburo, the hundreds of guests dressed themselves for a formal function that for them was unprecedented. Some of the men wore black tie. In some cases, the tuxedos might have dated back to the czarist era. Others came either in military uniforms or dark suits overflowing with the obligatory rows of communist medals from their past glories.

The women were clad in a myriad of outfits ranging from ball dresses with fox and mink stoles, to micro-mini skirts and see-through tops. One lady even came in a large black funeral dress and sported a canopy-like hat adorned with drooping black ostrich feathers, as if a depressed vulture had landed upon the head of a contrite mourner.

A band dressed in military uniform played in the background. Then a procession of young girls dressed in white debutante gowns entered. We were ushered into the theater and seated a row away from Gorbachev. The film itself was a celebration of pre-revolutionary Russia, produced by a man who advocates the return to a benevolent, enlightened monarchy.

After the premiere, Umar took us back to his elegant hotel and the party he organized for the actors and producers of the film. We were seated next to Shirley MacLaine, who had just flown in. I made small talk with her about my life and this book. She told me that her own eight books that featured her beliefs in reincarnation had sold millions of copies.

'You must have made a lot of money,' I responded.

'Massimo, from what you have told me about your earlier life, particularly about Lydia, I think that money is too important to you. After all, you can't take it with you.'

Allan came to my defense by quickly responding, 'Shirley, that sounds awfully funny coming from you!' At which point, she had to laugh.

The trip was quite interesting, but reinforced my old belief that there still is a human need for elegance in this world. Maybe we Jet Setters had taken it too far, but when one sees a culture that has been starved for generations, it seems that people really crave a form of social aesthetics. I became convinced that there was some role for the Jet Set, a way of passing down the old

370

traditions and even the old etiquette before they become extinct.

My trip to Russia reinforced the feelings that I had developed since my incarceration. Perhaps what I was trying to do with my award and my social network seems obvious and even naïve. But I wanted to show that the Jet Set and its components of aristocrats and wealthy industrialists had a purpose. We could use the privilege of rank and resources not just to compete over which socialite could throw the most lavish party or wear the most expensive gown and jewels. We were in a position to recognize that times have changed, and the time has come for us to stop ignoring the suffering in the world and do something to alleviate it.

Fine talk coming from a man who spent his life this superficially! Yes, perhaps it sounds funny coming from me. But my imprisonment, the reactions of my former friends, and the benefit of having the chance to really study my own life had changed me.

Two weeks after the ceremony, I went back to Gstaad for New Year's Eve. I invited Allan along, and we went to a wonderful chalet party where some of the friends who had remained loyal to me were present. Among them was Victor Emmanuel, my exiled king. At exactly the stroke of midnight as the sky around the turreted tower of the Palace Hotel exploded with fireworks, Victor Emmanuel embraced me and told me that he wished to restore to me the rank of marquis that had died out with my mother's line of the family.

All my life I had so admired the aristocracy, and now I was to be made a member of it. Not in the fake way of purchasing a title from a destitute heir, but by the restoration of a hereditary title that even an exiled king was permitted to reinstate.

That evening, I was filled with great emotion. We were due to go to the Palace Hotel to finish our celebrations, but there was something I had to do first. It's funny because as I was leaving, Allan caught my eye and smiled. He knew where I wanted to go and said later on, 'Man is only ever really understood by three people — his spouse, his therapist, and his biographer.'

I drove my car through the now snowy streets to the neighboring town of Gsteig. Parking in front of the Hotel Viktoria, I walked into the little paneled bar. It was exactly the way I remembered it — rustic, warm, and cozy. Guests were celebrating the New Year in their own casual fashion. I felt out of place in my tuxedo, but this time I was not ashamed to meet their gaze. Exactly twenty years had passed since first I walked into that room, convinced that I would end life as a charming parasite. Now, two decades later, I had become a man who lived from his own efforts and his own strength. I had been abandoned by many, but in the intervening years had rediscovered myself.

I felt that I could look back at those endless parties and at the pantheon of faces of those whom I loved and know that somehow they are each a part of me, but also that I am an independent human being who earns his own passage through life. I was filled with pride at the freedom, independence, and self-esteem that such a simple realization gave me.

That night I had learned that I was to be made a nobleman, but in the years since I had last been in this room I had learned something else. We are all either noblemen or knaves, not by virtue of our birth, but as the result of our actions and the nobility of our souls.

I have a long journey ahead and a great distance still to go, but I have rediscovered the right direction.

I glanced at my watch. It was time to get back. It would be a pity to miss the next party.

THE END

THE LADY ON MY LEFT

Catherine Cookson

Alison Read, orphaned when she was two years old, had for some years lived and worked with Paul Aylmer, her appointed guardian. Paul, an experienced antique dealer whose business thrived in the south-coast town of Sealock, had come to rely on Alison, who had quickly learned the trade. But when he had asked her to value the contents of Beacon Ride, a chain of events was set off that led to the exposure of a secret he had for years managed to conceal. As a result, Alison's relationship with Paul came under threat and she knew that only by confronting the situation head-on would her ambitions be realised.